"I AM A CITIZEN OF ISRAEL.

But I am, in a sense, a Russian Jew as well. For I drew my first breath in Russia . . . My childhood and adolescence were spent in tiny Tel Aviv, which was then being built on the sand dunes by the sea . . . During the past few years, I have had opportunity to make a number of lengthy visits to the Soviet Union. I have seen Soviet Russia and its life from many and varied angles. . . .

The situation of the Jews in the Soviet Union concerns me deeply . . . I regard myself as a partner sharing the fate of the Jews who live there, for there my ancestors are buried: there I was born: there my cradle stood: there my cousins live to this day.

And there, among the Jews, I left a portion of my life and my heart."

—Arie L. Eliav

Other SIGNET Books of Special Interest

BETWEEN HAMMER AND SICKLE

by Arie L. Eliav

UPDATED EDITION

A SIGNET BOOK

Published by
THE NEW AMERICAN LIBRARY

Published as a SIGNET BOOK by arrangement with The Jewish Publication Society of America.

SIGNET TRADEMARK REG. U.S. PAT. OFF. AND FOREIGN COUNTRIES
REGISTERED TRADEMARK—MARCA REGISTRADA
HECHO EN CHICAGO, U.S.A.

SIGNET BOOKS are published by
The New American Library, Inc.,
1301 Avenue of the Americas, New York, New York 10019

FIRST PRINTING, JULY, 1969

PRINTED IN THE UNITED STATES OF AMERICA

Yes, I saw the Plain of Sharon!
In my dream of it I hold my head high . . .

An anonymous Russian Jewish poet*

* From *Don't Ask,* a collection of poems of Zion by D. Seter

Contents

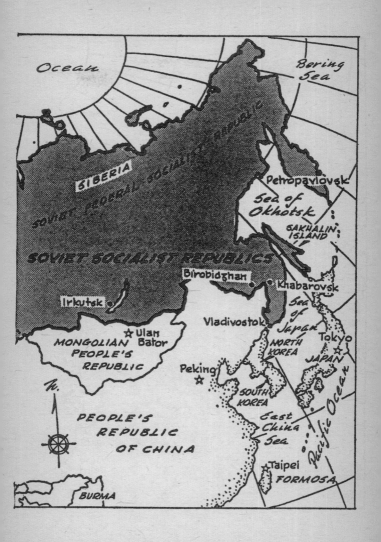

1

Encounter

The old bazaar of Samarkand

The ancient bazaar of Samarkand is one of the most colorful and noisy spots in Uzbekistan, even on an ordinary weekday. But imagine the excitement that takes place on the eve of the First of May, the great national and spring festival of the Soviet peoples. The year I was there the parade attracted thousands from the furthest reaches of the Republic of Uzbekistan, and the market places were filled with a multicolored throng.

The bazaar itself is a unique medley of Bukharan and Persian architecture: arched domes and minarets dotted with mosaics in blue, turquoise, and green dominate the markets and squares of the town. A riot of red flags, posters, and slogans added a new touch to the ancient scheme. Pictures of Marx, Engels, and particularly Lenin covered entire walls; alongside them were photographs of the Soviet leaders of the day, all grouped in a prearranged hierarchic order that suggested an unbroken continuity.

I loved walking through this tumultuous crowd. Heavy-footed Uzbek peasants wandered between the stalls, their wives dressed in yellow, speckled, artificial silks that fluttered in the breeze. Slanty-eyed, bushy-bearded Tajiks walked about in groups, talking loudly in a strange idiom. Thickset Bukharans engaged in smiling conversations with tall, slim, stern-looking Turkmen. Russian and Ukrainian *kolkhoz* members moved through the crowd, tall, broad,

13

blue-eyed, and yellow-hatted, their thickset Slavic wives wearing colored kerchiefs on their heads. The sound of Turkish, Persian, and Mongolian dialects, mingled with Russian and Ukrainian, echoed through the market place. At sunset, as the blue mosaics and the glass covering the red pictures reflected the sun's yellow rays, the bazaar and its throng looked as though it had been cut out of the colored frescoes which adorn the palaces of the Persian princes or the emirs of Bukhara.

I was certain that many of the people selling rugs, cloth, and colored cotton material were Bukharan Jews, descendants of that remarkable and ancient Jewish group who had handed down the profession to their descendants. Now, under the Soviet regime, their private enterprise had become a nationalized trade; but nothing else about it had changed. For all the uniformity imposed by official policy, this place, far away from Moscow, had retained intact much of the special flavor of the bazaars: the loud bargaining and the give-and-take that made commerce a rite and an art.

Walking through the alleyways of the market, I suddenly came across a Jew who seemed to have dropped from another world. He stood facing me on the narrow sidewalk, an old man of seventy or more, above average height but bent with age, his beard white and short, his face furrowed with wrinkles, his eyes deep blue. He wore a long black coat, old and faded, and shabby half-length boots. He stood behind a little valise-like table which rested on a tripod and was attached to a wide leather belt which hung loosely over his shoulders. The table was filled with an assortment of little things—all sorts of haberdashery.

I felt sure that this was no native Bukharan Jew, but an Ashkenazi Jew from Europe. My curiosity changed to eager excitement as I came close to the peddler. The man suddenly reminded me of my late father. The build, the beard, the features and, above all, the wonderful blue eyes were all the same. He seemed so out of place in this Oriental Samarkand bazaar that his very presence there aroused pity. Nobody stopped to buy his wares. He stood there, lonely, sad, and foreign, amidst the noise and tumult around him.

I came closer and greeted him in Yiddish: *"Sholem aleichem, Reb Yid."*

So absorbed was the old man, that he started when I

spoke; and when he saw before him a man much younger than himself, dressed as a foreign tourist, he seemed utterly amazed. He peered at me with suspicious eyes and answered in a whisper: *"Sholem aleichem."* I asked him: *"Reb Yid,* what have you got to sell?" He showed me his wares: shoelaces, hairpins, cheap bottles of perfume, combs, matches, tacks, and the like. I picked up a pair of shoelaces and, while examining them at length, asked: "Well, and how is my fellow Jew?" He countered with a quick question. "Please tell me, sir, where do you come from, and what are you doing here?" I answered slowly: "I come from Israel and I am here on a pleasure trip."

Beside himself with surprise, the Jew leaned on his tripod and breathed a long "Oy!" I bought the black laces as the old Jew held my hand and looked deep into my eyes. Then he suddenly started speaking quickly: "Please buy something else so that you do not seem conspicuous. You are the first Israeli, probably the last, I'll ever see. I must speak to you." I examined the things on the little stand and bought a brown comb, all the while listening to the man's life story, which he told in short, broken, breathless sentences.

He was born in a little town near Vilna in Lithuania, and attended a *heder* and a yeshiva. When he reached adolescence, he joined a religious Zionist youth movement in his town; then he moved to Vilna, the big city. He made good in the textile trade, married, prospered, and raised a Jewish family; he had sons and daughters, was an active Zionist, contributed to all the drives for the pioneers in the Land of Israel. He did not emigrate to the Land of Israel because he did not want to leave his thriving business. Then came the war. . . .

I bought another comb and two more pairs of laces. . . . "Yes, war broke out." Two of his sons died at the Red Army front. He, his wife, and his little son wandered to Siberia. There he was accused of being a "former great merchant and active Zionist." He was arrested and deported to a prison camp in the far north.

I bought some buttons and safety pins. "The camps, yes. . . . They are in the land of the white bear, as the saying goes. I lived there thirteen years, working like a slave, chopping trees, mining coal, and laying railway ties. Look at me, I'll be sixty-four next year."

I looked closely at him.

"Yes, yes, I know. I look like an old man of eighty.

This is the price I paid for what I learned in those camps. After that barbarian died, I was liberated. My wife and I were given permission to live only in Samarkand. And this is how I make my living."

I picked up some boxes of matches and two packets of candles and added them to my stock of purchases. "I have relatives and friends in Israel, but it is many years since I wrote to them. My heart is with them and, do you know, my son works as an electronics engineer in some large plants in northern Siberia. He came to see me once in Samarkand and told me how easily he can pick up Israeli broadcasts and get the news. Don't be so surprised. I educated him myself and taught him to love the Land of Israel and the Jewish people. He also told me that someone with the same name as mine was appointed to an important position in the Israeli government. I worked out my family tree and told my son: 'Do you know, son, I am sure this is my cousin who emigrated to Palestine and was one of the first pioneers forty years ago.' What do you think, sir, could that be true?"

I bought a little bottle of scent and some more haberdashery, then learned the full name of the peddler. I told him: "Yes, my friend, I do believe that your cousin is now something like a minister in Israel." The Jew looked at me with his beautiful sad eyes and as his tears fell slowly, he murmured: "Nu . . . that He has kept us alive and preserved us and enabled us to see this day."

He wiped away his tears with a tattered handkerchief and added: "When you return to Israel, greet him for me. As for me, if I perish, I perish! I am afraid to write to him, not for my own sake, but for that of my son. He has such a responsible job and his position is so delicate—I may hurt him."

I asked whether he had a specific message.

"Yes," he answered. "When you get back, please tell my cousin and all other Jews. . . . Nu . . . this is what you'll tell them." And here the peddler began to hum the opening bars of the *"Hatikvah,"* the anthem of the Zionist movement and, now, of the State of Israel. But he could not go on, for tears choked him.

I gathered up all the things I had bought, paid him, doubling and trebling the sum, wrung his emaciated hand, and told him: "I shall bring your cousin and all the people of Israel your greetings and those of your wife and of your son the engineer in northern Siberia."

That night, after watching the fine performance of the national Uzbekistan folk dance ensemble, and then the fireworks display, I returned wearily to the Intourist hotel. I could not sleep. I was obsessed by the face and the story of the old peddler—the more so because of his amazing resemblance to my father. A strange thought haunted me: It is mere chance that brings me, a foreign tourist, to the market places of Central Asia, wandering without a care in the footsteps of Marco Polo. Had my father not been a Zionist, had he not decided to leave Russia forty years ago and travel to Israel, I would now be another resident of the Soviet Union, provided, of course, I had survived all that had befallen my generation, the hunger, the liquidations, prison, war, and—worse than all—the Holocaust. Who knows but that I might also be working now as an electronics engineer in northern Siberia.

I should, at this stage, tell the reader who I am and how I came to be in Samarkand on the eve of the First of May.

I am a citizen of Israel. But I am, in a sense, a Soviet Jew as well. For I drew my first breath in Russia where I was born on a winter night in the early nineteen-twenties. There I learned to walk and to utter my first word, "mamma"—in Russian.

My father was a native of a small town in western Russia. He lived for a long time in Vilna and dealt in timber. At the end of the First World War, he wandered away, together with other groups of refugees, and arrived in central Russia during the Bolshevik revolution. There he met my mother. Shortly after they were married, and while my mother was pregnant with me, my father went into hiding in the city suburbs, having learned that he was wanted by the G.P.U. (Soviet Secret Police) on a charge of being a "merchant and Zionist." At the time of my birth our home and our town were in the grip of severe hunger and cold. Life was precarious. Occasionally, my father would secretly bring home some potatoes and other meager foodstuffs which he had somehow gathered in the suburbs or villages.

When I was about three years old, my father decided to take his life in his hands and attempt to escape from the Soviet Union. He had been a member of the Zionist movement since youth, and he now decided to save himself and his family at all costs, and to start a new life in Palestine. One night he crossed the Soviet border illegally into Latvia and from there he made his way to Palestine. My mother, who earlier had gone through a mock divorce, secured a permit to emigrate to Palestine with her little children. In 1924 we boarded the Soviet ship *Lenin* at Odessa, and arrived at Jaffa a few days later. Father was waiting for us there.

My childhood and adolescent years were spent in tiny Tel Aviv, which was then being built on the sand dunes by the sea. I grew up as a sabra. At fifteen I was already caught up in the first of the series of wars that my generation was to live through. I was enrolled in the Haganah, was taught the use of firearms, then sent to protect Jewish settlements against Arab attacks.

At the beginning of the war against Germany, I enrolled in the Jewish Brigade of the British Army and served in Egypt, the western desert, and in Italy. At the end of the war, we established contact with the Jews who had survived the extermination camps.

During the past few years, I have had the opportunity to make a number of lengthy visits to the Soviet Union. I have seen Soviet Russia and its life from many and varied angles. My deepest experiences, those that are uppermost in my memory, were Jewish experiences. I shall never forget them as long as I live. The situation of the Jews in the Soviet Union concerns me deeply. I read, listen to, and study all that is available on the subject; indeed, I regard myself as a partner sharing the fate of the Jews who live there. For there my ancestors are buried; there I was born; there my cradle stood; there my cousins live to this day. And there, among the Jews, I left behind a portion of my life and my heart.

"Why have you forgotten us?"

When I returned from the Soviet Union, I told my family and friends about the condition of the Jews there. Invariably, I was asked the same questions. On whose behalf do you speak? Who authorized you to describe their condition and say "they" want, "they" feel? By what criterion do you evaluate their situation? Is it true that you met only old Jews in the synagogues and that it was from them you gathered what was going on? If that is the case, then your criterion is inherently wrong. Where, indeed, are the rest of the Jews, those who do not go to the synagogues? On your own admission, those who attend the synagogues are only a small minority of the Jews there.

I had no ready answer to these questions. Such answers are not easy to come by even for a person like myself who has made several trips to the Soviet Union and has lived there, all told, quite a lengthy period of time. Needless to say, they are that much more difficult for one who has been there only briefly.

I must admit that it is, and will remain, impossible to make a systematic and scientific social survey of the state of the Jews in the Soviet Union, just as it is impossible to conduct such a survey on the various other social problems of that country. The scientific area of study now known in the West as Sovietology rests on the analysis of data published on specific topics in the Soviet Union, and is supplemented by impressions gained during tours, visits, and conversations, as well as by various guesses, opinions, analogies, and conclusions. These observations are not intended as a derogation of Sovietology in any way. Rather, they are meant to give some idea of the difficulties and obstacles encountered in dealing with Soviet Russia.

If this is the case with regard to subjects about which the Soviet Union publishes a great deal of information— such as economic matters, the situation in agriculture, literature, art—how much more so is it true in the case of the Jewish problem, where the Soviet authorities do not even acknowledge that a problem exists, or else claim that the problem has been completely resolved and that they have little or nothing to publish on the subject. Hence, to gauge the precise value of cumulative personal impressions gathered through direct contact with Soviet reality, is a far more difficult matter in the Jewish sphere than it is in any other.

My survey is of a collective and cumulative nature. I was not the only one to travel the length and breadth of the Soviet Union, from Birobidzhan to Brest, from Leningrad to Sochi. Nor was I the only one to meet old and young Jews, men and women, scientists and ordinary folk, wherever they happened to live in the fifteen Soviet republics. Before me, during my stay, and afterwards, Jews from the "outside" had met many of the Jews "inside." In past years thousands of Jews from the West visited synagogues and relatives, beaches and resorts, festivals and congresses. This is true of tourists from America, businessmen from England, visitors and delegates from Israel, scientists from many countries, sports groups, musicians, or just "folk" who came from Western lands to meet a brother or cousin whom they had not seen for decades. All of these brought back with them a rich store of impressions, conversations, and experiences. They spoke at length or briefly with countless Jews throughout the Soviet Union. This extensive sampling must form the basis of any description or analysis of the situation.

One summer evening I was sauntering along the walk of a Black Sea resort in the company of an Israeli family. The resort was crowded with thousands of holiday seekers from every corner of the country. It was not difficult to identify us as foreigners, and our clothes, bathing suits, and the beach balls of the children—all of foreign manufacture—made us the center of natural and lively interest on the part of the people on the beach. The Jews on that beach recognized us immediately as Israelis, what with the noisy sabra Hebrew of the children and the El Al flight bag my wife was holding.

We sensed hundreds of eyes following us as we walked along, and these included many Jewish eyes (bear in mind: in the Soviet Union there quickly develops inside one a special sixth sense that helps him to tell, by looking in a person's eyes, whether or not he is a Jew). Then a Jew got up from a bench, came to us hurriedly, and, as though meaning to ask casually, "Excuse me, what time is it?" asked: "Why have you forgotten us?" Still walking, and as casually as if we meant to say, "It is ten after five," we answered just what he expected to hear: "We have not forgotten you." That was the end of it. The Jew went back to his bench and we continued sauntering along the walk.

When I relate this little incident to someone else who has also visited the Soviet Union, he smiles and says: "This happened to me at the Kiev railway station," or "at the Tashkent airport." Another tourist describes how he was asked the same question by a Jew at the exhibition held at Gorki Park, and still another in the lobby of the Bolshoi Theater. And this makes me think that the restless Jew at the Black Sea resort and others like him are, in a sense, wandering Jews who, while rushing from one town to another, between train and plane, between festival and theater, manage to spot Jews "from there" and ask them the same question: "Why have you forgotten us?"

This Jew is one of the mosaic stones in my cumulative model or image. But there is another kind of Soviet Jew. When he recognizes an Israeli he presses his nose closer to the book he is reading, or veils his face more closely with the paper he is scanning; and when, at some international congress, he sees "Israel" on the identity tag pinned to a delegate's coat, he turns away.

He is also one of the components of the mosaic. And so are the young Jewish students who clasp hands with an Israeli tourist in the dark, amidst a crowd of thousands, in the open space before the synagogue on Simchat Torah, and who awkwardly dance the *horah* with him and his children, and join him as he sings.

Thus, after lengthy visits to the Soviet Union, after traveling thousands of miles by train, boat, and plane from one end of the country to the other, after hundreds of conversations and meetings with Jews, one manages to collect in his bag a varied assortment of mosaic stones from which he tries to reconstruct the collective face of the Jew in the Soviet Union.

2

A Nation Among Nations

Who is a Jew?

The key to a proper understanding of the Jewish situation in the Soviet Union hinges on this question: How does the Soviet regime regard the Jews?

Despite its pragmatism in daily life, the Soviet regime rests essentially on a set of doctrines and dogmas derived from an ideological text. This text, by its very nature and substance, must provide a dogmatic answer to every significant social, economic, or political problem. These answers must all grow out of a single ideology. The Soviet regime cannot avoid any issue by failing to provide the answers, or by saying, "I do not know," or "This is not clear enough," or "It may possibly be so," for such equivocation might cast serious doubt upon the basic tenets on which its doctrines rest.

Blatant contradictions may be detected at times between the answers to various questions. But like other doctrinaire regimes, the Soviets manage, through Marxist dialectic or by other means, to close the gap between the contradictions by means of a bridge of words. However insubstantial such a construction may seem, it must at least convey the impression of being a monolithic edifice.

This is how the Soviet regime, from its earliest days, approached internal Jewish problems. It had to define both the Jew and his Judaism. The answers were: A Jew is one who belongs to the Jewish nationality, one of the many nationalities of the Soviet Union; and Judaism is one of the religions practiced in the Soviet Union. Because these answers determine all that there is to be said about the fate of the Jews in the centralized Soviet regime, an evaluation of the Jewish situation in the Soviet Union must start with an appreciation of these two elements, the national and the religious. Only against the general background of the national and religious problems in the Soviet Union, can it be seen that insofar as the Jews are concerned there exists between these problems an indissoluble link, and that they have tremendous reciprocal impact upon the Jews both as a group and as individuals.

Soviet Russia is composed of many nationalities, a natural consequence of the geography and history of this great land, a history going back a millennium. From earliest times, Russia was penetrated by invading hordes and by migrating peoples. The tribes and peoples that came through it left indelible marks. In the last few centuries, the Russians began to consolidate themselves into a powerful, unified state. At the same time, they expanded over vast areas of Europe and Asia, engulfing nations, large and small, and incorporating them into their empire. Thus, since its inception, the Soviet regime has been faced with the knotty and complicated problem of how to handle its minorities. The Soviets defined the many large and small peoples living in their midst as "nationalities" *(natsionalnosti)*; but the fifteen large nationalities, whose areas bordered on neighboring outside countries, were organized as "Soviet republics," and each was recognized as a "nation" *(natsiia)*. Others are recognized as "autonomous republics," and still others, as "autonomous regions." They are all headed, naturally, by the Russians themselves, who represent the backbone of the Soviet Union. The Russians make up about half of the total population, and the Russian Republic (R.S.F.S.R.), where Moscow is located, is by far the largest of the Soviet republics.

In terms of size, the Russians are followed first by the Ukrainians, then by the Belorussians (White Russians). All three possess a common historic and ethnic denominator—they are Slavic peoples whose languages bear a resemblance to one another (though they are not identical). These republics are followed by the other nationalities, both of Europe and Asia, which are not of Slavic origin. In Europe there are the Estonians, Latvians, Lithuanians, and Moldavians. In the Caucasus: the Armenians, Georgians, Azerbaijans. In Central Asia: the Kazakhs, Uzbeks, Tajiks, Turkmen, and Kirghiz. Each of the fifteen nationalities enumerated here has its own republic and is part of the Soviet Union. But the people of any given nationality which lends its name to the respective republic do not necessarily constitute a numerical majority within the republic. Outstanding examples are Kazakhstan and Uzbekistan. As a result of large scale colonization by Russians, Ukrainians, Belorussians, and others, the original nationals in these republics have either already become or are on their way to becoming a minority.

In addition to the fifteen great nationalities, there exist, by Soviet definition, many other nationalities throughout the Union. Some are concentrated in more or less well defined territorial areas, while others (for instance the Jews, Poles, and Germans) are scattered over wide areas of the country.

There are no Soviet citizens

Soviet law and usage require everyone living in the Soviet Union to be recognized as a member of one of these nationalities. No person is merely a "citizen of the Soviet Union" without his nationality being known generally, or at least to the Soviet authorities. Every member of the Union is registered in his identity card as belonging to a specific nationality. We shall not discuss here the problem, interesting in itself, why of all people it is the Soviets who, though opposed from the start to every form of discrimination, have introduced a system which requires the registration of nationalities within their own country. It is a fact, however, that citizen Ivanov, registered in his identity card as Russian (*russkii*), and citizeness Ivanova, registered as Russian, must register their offspring as Russians. The same holds true for citizen Muhamadov, registered as an Uzbek, and for citizeness Muhamadova, registered as an Uzbek, and for all the other numerous nationalities. Incidentally, it matters not whether citizen Ivanov resides in Moscow, which is in the Russian Republic, or in Tbilisi, the capital of Georgia, for he, and his children as well, must register in Tbilisi as Russians. And if Muhamadov moves from Tashkent to Leningrad and settles there, he and his offspring are required to register as Uzbeks. The only means whereby a man can break the connection with his original nationality insofar as his children are concerned (but not in his own case) is through intermarriage. If comrade Kirichenko, registered as a Ukrainian, marries Tefildze, a Georgian, they are entitled to register their offspring as Ukrainians or Georgians, as they wish.

In order to understand this situation completely one must not only consider the formal aspect of registration, as indicated, but also the advantage the nationals derive from the authorities in exchange for their national identification.

The Soviets have always proudly claimed that they have found the formula which enables them to handle their national minorities. This formula was expressed by Stalin as follows: Culture is "national in form and socialist in content." And so the Soviets tackled the problem of nationalities from these two angles, form and content. By form they mean the various elements that comprise a national culture, the primary element being the national language. Actually, however, Russian is the *lingua franca* of the Soviet Union and dominates everything, everywhere. It is the idiom of science, technology, administration, and so on, not only in the Russian Republic, but throughout the other republics as well. It is inconceivable for a scientist or tractor mechanic in Armenia or Latvia not to know Russian. It is a must for most members of the Soviet Union, regardless of nationality or place of residence. At the same time, it is an undeniable fact that, far from being obliterated, the dozens of national languages of all nationalities (except in the case of the Jews) are preserved and deliberately encouraged. A child born of Georgian parents starts speaking Georgian at home. As he grows up, he will go to a kindergarten where the language of instruction is Georgian, then to school where it remains Georgian (a language totally different from Russian, both in origin and alphabet). If he goes on to the university in Tbilisi he will be taught a profession in Georgian. But the youngster will pick up Russian as a second language along the way. One simply cannot move without it. It will, however, remain essentially his second language, while Georgian will be his first, one he will be proud of all his life. This applies equally to Armenian, Lithuanian, Latvian, Ukrainian, and so on.

But the form of a national culture does not consist solely of a language and an educational system. To these must be added the encouragement given to the culture by means of the communication media: the press, radio, and television, all in the nationality's idiom, as well as poetry, literature, art, music, folk dances and folklore, architecture and archeology. These are all encouraged to augment the spirit of the respective traditions (except in the case of Judaism).

Considerable talent and large sums of money are proudly invested by the government in promoting the national troupes of the Uzbeks, Kirghiz, Armenians, Moldavians, and others. They are brought to Moscow; a "week" is organized for each nationality—an Uzbek week, a Kazakh week, and so on—in which hundreds of thousands of people participate. They are shown to every foreigner and visitor and they are of high export value abroad. But even these do not exhaust all the aspects of the notion of form. Each nationality teaches its own history with love and pride in its schools and in its national idiom. The Georgians are proud of their erstwhile kings and princes, poets and writers, wars and victories (even those won over the invading Russians). And the same is true of other nationalities (except the Jews). Monuments and squares are erected in honor of national heroes, from Khmelnitskii in Kiev to Nizamiy in Baku. Towns and streets are named after them.

Alongside the form of a national culture there exists at all times the underlying socialist content. It must be borne in mind that this important and vast framework of national culture was like a vessel which the communist authorities had to fill with a homogeneous ideological content. The national and cultural context which the centralized regime helped to preserve, and occasionally to create, served as an excellent medium for conveying its concepts and ideology, in a uniform manner, to all age levels of the population. The government managed to inject no small part of its aims and values into the mother's milk drunk by children of every nationality.

The history of each separate nationality must also conform at times to the rigid criteria of Soviet dialectics, and this occasionally results in considerable absurdities and in the rewriting and reconstruction of a culture's history. The children of Lvov are taught that a thousand years ago, the people of Lvov wished to integrate fully with their Ukrainian brethren, and that the "liberator" Khmelnitskii almost achieved this desired goal. The Austro-Hungarian regime is briefly glossed over and the Polish regime is mentioned merely as an afterthought. Latvian and Estonian children are taught that their ancestors had always dreamed of living under the protection of the big Russian "brother," and only the reactionary policies of their German and Swedish conquerors, and the bourgeois regime that prevailed there between the two world wars, prevented the attainment of this "voluntary union"; and that the conquests of Ivan the Terrible and Peter the Great in the Baltic lands were "progressive trends." Soviet dialectics has even convinced the natives of Bukhara and Samarkand that the czarist conquests were actually "wars of liberation from the oppressive yoke of the cruel emirs"; that these conquests were an essential and desirable stage toward Soviet and communist rule. In Bukovina it is standard practice to teach that the people's true national link has always been with the Ukrainians, and that Rumanian rule was no more than a passing episode, and so on. Here, the socialist content operates within the national form by explaining it, by justifying the status quo, by enhancing the stature of the Russian people in the eyes of the national minorities, and, as explained, by injecting and reinforcing communist ideology. The Soviet authorities claim that this formula of form and content works effectively. And in truth, this policy has been firmly maintained for more than two generations. The question is, of course, whether such a system could have existed for any length of time without the big stick of the centralized authority, the presence of which is experienced by all the nationalities despite the fact that it is not wielded very often.

Against this general background and within this framework the Soviets have defined the Jews as a nationality (and not one of the smaller nationalities, either; for according to Soviet statistics the Jews occupy eleventh place among the large nationalities). In other words, comrade Benjamin Rabinovich, registered as a Jew (*evrei*), and his wife Fania Rabinovich, registered as a Jewess, are required to register their little son Grisha Rabinovich as a Jew. Paradoxical though it may sound, it may be said that the Soviets are the only people who have given an unequivocal answer to the vexing question: Who is a Jew? And the great arbiters in this matter were Lenin, Stalin, and Khrushchev. They stipulated that a Jew in the Soviet Union is a Soviet citizen of Jewish nationality, born of a father registered as a Jew and a mother registered as a

Jewess. And it must be kept in mind that, in line with such usage and procedure, no Jew can divest himself of the stamp of Jewishness (as a nationality), either by changing his name (from Abramovich to Popov, for instance), or by changing his faith (for the question of nationality has no bearing on religion which, according to Soviet law, need not be registered anywhere), or by the fact that the person registered was not cercumcised (circumcision has no bearing at all on this situation). Theoretically—and on occasion not so theoretically—there may be a young man in the Soviet Union whose name is Ivan Popov, who is not circumcised, who claims that he wishes to be a Catholic, or may even have been baptized by a priest of the Catholic Church, and who, despite it all, will remain registered in his card as a Jew. And if his wife is likewise registered as a Jewess, Popov would be required to register his sons and daughters as Jews. As with other nationalities, Jews are also able to have their children registered as non-Jews by means of the intermarriage of a Jew with a non-Jewess, or of a Jewess with a non-Jew. We shall return to this at a later point.

The shadow people

The Jews are therefore registered as Jews insofar as nationality is concerned. But if we evaluate their status by the criterion of form (in other words, by that complex of cultural advantages we discussed above), they are in fact a shadow people, because in exchange for their assigned nationality they have been given nothing. They have no recognized language, no educational system of their own, no press, radio, poetry, literature, or history; in short, nothing at all. The few Yiddish booklets and newspapers, and the two or three Yiddish singers who appear today in the Soviet Union, will be dealt with in another context, for they are maintained mainly for display and foreign consumption.

The most important of these missing elements is, of course, the language and educational system. In this respect Jews live in a total wasteland. About three and a half million Jews in the Soviet Union (half a million of whom speak Yiddish, according to the Soviet records, and tens of thousands of whom had a Hebrew education in their youth) are deprived not only of schools where the Hebrew alphabet is taught, but even of a class where Yiddish or Hebrew teaching is allowed, if only once a week, or once a month.

Whenever someone asks a top Soviet official, who might be visiting the West, to explain this astounding situation, the immediate response given is that the reasons are to be sought among the Jews themselves, as "they simply do not want to learn, and certainly do not want to teach their children, Yiddish or Hebrew. Otherwise they would merely have to do a very simple thing, namely, collect a few dozen signatures from parents who really want their children to learn these languages and present their petition to the Ministry of Education. The latter would then be required to grant their request, and everything would be in order. Why, therefore, blame the Soviet authorities?"

The fact is, however, that among all the thousands of Jews living in Kovno and Vilna, in Bukhara and Samarkand, in Riga and Chernovtsy, in Kishinev, Tbilisi, and in the numerous other centers where Jews grew up and were educated in Yiddish or in Hebrew, there cannot be found twenty or thirty Jewish parents who would dare to sign such a petition. For they are simply afraid. They know only too well that the government is unequivocally opposed to such a step. Jewish parents, like other citizens, are well aware that in the land of the Soviets no one dares do anything that opposes the will of the government.

The government did not always adopt such a negative attitude to the exercise of all these rights, or oppose this form of Jewish culture. Its attitude toward the Jews as a nationality and a culture (or, at least, to what it defines as Jewish culture) was once altogether different. This is not the place to go into the history of Jews and Judaism in the early days of the Soviet regime, but it must be remembered that for about thirty years there existed in the Soviet Union a Jewish culture on a communist pattern. In the twenties, the thirties, and, to a certain extent, even in the early forties, throughout the Soviet Union, but mainly in the heavily Jewish areas of the Ukraine and Belorussia, there were still hundreds of Jewish schools whose language of instruction was Yiddish, and which were attended by tens of thousands of students. A flourishing, widely read Yiddish press existed, which included dailies, weeklies, monthlies, and so on. There were dozens of Yiddish theaters where both original and translated plays were staged and in which many talented actors performed. There were Jewish choral ensembles, as well as dance and musical groups. Thousands of Yiddish books, printed in hundreds of thousands of copies, were published, some of them written by very gifted authors. There was Yiddish poetry penned by great poets. In short, the Jews of the Soviet Union possessed all the main ingredients of a national culture, almost equal to that of the other nationalities. Admittedly, the Jews of the world outside the Soviet Union did not relish this type of literature at the time, as it was blatantly one-sided and communist. Its authors were careful to omit any mention of the great Hebrew heritage, of Zionism or the solidarity of the Jewish people. Moreover, many of them despised the Land of Israel, the Jewish religion, and the tradition and history of the Jewish people. They wrote paeans of praise to the "father of nations," to the "rising sun," in a style that made one's gorge rise. The Yiddish textbook seemed shorn of any sense of Jewish continuity. But it is well to remember that this was also the manner of the writers and poets of other national groups in the Soviet Union. Everyone sang, each in his own idiom, of Stalin's grandeur, and all gave fulsome praise to the regime and its dictator. Evaluating this period twenty years later, one must admit that it flourished quantatively and, further, that it did not lack true signs of talent and quality. It is wrong to look with contempt upon the often desparate efforts of Jewish men of letters to create and keep alive a literature while hedged in and choked by the Soviet regime. And, indeed, many of the best among them paid with their lives for having identified themselves as closely as they did with Jewish culture.

This entire Jewish culture has disappeared—first in gradual stages, then all at once and totally during the last years of Stalin's life. Some people, including Jewish communists in the West, Soviet sympathizers and those who can find no fault with Russia, argue that the gradual disappearance of the Yiddish language and of Jewish education is prevalent throughout the Diaspora. "It is the same in the United States," they say. "How many Yiddish newspapers do you still have in New York?" Or, "How many Yiddish theaters are there in London? Both there and in Moscow Yiddish is the language of the oldsters, and is dying."

This argument is based on a half-truth that is worse than an outright falsehood. It is true that Yiddish is rapidly fading out as a live medium in the United States, England, and other centers of the Diaspora. This, no doubt, is unfortunate, but it is part of a gradual sociological procsss. But during the decades when Yiddish still prevailed, the Jews in these countries managed to absorb the new language of their country of adoption and to use *it* as a dynamic medium whereby they were able to express their individual culture. This is in no way comparable to the "process" used by a ruling power which forcibly cuts down a culture and a language. And this is precisely what occurred in the Soviet Union.

What actually happened to Jewish culture during the Stalin regime? Why was it subjected to restrictive decrees in the thirties, and why was it condemned to the gallows in his last years? We must look for the answer in the dark world of Stalin's private suspicions, a world that transformed Stalin during his last years into a demented tyrant. It is doubtlessly here that some of the origins of the present tragedy confronting Soviet Jewry may be found.

It seems that certain processes and events led Stalin, in the thirties and especially toward the end of his life, to suspect that the Jews of the Soviet Union were not totally loyal to him and his regime and that they had to be regarded collectively as a threat to the security of the nation. During the thirties, at the time of the sweeping liquidations, some of whose chief victims were Jews from the top leadership of the Bolshevik party, there began a systematic shutting down of Jewish schools and an undermining of Jewish theaters and publishing houses. During the Second World War, however, while Stalin sought every available support and assistance from the peoples of the Soviet Union and the Allies, Jewish culture—now close to the brink—was given a short reprieve. Stalin gave impetus to the organization of the Jewish Anti-Fascist Committee, which included some of the best Jewish writers and intellectuals. The Committee tried to gain Jewish sympathy among the Jews in Russia as well as those outside, particularly in the United States. The Jews were again granted the opportunity to express themselves through their own press, literature, and poetry, though these opportunities were meager compared to what they had enjoyed before the liquidations.

Two years after the end of the war, the old tyrant's suspicions appear to have been aroused once again. Some of these suspicions may have been caused by Jews who had served in the Red Army during the war. Jewish soldiers fought the Nazis with great courage and were often brave to the point of recklessness. As the Red Army broke through to the West, Jewish soldiers established contact with those who had survived the war. They threw open the death camps and met relatives and brethren who had somehow lived through the Holocaust. Amid the ruins of European Jewry, they also met Jewish soldiers of other armies, as well as the men of the Jewish Brigade and other Jewish units in the British Army who had come from Palestine. There is no doubt that these dramatic and tragic encounters were charged with an intensity of feeling far greater than that which typified the mere chance contact between a Soviet and an American soldier in the line of duty. This was the meeting of brothers over the family grave. It is not at all unlikely that distorted accounts of these encounters containing anti-Semetic undertones found their way to the dictator's ear. And thus was created a fertile ground for the suspicion that the Jews entertained some kind of double allegiance. They were not merely Soviet soldiers but, deep in their hearts and souls, they were also Jewish soldiers concerned with their own people and its fate; and their attitude toward their Jewish brethren, even though they came from the friendly West, had overstepped all permissible bounds.

Another characteristic of Russian Jewry, which had undoubtedly been taken for granted all along by the government, was now brought glaringly to the fore with increased sharpness: the Jews of the Soviet Union had millions of relatives throughout the Western world—brothers, parents, uncles, cousins, and so on. And right then, at the end of the war, and immediately thereafter, these relatives began to seek each other out. Hundreds of thousands of Jews attempted to locate those members of their families who might have survived. Jews began to wander from place to place, both within the Soviet Union and outside. And thus it was said that the Jews were "wandering around too much" from town to town, from village to village, with the Red Army and in its wake, and that they "poked and sniffed around too much."

Furthermore, with the end of the war and the final annexation of the Baltic states, eastern Poland, and northern Rumania, "new" Jews by the hundreds of thousands were added to the Jewish population of the Soviet Union, and these had even more relatives in and family ties with the "outside," the West. They stormed every barrier in an effort to escape; they beat their fists relentlessly on the barred doors; they corresponded avidly with their relatives. And they brought with them a new burden of a "perverted" national Jewish culture which would "poison" the established Jewish residents in the Soviet Union.

The events which followed, beginning in 1947, intensified the suspicions already aroused against the Jews of the Soviet Union: the struggle for the establishment of a Jewish state and the Israeli War of Independence had begun. One can hear, to this day, echoes of the excitement that gripped the Jews of the Soviet Union as they heard about the war of the Jews against their enemies and about the establishment of the new State of Israel. It is well to remember that the Jews of the Soviet Union were still in shock: they had just emerged, broken and shattered, from the Holocaust. Virtually all of them had tasted during the war years the bitterness of being a Jew.

The Golda demonstration in Moscow

It need not surprise us that dormant national feelings were aroused in many Soviet Jews, possibly stimulated at times by the government which allowed the Jewish Anti-Fascist Committee to proceed with its propaganda. Further, the Soviet Jews interpreted their government's support of the Jews of Israel and its favorable vote at the United Nations as permission to identify themselves more closely with Israel in its fight for existence. It must also be remembered that many tens of thousands of Jews, most of whom had been raised on Zionism and the Hebrew language, were added all at once to the population of Russia as a result of the annexations that took place after the war.

All of this accounts for the rising tide of excitement among Soviet Jews in the years 1947–48. The crest of this excitement was reached during the spontaneous demonstration that took place near the Moscow synagogue (during Stalin's darkest days!) when thousands of Jews came to greet Golda Meir, the new Ambassador of Israel, and the *"Hatikvah"* burst out from the throng, and the cry "The people of Israel is alive" echoed through the air. We know that some naive Jews even went so far as to petition the authorities to let them join the Israel Defense Forces as gunners, tank drivers, sailors, and pilots.

The dictator was made aware of these extraordinary events, and his dark suspicions were intensified. Now, after thirty years of communist rule, the regime had not succeeded in severing the Jews, spiritually and psychologically, from their ethnic and national roots and from the course of dramatic developments in the Jewish world outside the land of the Soviets. The dictator then decided that in order to put out the flame that had begun to blaze again from the dormant Jewish embers, he would have to extinguish their cultural and national feelings with "freezing water."

First, it was necessary to cut off all contact with Western Jewry. Those concerned had to be made aware that the maintenance of contacts would be regarded by the authorities as an act of conspiracy and espionage directed against the regime. This accounts for the numerous articles that appeared in the Soviet press on the subject of Zionism, the American Joint Distribution Committee, and other international Jewish organizations, all exposed as enemies of the Soviet Union. They were dubbed as agents of the imperialist powers and as the spearheads of the dark forces that were attempting to undermine the Soviet Union and destroy its foundations. But that was not enough. In order to make certain that such demonstrations of Jewish solidarity would not recur, it was imperative to drain the morass, called Jewish culture, which had bred the mosquitoes that generated the sudden fever which seized the Jews. It was necessary to dry up the mainsprings of Jewish culture—language, education, and literature—and leave its adherents absolutely naked and sterile, so that they could be taken in hand again and made into faithful citizens of the Soviet Union.

These decisions were quickly enforced in the manner and style typical of Stalin. All Yiddish schools were shut; the newspapers were discontinued; the few theaters still performing in Yiddish were closed and their personnel scattered; writers and poets were at first silenced, and then taken away. For in order to make doubly sure, Stalin had decided to have the flag bearers of the communist Jewish culture liquidated.

Many thousands of leading figures of the Jewish intelligentsia were thus arrested and deported to concentration camps. Many were leaders of the autonomous Jewish region of Birobidzhan; others were theatrical people, journalists, authors, poets, active members of the Jewish Anti-Fascist Committee, or simply important Jews. The best of them were executed—Markish, Pfeffer, Bergelson, Der Nister, and a host of other gifted and capable personalities. They all paid with their lives for their only sin: the writing of stories and songs, some even praising the regime and the dictator, in a language that read from right to left.

This insane treatment of Jews and their culture had a logical sequel. It was not enough to frighten the Jews away from maintaining any contact with their brethren or to block all the streams of their culture; they also had to be exposed to the eyes of all Soviet peoples as dangerous and obnoxious elements, as bearers of the sign of Cain. This explains the attacks against Jews as cosmopolitan parasites battening on the healthy Soviet society. This was only one step away from the next phase initiated by Stalin in the last months of his life: the staging of the "doctors' plot," as a result of which some of the leading physicians in the Soviet Union—all of them Jews—were charged with plotting the murder of top Soviet government officials.

By dint of such logic Stalin sought to sterilize the Jews spiritually, to remove their fangs, and at the same time to prevent them from assimilating completely with the peoples of the Soviet Union—to make it difficult for them to disappear into the masses—for who knew what they might be capable of if they hid and became anonymous inside Soviet society. It was therefore seen to be essential to bar their way to complete assimilation and to prevent them from erasing the sign of Jewish nationality that was stamped on their identity cards. Stalin's Jewish policy during his last years may be characterized as cultural bloodletting. He created a shadow people who had no territory of their own, no culture or language, and no organization with which to identify themselves.

Thus the Jews of the Soviet Union were plunged into the seven years they describe as "the black years" (*die schvartse yoren*). You can still hear to this day, from Jews in every corner of the land and from every class of society, that had "the mustached fellow" (many do not dare breathe the name Stalin even today) lived and ruled a few more years, he would undoubtedly have followed this policy to the end. He intended to turn the trial of the doctors into a show trial to end all show trials, and then to start banishing thousands of Jews to forced labor in Siberia and to physical annihilation.

Stalin died and the people of the Soviet Union, especially the Jews, awoke from the long night of terror. After the initial shock, the Russian people hoped that the new rulers, especially Khrushchev, who was the leading figure in the hierarchy, would bring about a change. And indeed "the great thaw" began. The stream did not always flow in one direction. It took a crooked course with sharp angles, and, at times, stopped and froze over. Nevertheless, hundreds of thousands were liberated from the concentration camps; the reputations of thousands, alive or dead, were rehabilitated. Whole peoples and regions were favored with rehabilitation, and the hand of death placed over their heads by Stalin was removed.

The Jews—individually, of course, for they did not have any representative organization or any organs of expression—began hoping secretly, within their own four walls, if not for deliverance or a miracle (they were too downtrodden and pessimistic to expect miracles), at least for a return to conditions that had prevailed before "the black years." They hoped that a school would be opened here or there; a few newspapers published, an occasional theater created; that some contact would be established with Jews outside Russia and with Israel; that they would, in short, be given an opportunity to identify themselves once again with their Jewish nationality. But nothing of the sort happened.

Khrushchev, who had inherited Stalin's scorched earth policy in relation to the Jewish problem, gave the Jews no sign or indication that they would be permitted to cultivate this burnt land, seed it, uncover new springs of spiritual life, irrigate it, and develop on it, once again, their language and culture. In the absence of such an indication, or, more accurately, in the presence of signs that clearly said, "Do not touch," the Jews of Russia did not dare, and still do not dare, to do a thing.

It is true that some Jewish singers are now touring the Soviet Union and are appearing at Yiddish concerts before packed halls. It is true that about half a dozen Yiddish books and pamphlets have appeared since Khrushchev's advent to power. It is true that two Yiddish periodicals (*Birobidzhaner Stern* and *Sovietish Heimland*) are now being published. We will deal further with the causes and motives behind these phenomena. We shall at this point merely state that these are not even oases in the wilderness, but only mirages toward which the thirsty person runs and finds nothing, while his soul dies all the more quickly from disillusion.

"Where did you buy these medals?"

We shall devote a later chapter to a discussion of the obliteration of the Jewish past and the uprooting of its ancient tradition. But while on the subject of the Jews of today who live as a nation in the Soviet Union, it must be emphasized that despite their lack of connection with their people's past, they managed to create a culture and value system of their own during the thirty to forty years they participated actively in Soviet society. They fought in the Second World War and shed their blood not only as the slaughtered victims of the Nazis and their followers but also as partisans fighting in the forests and as soldiers in all units of the Red Army. Even if one were to assume that the Soviet disregard of all the Russian Jewish history that occurred up to the Bolshevik revolution is "natural" —that history is officially looked upon as totally reactionary, growing out of an obscurantist religion and steeped in the narrow horizons of Zionism and nationalism—even so, what of the three generations of Jewish history that have taken place in the Soviet Union itself? Actually, according to the cruel logic of Stalin and his heirs, it was necessary to eradicate this history as well; it too was suspect. That is to say, it was not enough to shut down the Jewish schools, theaters, and periodicals, it must also never be mentioned that they even once existed. It was not enough to arrest and exile to the camps some of the bravest Jewish soldiers, it must also not even be acknowledged that they had once lived. Moreover, it must not be said openly that Jews perished as Jews at the front. Russians, Ukrainians, Latvians, Lithuanians, Belorussians, Moldavians, and others—all of them fell in the war against the fascist invaders as faithful sons of their respective peoples. Monuments were erected in their honor throughout the land. But let no mention ever be made of the Jews. Is it surprising that to this very day no memorial has been erected to the victims of Babi Yar, the slaughter field near Kiev, where eighty thousand

Jews were liquidated all at one time? And even now that the bold poem of Yevtushenko has been heard, and in spite of it, Babi Yar remains desolate while residential buildings rise around it. Soon it will be blotted out. Western tourists may still nag the Intourist guides and ask where Babi Yar is, but the latter will evade the question. Only a taxi driver will perhaps take the determined tourist to the place of slaughter, and then will watch as he leaves the cab and stands in silence and sheds tears by the deserted and desolate spot.

And what of Fonar, the collective grave of Vilna's Jews? When the huge monument to the murdered thousands was erected, the Jews of Vilna engraved on it an epitaph written both in Russian and Yiddish. Shortly thereafter, the local authorities began urging the heads of the Vilna community to obliterate the Hebrew letters. When they refused, the authorities sent workmen who poured cement over the epitaph, then engraved on the monument a new inscription in Russian which does not indicate even by a word that the victims were Jews. This is only one step removed from defamation of the Jews and their share in the war: it is claimed that not only did the Jews fight poorly against the Nazi foe, they also tried to evade combat and fled from the front. Soviet Jews repeatedly confess, with pain and shame, that when they wear their medals they are mocked with, "Where did you buy these medals, in the Tashkent market place?" These "medals of the Tashkent market place" are a taunting accusation that most Jews fled to Central Asia far away from the dangers of war, and there, in the bazaar, purchased the military medals and decorations which they now dare to wear on their chests.

I visited the city of Bobruisk in Belorussia. The Intourist people arranged a meeting with the mayor. I told him that his city is famous in my country, as some of the founders of the State of Israel were born and raised there. I mentioned the names of Berl Katznelson ("a great labor leader"), David Shimonovich ("a great national poet in my country"), Kadish Luz ("the Speaker of our Parliament") and others. The mayor listened, even took down the names, without moving an eyelid. I asked how many Jews lived in Bobruisk. He answered: "There are Jews but we have no specific statistics." I asked if there was a synagogue in town. "No," he answered. "The Jews have no synagogue because they do not need one." Led by a guide who was no doubt a Jew, I visited the city museum. I went with him from room to room until we came to a display of pictures, drawings, and documents which illustrated the participation of the people of Bobruisk and its surroundings in the Second World War. In this entire display there was not a single word about the Jews. I remarked: "Both of us know there was once a large Jewish community here with a proud past; we both know that there were thousands of Jews among the soldiers and partisans who died here; and we know that several thousand Jews still live here. Why isn't any of this mentioned in the display?" The guide looked at me sadly (he himself limped on one leg as a result of war injuries) but said nothing.

Next day I visited a neighboring town and, together with an Israeli family, rowed across the famous Berezina River, which flows through the town, to the public beach on the opposite bank. When we came ashore, a man of about forty-five got out of the water. The upper part of his body was muscular, handsome, and athletic, but his legs were disfigured as a result of surgery and he waddled like a duck. He identified us at once as Israelis and in front of everyone fell on our necks, shouting: "Take me away with you, let me join the Israeli Army and die in its ranks. Look at me. I was wounded three times in battle and kept on fighting. I am now a building workman and I can hardly climb the scaffolding; and whenever the workmen taunt me about the Tashkent medals, the blood rises to my head and I hit anyone who says it, and get beaten in return. I have no more strength! Take me with you!" Other Jews who were nearby tried to pacify him because he was getting more and more excited as he went on. He pushed them aside and cried: "What have I to fear? From whom? Go to hell!" When he calmed down somewhat and we had moved on, the others said to me: "You have to forgive him. After everything that had happened to him, his young son was murdered, and he had a nervous breakdown."

This is what happened to the son. Handsome and very talented, he had succeeded in becoming a teacher and sports instructor in the city school. He was very much liked by his pupils. One day, some two years before, he went out of the school building to the main street and saw a policeman stop one of his pupils, a non-Jew, who was riding a bicycle, for a traffic offense. The young instructor went over and asked the policeman what was wrong. The latter answered rudely that it was none of his business and told him to leave. The teacher said that he wanted to go with them to the police station and testify to the boy's good character. The policeman told him to get out of there at once, and added a foul remark. As the teacher argued with him, the policeman suddenly cursed: "Dirty Jew!" Losing his temper, the instructor approached the policeman threateningly. The policeman took out his pistol and shot him dead on the spot. He was sentenced to two years in prison but was released a few months later for good behavior. "You must understand the father's feelings," said the Jews, "and overlook his outburst."

Paul Robeson and his Yiddish songs

The ways Jews feel when someone tells them that not all of them bought medals in the Tashkent market place, but that there were also Jews who fought heroically, is illustrated by the episode of Paul Robeson's appearance. Early in 1959 the Soviet authorities decided to demonstrate their good will toward the Jews by celebrating Sholem Aleichem's centennial birthdate. A series of Sholem Aleichem evenings was organized in the major cities of the Soviet Union. This act, which was followed by the publication of three Yiddish booklets, portended a fresh start in the minds of some Jews; but even those who had no illusions about these Sholem Aleichem evenings would not have missed attending them.

The crowning feature of this celebration was a great festive evening in Kolonnyi Zal, Moscow's famous colonnaded hall. The gala performance was presented under the auspices of the Writers Union of the U.S.S.R., the most prestigious body in Soviet literature. I obtained a ticket by mere chance. The hall was packed when I got there and many people could not be admitted for lack of seats.

On the stage were seated some of the surviving Jewish writers, and among them, in the center, the Russian writers Surkov and Polevoi, leaders of the Union. At the center of the speaker's table on the stage, sat Paul Robeson, the American Negro singer, a famous figure in the Soviet Union who happened to be in Moscow at the time.

The evening was opened by some of the Jewish writers, who repeatedly described Sholem Aleichem as one of the greatest Jewish writers of all time. They stressed time and again that he had defended the humble and poor Jewish proletarians against the exploiting bourgeois Jews who had thrived in the Jewish towns. In their view, Sholem Aleichem had really heralded the development of socialist and communist literature, just as Gorki had done in Russian literature.

Some artists then read selections from Sholem Aleichem, to the great delight of the audience. Then came Robeson's turn. He was greeted with wild applause, for it was no small matter for a Jewish audience to be honored by the presence of the great Robeson. He does not speak Russian and was assisted by a female translator who stood by his side. He did not use notes and I am certain that his remarks were neither censored nor edited beforehand. He started out by saying that, actually, Jews and Negroes share a similar fate, and when this was translated into Russian, it was greeted with enthusiastic applause. But I noticed immediately that the organizers, Polevoi in particular, looked embarrassed. Robeson went on to say that his grandchildren in the United States were half-Jewish and half-Negro and that he loved to sing them lullabies in Yiddish, a rich and wonderful language (another storm of applause). Then he told the audience how impressed he had been several years ago, by the Sholem Aleichem performances in the Jewish theater in the Soviet Union; and not only by his plays but by the high standard of the great theater and, in particular, its greatest actor, Schlomo Mikhoels (a name that was avoided until that moment, especially in a Jewish gathering, for, having been a victim of Stalin's liquidations, Mikhoels brought back memories of past guilt). He then described how Mikhoels had played Shakespeare's King Lear, and said that it had been one of the finest Shakespearean performances he had ever seen. Robeson continued: "But don't imagine that you are the only ones who love Jewish literature and culture. In the United States the Jews have great cultural institutions, seminaries, teachers, schools, academies of literature, poetry, drama and Jewish song." As he continued in this vein, with the crowd applauding every sentence, I saw that the interpreter was virtually choking over her translation and that Polevoi was shooting furious looks at the unfortunate woman and at Robeson.

When Robeson finished his complimentary remarks about Jewish culture, he concluded: "Fine, now I will sing some songs in Yiddish, a language I love." In his deep and wonderful voice, he opened with some folksongs—*"Suntig bulbes,"* and others—and the audience, spellbound, enjoyed every minute of it and responded with peals of laughter and applause. Then Robeson raised his hand and said: "I shall now go from folksongs and cheerful tunes to a special kind of song, sad but wonderful, which I heard from Jewish partisans when I visited the ruins of the Warsaw ghetto. As you all know, the Jewish heroes of the ghetto fought a battle which was probably the most desperate and courageous of all peoples' wars for independence and honor. I learned this partisan song from the survivors who sang it on the barricades and in the bunkers as they fought their people's war. I'll sing for you 'The Song of the Jewish Partisans'!" As the words were translated, I felt an electric current coursing through the audience. The people froze in their seats, stunned. Jewish fighting songs, Jewish partisans fighting for their people—these were concepts every Jew in the Soviet Union carried deep in his heart; but they were never to be mentioned aloud, because they did not exist in the eyes of the authorities. And here, one of the greatest singers in the world, a man who was loved by the Soviet people, was talking about it openly and with such pride!

In a spellbound hall, Robeson sang in Yiddish: "Never say this is the final path I tread." I shall never forget those moments, nor will the thousands who were present. It seemed as though Robeson sensed the significance of the unusual tension in the hall and that he utterly surpassed himself in the power of the feeling he poured into this superb war song.

When he finished, there was a long moment of silence. The audience was too deeply moved. Then, all of a sudden, like an approaching storm, there arose a thunderous wave of applause, and it went on and on, and it would not end, it would not end, it seemed as if it would never end. All their suffering, pain and humiliation, all their yearnings and longings, were put into their clapping hands; and in the rhythmic pounding of thousands of hands, the audience let everyone know what they bore in their hearts and minds.

Robeson repeated the last bar of the song again and again until the crowd grew calm.

He was the last to appear that evening. But since it was impossible to conclude on such a note, Boris Polevoi, pale with fury, got up, and, turning to the Negro singer, asked him, demanded of him: "Will you please now sing a Russian folksong, and may I request that you sing one which we love so much, *'Broad and Wide is My Homeland.'*" Robeson obliged and sang the beautiful Russian patriotic national song, which ends, "For like ours, there is no other where man draws his breath so proud and free." And when Robeson concluded the last stanza, Polevoi rose again and repeated it with emphasis. He directed his hand at the people, and, pointing a finger which was almost threatening, said: "For like ours, there is no other where man draws his breath so proud and free." The Jews understood the inference.

I don't know whether anyone conveyed to Paul Robeson what he had done that wonderful night, what chords he had touched, what springs he had opened, if only for a few minutes, in the hearts of his Jewish audience.

Why did Khrushchev and those who followed him retain the wasteland policy they had inherited from Stalin? What are the motives that caused him and his successors to perpetuate that policy to this day, though without resorting to Stalin's threats of physical terror. In order to answer this we must leave aside for the moment the national aspect, the millions of solitary Jews who are registered as Jews despite the fact that they have no real basis for their nationality, and take up another aspect of the problem—Judaism as a religion in the Soviet Union.

3

A Religion Among Religions

Judaism is not merely an opiate

As already noted, the Soviet authorities regard the Jewish faith as one of the world religions which has adherents among its citizenry. Its situation is therefore not different from that of the Russian Orthodox, Catholic, Moslem, Buddhist, or other faiths in the Soviet Union. Militant atheism has been, and remains, one of the main pillars of the communist credo. As Karl Marx said: "Religion is the opiate of the people." Churches of all denominations are regarded as instruments wielded by the capitalist system to exploit the ignorance of the masses. It is the duty of communism, which epitomizes knowledge and progress, to combat religion to the bitter end. This is one of the main dogmas which the government of the Soviet Union has tried to realize since its inception. In fact it has managed to destroy the powerful organization of the Russian Orthodox Church, leaving only a skeleton which it uses for its own needs. The government has also fought the Moslem religion and its institutions, the Catholic faith and its churches, the Protestant sects of the Soviet Union, as well as the Jewish religion.

It is clear that up to this point there is at first glance no discrimination in the treatment of the various faiths. But when we come to examine the problem as it affects only Jews and Judaism, there is a semantic factor which differentiates the status of Jews, whether religious or not, from that of all other faiths.

It would not be playing with words to say that the meaning of the term "Jew," in the Russian *evrei*, points in two different directions: to the Jewish people as a nationality *(evreiskaia natsionalnost)*, and to the Jewish religion *(evreiskaia religiia)*. This fateful link has pursued the Jew in all lands throughout the centuries. The Soviets are not the first to face the problem and ask: Is Judaism a religion? Is it a nation? Is it a national religion? Or are the Jews a religious nationality? This philosophic-historic problem has been debated by Jewish and non-Jewish thinkers and scholars everywhere, and the answers have been as diverse as those who pondered the questions. Obviously no answer can be found until there is agreement on the definition of the terms "nation," "people," and "religion." We are giving this problem serious attention in Israel, as are the best Jewish thinkers in the United States and other centers of the Jewish Diaspora. But we have not been, and I doubt if we ever will be, able to define precisely who we are. Perhaps this uncertainty is in itself an indication of our unique status. Perhaps the feeling of being Jewish, together with our awareness of the great history of the Jewish tradition and its spiritual heritage, as well as the common memory of persecution and, at present, the concrete link with the Jewish State of Israel—perhaps all of these, together, serve to unite the Jews of the world.

In the Soviet Union, however, the peculiar semantic link between the term "Jewish religion" and the term "Jewish nationality" has had the most grievous impact on the Jews. It must be borne in mind that when the Soviet regime persecutes the Russian Orthodox faith, it does not aim at the Ukrainian nationals of this faith; on the contrary, the two are completely separated. The Ukrainian national is proud of his rich background and history, and when Orthodox priests and churches are persecuted, no harm is intended to Ukrainians as such. When a Lithuanian youth reads an atheistic manifesto which damns the Catholic Church and the Pope, he does not feel that he is being discriminated against as a Lithuanian national. The two are unconnected. On the contrary, his feelings as a Lithuanian are kindled and so is his pride in belonging to that nation. The fact that his uncle attends a Catholic church in Vilna and that the authorities do not look upon this kindly, does not trouble him too much. When an anti-religious tract is published in Uzbekistan containing derisive remarks against the Moslem religion, the Uzbek national is not upset. He remains a proud and self-respecting Uzbek and is not at all concerned by the fact that his grandfather's attendance at the mosque is regarded with displeasure by the authorities.

We are not going to discuss the question, interesting though it may be, of the Soviet Union's success or failure in its anti-religious drive. Much has been written about whether or not a half-century of atheistic rule has managed to uproot the traditional religious beliefs of the people. The point we wish to make is that, except in the case of the Jews, a complete distinction is made between religion and nationality. For when the Jewish religion is debased, every Jew, by the mere fact of his identification with the word "Jew," senses that this attack affects him and is aimed at him, directly or indirectly.

We must stress again that as a member of the Jewish nation every Jew in Russia today feels as if he is standing with his back to the wall, or, rather, with his back to an abyss of ignorance as to what constitutes Jewish nationality, an ignorance born of his own lack of knowledge of the Jewish language and culture. Let us remember that under present conditions, the Jew, as a member of the Jewish nation, is offered no reciprocal benefit or positive value that will symbolize his Jewishness. Because of the semantic affinity between the term "Jewish religion" and the term "Jewish nationality," the Jew in Russia is the butt of endless attacks against the Jewish faith. He reads continually that the Jewish religion is barbaric, polluted, exploitative, and reactionary. These negative attributes, related to something to which he is willy-nilly attached, are the only traits by which he can identify himself, his origin, and his past. Were he to believe all that is said about the Jewish religion, he would be bound to regard himself and his forefathers as being of doubtful, corrupt, and tainted origin. It is not difficult, therefore, to picture his moral situation.

But that is only one aspect of the situation. Actually, the Soviet authorities persecute the Jewish religion to a far greater extent than they do the other religions. To paraphrase Orwell, the regime claims that "All religions are equally reactionary, but the Jewish religion is more so."

What is the reason for this greater persecution?

The numerous atheistic booklets against Judaism seem to provide a clear answer. First, the Soviet ideologists argue that the Jewish religion is the mother of the great religions, namely, Christianity and Islam. Christianity was actually conceived in the womb of Judaism and was nursed at its breast. Islam was, at its inception, deeply influenced by Judaism. If one must fight the great religions, the first to be fought should be the one that gave rise to all the others. Second, the Soviets argue that though all the other religions are evil and corrupt, at least they do not encourage emigration from the native land of their followers. The Russian Orthodox Church preaches the Kingdom of Heaven, the transfiguration of the soul and the trinity, but it does not enjoin its believers to abandon Zagorsk or Moscow. The Catholic Church does not encourage its followers in Vilna, for instance, to go and live in the Vatican. The pious Moslem must pray facing toward Mecca, and a pilgrimage to Mecca is a meritorious deed; but Islam does not request that its followers emigrate and settle in Saudi Arabia. But Judaism, the Soviet ideologists say, is not only a reactionary faith, it also encourages the belief in a second spiritual motherland and in actual emigration to a country outside the Soviet Union. The Jewish religion, in short, is first of all Zionist, and its prophets are Zionist proselytizers: Isaiah, Jeremiah, Amos, Ezekiel, and others like them are propagandists for Zion and Jerusalem. The Jewish prayer book requires the faithful to pray three times a day for a return to Zion. Why should a Jewish citizen living in Kharkov or Bukhara go to Jerusalem? Why should he pray to his God to take him out of the Soviet Union and bring him to some little country in the Middle East?

Moreover, such a Jew also wants to educate his children —who are faithful citizens of the Soviet Union nurtured by the communist regime—to pray for emigration to Jerusalem. This is clearly anti-Soviet propaganda which, under the guise of religion, calls on people to run away from the Soviet Union. Assuming that one could buttonhole a Soviet emissary while he is visiting the West (for it is impossible to reach him, or anyone else with whom such discussion would be fruitful, inside the Soviet Union), it might be explained that, for pious Jews, the Jerusalem in question is the one referred to in the Bible or the prayer book, and means the heavenly Jerusalem, a concept related to the Kingdom of Heaven and the End of Days; that not all

Jews identify their religion with emigration to Israel; that in Brooklyn there are many orthodox Jews who fervently pray "May our eyes behold Thy return to Zion in mercy," but who do not, after their services, rush to the booking offices of El Al or Zim to buy a ticket to Jerusalem. Actually, only two million Jews live in Israel, while at least four times as many (not counting the Soviet Jews) live in other lands. The Bible and prayer book do not prevent their staying where they are, without any qualms, as faithful citizens of their respective lands.

But the whole argument is pointless, since the Soviets retort that they are the only ones who can see through the deceit and hypocrisy of the Jewish faith which enjoins the faithful to run away to Israel after having extorted all they can from their present homes. The Soviets argue further that the Jewish faith is particularly dangerous because it proclaims that Jews are responsible for one another. The saying "All Israel are brothers" indicates a mystic tie that must exist between the Jews of Moscow and New York, between the Jews of Khabarovsk and Los Angeles, between the Jews of Leningrad and Johannesburg, and certainly between all of these and the Jews of Tel Aviv and Jerusalem

These and similar arguments can be read by anyone for a few rubles; they can be found in dozens of booklets, folders, atheist books and pamphlets which have been published and are still being published throughout the Soviet Union.

The big stick wielded by the regime against the Jewish religion takes many forms. Jews are forbidden to organize; they cannot maintain a line of continuity for religious leadership (training of rabbis); synagogues are shut down gradually but relentlessly, and those still open are defamed; the government also tries to interfere with, or prevent, the observance of the fundamental religious practices of Judaism.

How does the problem of organization or the maintenance of continuity affect other religions? Even after the government stripped the Russian Orthodox Church of its power, it still granted it sufficient strength and vitality to carry on, and left intact its organizational structure. Zagorsk, the capital city of the Russian Orthodox Church, is still the seat of its titular head and his subordinates. All local churches are directly linked to the central headquarters and all priests are firmly established in a well-regulated hierarchy. Printed material is distributed by the central headquarters, which has permission to publish prayer books as well. It also maintains a government authorized seminary for the training of priests. The heads of the Russian Orthodox Church are welcome figures at various national functions; where it suits the needs of the central authorities they even appear in all their splendor at cocktail parties given by foreign embassies in Moscow. They show up frequently at denominational or interdenominational Church conventions throughout the world, and one meets their delegates at congresses held in Constantinople, India, Rome, Athens, and other places where the heads of the world's major religions gather. This activity is conducted, naturally, under the strict control and supervision of the Soviet authorities; but it is maintained and even encouraged.

The Islamic religion in the Soviet Union possesses a widespread organization, headed by a Grand Mufti who lives in Tashkent and presides over a hierarchy of *Ulema* (priests) who officiate in the mosques of Azerbaijan, Uzbekistan, Tajikistan, Turkmenistan, and other parts of the Soviet Union where Moslems live. A seminary in Bukhara trains Moslem priests from early youth and bestows upon them the title of *mulah* after a six year period of study.

I happened to visit this seminary, which is housed in an ancient and beautiful Moslem-style building. The place is suffused with vitality and learning. The students use the Koran and other Moslem religious texts published in Tashkent. At the same time they are indoctrinated into the principles of Marxism-Leninism on a very high level. The end product is a blend of Moslem priest and communist propagandist. Leading Islamic figures from the Moslem countries of Asia and Africa are occasionally brought to Bukhara, and there is no doubt that this constitutes good export propaganda material. Moslems, particularly the priests, have no difficulty arranging their pilgrimage to Mecca, and the Russian authorities find it to their advantage to have prestigious delegations from the Soviet Union participate in these pilgrimages.

The Buddhists also have a hierarchy of monks and priests in Siberia, in the borderlands of Mongolia and China, as well as in the Central Asian regions that border on China. I was told that when Dr. Malalaskara, the Ceylonese ambassador to Moscow, married his daughter to a young man of Colombo and arranged an imposing ceremony at the embassy, the Russian authorities flew in groups of Buddhist monks, complete with yellow robes, scrolls, and musical instruments. It was the talk of the day in the diplomatic colony of Moscow.

In the Armenian Vatican

The Armenian religion is in a particularly advantageous position. The Armenians, as is well known, have their own republic in the Soviet Union, but there are also a large number of them scattered throughout the world. They were among the first peoples to adopt Christianity, and they are very proud of this fact. They are now split into several factions; the headquarters of the most important of these factions, the Monophysite-Gregorian, is in Echmiadzin, not far from Erevan, the capital.

Echmiadzin is like a Vatican to the Armenian faithful, and I had the pleasure of visiting it. I was received at the entrance to the church (or rather a large aggregate of churches, monasteries, and schools) by a young Armenian priest into whose care I was entrusted by the Intourist guide. The guide did not interfere from that moment. Quite the contrary, he walked around the place as if on tiptoes. Our host showed us around the well-maintained, neat churches and monasteries, and proudly pointed out the beautiful objects inside them. "We received this marble altar from the Armenians in Italy," he said. "These rugs came from the Armenians in India. That large organ was sent three years ago as a gift of the Armenian congregation in London"; and so on. When we got to the printing house, which was in one of the adjoining buildings, our host pointed to a number of large crates and told us that they contained modern printing presses which the Armenian community of the United States had just sent over.

At the head of the Armenian Church is the Chief Patriarch, who is called the Supreme Catholicos of the Armenian Church, and whose authority is similar to that of the Pope. I requested an interview with him and after waiting for half an hour in a wonderfully kept garden, another priest appeared and told me: "His Holiness, Catholicos Vazgen I, will be glad to receive you."

Vazgen I, a youngish, handsome man, greeted me in his

sumptuous office. The subject of our conversation was the state of the Armenian community in the Holy Land. The Soviet government encourages Armenians in every part of the world to make pilgrimages to their religious and spiritual center in Armenia. Thousands upon thousands of Armenians flock to Echmiadzin, carrying gifts, and the authorities encourage the bringing of contributions to this spiritual center from all parts of the Armenian dispersion. I believe the only "private" place of business in the Soviet Union is the shop that the Armenian Catholicos has opened in Erevan with the permission of the authorities. There, all kinds of gifts which have come from overseas are sold. The proceeds, I was given to understand, are used for archeological excavations, for the maintenance of historic sites of the Church in Armenia, for the repair and construction of buildings in Echmiadzin itself, and for churches and monasteries in other parts of Armenia.

This is what happens when the government believes that it can profit not only from the preservation of an existing Church organization but also from the further development of it for the benefit of a religious group which, though scattered the world over, acknowledges its spiritual center as lying within the Soviet Union.

With this as a background we can now discuss the state of the Jewish religion in the Soviet Union.

To begin with, it has not even the semblance of an overall organizational structure. This constitutes the first big stick wielded against it by the authorities.

Readers of the Israeli or Western press sometimes get the impression that there is a Chief Rabbi of Russian Jewry. This title is sometimes used to describe the rabbi of the Moscow congregation. But this is only a euphemism used by Jews living outside Russia who look for some sort of consolation in the face of the tragedy of Russian Jewry. It is they who bestow this honorific title, which has no basis in reality. The Soviet government recognizes neither a Chief Rabbi nor any rabbi whose authority extends beyond the boundaries of the religious community of the large city or small town where he officiates. The Jewish faith has no hierarchy and the rabbi of the religious Jewish congregation in Moscow is equal in Soviet eyes to the rabbi of Batumi in Georgia. And not only is there no hierarchy, there also does not and cannot exist any recognized and permanent link between the rabbis and the leaders of the various religious Jewish communities.

The situation is due to the nature of the "religious Jewish community" (*evreiskaia religioznaia obshchina*), the only Jewish religious body recognized by the Soviets. This institution is always connected solely with the one local synagogue of a city or of a section of a city, and never with an area that is more extensive than the town in which it is located. The government stipulates that twenty Jews, known to and authorized by the authorities, shall be responsible to it for all activities in a given synagogue. When we speak of the authorities in this instance, we refer to the responsible official (*upolnomochennyi*) appointed by the Department of Religions in that town. This department is a special official body, an extension of the Committee on Ritual and Religious Affairs of the Council of Ministers, and its task is to supervise all religions and religious institutions in the Soviet Union. Close ties no doubt exist between the Committee, or its allied bodies, and the central security organization of the Soviets (K.G.B.); it may even be an integral part of the security organization. The law requires that these Jews, called *dvadtsatka* (the twenty), be elected in accordance with a plan predetermined from above, and must include a chairman, finance committee, auditing committee, and so on. They must conduct meetings and keep minutes, which they are required to present to the Department of Religions at fixed intervals. The *dvadtsatka* includes the *gabbai* (director) of the synagogue and the heads of the congregation. When they select a rabbi for the religious community his appointment must first be confirmed by the authorities. Consequently the "religious Jewish community" in any given town is only a body representing one synagogue directed by twenty Jews.

Thus, for example, Leningrad, with a Jewish population in excess of a quarter of a million, has one religious community and one synagogue. Kiev, with its two hundred thousand Jews, has one religious community and one synagogue. Odessa, with two hundred thousand Jews, also has one religious community and one synagogue. The same is true of dozens of other cities which still possess a synagogue. Only in Moscow and in a few towns in Central Asia and the Caucasus is there more than one synagogue. (In addition to its central synagogue, Moscow has two small synagogues located in distant parts of the city.) But even where more than one synagogue is maintained within the confines of a town, they are not together as one religious community but are entirely separate.

Insofar as the authorities are concerned, every community is therefore considered a completely separate unit, and no rabbi or *gabbai* of any given congregation can maintain any connection with another community. Jews meet, of course, and when the rabbi of a provincial town comes to Moscow, he calls on the rabbi of Moscow for a chat. But this is casual; no overall organization exists; nor are any regular rabbinic meetings ever held.

Another big stick which the authorities wield over the Jewish religion consists in the difficulties they create in the matter of training future religious leaders and in the way they maintain a stranglehold over the educational insitutions which could produce them.

At present the average age of rabbis officiating in the few dozen Jewish congregations in the Soviet Union is quite advanced. Most of these rabbis are old men, and there is no line of continuity in sight. Whereas the Russian Orthodox, Armenians, Moslems, and other religions are permitted to maintain seminaries and regular religious colleges, the authorities have restricted the Jews to one yeshiva affiliated with the synagoguge of Moscow, and its existence is more fictitious than real. Nothing could be poorer or more humble. The maximum number of students it has ever had was little more than a dozen. The average age of the Ashkenazi students is over forty. The few young Jews from Georgia or Bukhara who once managed, with great difficulty, to join the yeshiva, lived in fear of breaking the law and doing something contrary to the wishes of the authorities. Not much time passed before they were forbidden to attend.

Only three or four students attend this yeshiva today. Its standards of learning are very low; there are hardly any books, and it is simply unqualified to grant its students any sort of ordination. It is a wonder that this institution, which is so closely controlled and watched by the authorities, can exist at all. The fact that it somehow does exist may be attributed, firstly, to the wonderful spirit of sacrifice of some of the scholarly old gentlemen who maintain a class of Talmud and Responsa for its few students; and, secondly, to the desire on the part of the authorities to preserve this skeleton body and not let it desintegrate completely, so that they can boast to the West that "the Jews also have a religious seminary of their own," and that "the fact that it is attended by only a scant half-dozen students is striking proof that the Jews themselves are really not interested in this entire business of religion. Is there any sense to all these complaints against the authorities?"

In sum, if nothing occurs in the next few years to alter this situation, there will soon be no rabbi or *hacham* (rabbi of an Oriental Jewish community) or teacher of Jewish law anywhere in the entire Soviet Union.

Three stages in closing a synagogue

The government's third big stick is the rapid process whereby synagogues are closed, a process that goes hand in hand with the manner in which the Jewish religion is usually defamed. This procedure started, of course, with the very beginning of the Soviet regime, almost fifty years ago. The government at that time closed down hundreds of synagogues (and thousands of churches, too). But the closing of the synagogues that survived Stalin's rule continues to this day, though the operation is now carried out in stages, because there are not many left. If this process has been slowed down in recent years, I feel certain that it is due solely to the fear of causing repercussions in the West. The closing of synagogues proceeds from the marginal areas toward the center. The first to be taken in hand are small synagogues in the provincial towns of the republics, mainly in the Ukraine and in Belorussia. It is simpler, easier, and more natural to close a synagogue there than in Moscow, which is full of Western journalists, diplomats, and tourists who are sensitive to such things.

The pattern repeats itself in many cities and towns with remarkably little variation. In my opinion, this implies that not only is the general policy dictated from above but that the actual planning itself also comes from a central source. Only the details of the plan's execution are left in the hands of the responsible local officials.

There are three stages in the closing down process: the softening up stage—effected through the defamation of the synagogue and everything pertaining to it; the mobilization of public opinion; and the actual act of closing.

The closing down of the synagogue in Lvov a few years ago is one instance among many of how this process works. Lvov was a major Jewish center before the Holocaust. Nearly all of its Jews were murdered by the Nazis.

Other Jews assembled there after the war, including refugees from neighboring small towns in the Ukraine; others wandered to Lvov, which is near the western border of the Soviet Union, all the way from central and eastern Russia, possibly in the hope of penetrating beyond the Iron Curtain. About thirty or forty thousand Jews congregated there, arriving in small groups. A *dvadtsatka* was organized and the authorities permitted the Jews to open one little synagogue in a square behind the Lvov Opera House. I visited that synagogue and found it to be no different from any other of its kind in any provincial Soviet town. It was a poor, humble structure; a few dozen elderly Jews gathered for weekday services; a somewhat larger number of elderly Jews attended on Saturdays. The synagogue was not without the usual disputes and splits between the old Jews over "honors" and "functions." The authorities encouraged this with zest (as they do in all synagogues), by planting some "eyes and ears" of their own among the congregants, or by inviting individuals or groups to "tell everything" about their opponents. Then, suddenly, at the beginning of 1962, a series of seven articles appeared in the local *Lvovskaia Pravda* about this synagogue. It must be noted that a Russian feature story is a deadly weapon in the hands of the local or central authorities. Its purpose is to denounce people, groups, or some aspects of life in Soviet society which, in the view of the authorities, are due for criticism or must be expunged. The article usually contains the actual names of the people who are being denounced, and any individual or institution which is the target of the writer's attack is as good as doomed. Here are the approximate contents of the seven articles which appeared in *Lvovskaia Pravda:*

The first told the "dear readers" that in the heart of communist, progressive, and prosperous Lvov, there was an institution called a *sinagoga,* located at a certain number on a certain street, where rabbi so-and-so (name given) officiated. The story went on to give some details about Jewish rituals, using sarcastic and contemptuous terms. The writer than asked a rhetorical question: Does anyone really believe that the people of that synagogue busy themselves only with prayer when they come there? Then he provided the answer: Of course not. So what do they really do? He replied that they deal, first of all, in black marketeering: the synagogue is one of the centers of the black market in Lvov where foreign exchange is bought and sold, where gold rubles are changed into dollars, sterling, francs, and so on—all this under the guise of prayers to the God of Israel. This is how the first article ended. And the writer promised his public that a sequel would follow.

This appeared some time later. It opened on an intimate note: Do you remember the institution called *sinagoga* about which we wrote recently? Well, do you think that they deal there only in the black market under the guise of prayers? You're quite wrong. What else do they do, then, in this *sinagoga?* The writer answered: They encourage drunkenness. How so? It's very simple, he explained. The Jews conduct a rite which involves drinking wine and spirits. The rabbi who conducts the service sanctifies the alcohol and the whole congregation follows suit and drinks up. This goes on week after week. (Let it be noted that the newspaper readers of Lvov, in the Ukraine, are familiar with alcoholic beverages, and when they are told tales of drinking, they know what is meant, for they themselves drink their fill, and one sees many drunkards around Lvov, mainly on Sunday; but there is rarely a Jew among them.)

In the articles that followed, the writer told his audience that the synagogue in Lvov fulfills other functions. He related, for instance, that American Jewish tourists visited there, as did Israeli diplomats. None of them came there to pray. Their intentions were altogether different. The American Jews told the congregants how good it was in America (of course, everyone knows this is a lie) and the Israelis told fairy tales about the "Israeli Paradise" (and we all know this to be a falsehood, for Israel is a seething ground of imperialism and capitalism). These tourists left "presents" for the Jews, namely, prayer books and Bibles, which are, as is well known, Zionist propaganda and anti-Soviet tracts. The writer then ended his series of feature stories with a brief account about what goes on in Israel and how terrible life is there. According to him, the whole country is nothing but an armed camp, an advanced base of imperialism and neo-colonialism. It is ruled by obscurantist rabbis who are themselves connected with reactionary rabbis and institutions in the United States. These, in turn, work hand in hand with evil Wall Street (this derisive term is fed to Soviet children as one of the staples of communist education).

Here then is the entire picture: There is a synagogue in

Lvov in which a rabbi officiates. It is attended by old Jews who come there to deal in the black market and to drink. They are connected with the agents of capitalist countries who give them gifts and "spiritual nourishment" (and who knows what the givers get in return . . .). The Jews pray there every day to their God, begging Him to take them out of the Soviet Union and bring them to Jerusalem.

This is how the first stage, the softening-up process, was concluded. The distressed Jews of the Lvov synagogue waited in fear for what they knew was still to come. The second stage was not long in coming. Letters to the editor began to appear immediately after the series of articles. Young and old Jews showed up suddenly in the press, "impelled" by the articles to express their views in public. A young Jew wrote that he was a student at the local university and was scandalized by the articles. After the first shock, he consulted his Jewish friends in college (Jews, of course, are permitted to gather and consult for such purposes). On his own behalf and on behalf of his comrades, he appealed to the "dear comrade editor" and, through him, to the local authorities, to remove this blot from the fair city of Lvov—namely, to close the synagogue. Then an old Jew wrote that he was seventy-five years old, that he had attended such a *sinagoga* for decades, but that his eyes were opened only after he had read the wonderful articles in the paper. He admitted to having previously stumbled in the dark. He addressed himself, through the paper, to those attending the synagogue and asked them to consider the truth in these articles so that their eyes might be opened as well. And he requested the authorities to take steps to close the synagogue.

This is how the second stage, the mobilization of public opinion, was conducted.

The picture is now clear. Articles have been published on the synagogue, and they have aroused the protest of the citizens—*vox populi vox dei*. The Jewish citizens of Lvov, young and old alike, demand the closing of the synagogue (the gentiles of Lvov obviously will not object). What can the authorities do but close the synagogue?

This is of course the final stage. It does not require the use of the armed forces. It is enough for the *upolnomochennyi* of the Department of Reglions to send an order by messenger to the *dvadtsatka* to close the synagogue within a specified number of days, padlock it, and hand over the building to the authorities.

And this is what was done on November 5, 1962.

That is how it happened in Lvov and, in identical or similar fashion, in Kharkov, Chernovtsy, Bobruisk, Smolensk, and many other cities and small towns.

Occasionally the authorities couple the synagogues and illicit activity with show trials which end in heavy sentences or death by shooting. Again, we take what happened in Lvov as an example.

In March, 1962, the city put on trial a group of Jews who were accused of being profiteers and black marketeers. The two chief culprits were the ritual slaughterer Kantorovich and a Jew named Sapozhnikov, both members of the *dvadtsatka* of Lvov.

This is what *Lvovskaia Pravda* had to report: "The accused have dealt for years in speculation, purchase and sale of gold and diamonds. This traffic was conducted within the synagogue and its ringleaders were the *dvadtsatka* people, Kantorovich and Sapozhnikov. Speculators from other cities came there too, not to pray but to receive instructions from Kantorovich and then proceed on their travels to secure foreign exchange. In addition, the synagogue dealt in the illicit trade of penicillin and other drugs at prohibitive prices." Kantorovich was also convicted of conspiring against the national monopoly on wines: he made wine for "a religious rite" and he sold it at extortionist prices for "ritual festivals." Kantorovich and Sapozhnikov were sentenced to death by shooting.

The authorities not only persecute the officially recognized synagogues but, with still greater cruelty, the "gathering for purposes of prayer" of ten or more Jews (a *minyan*) in a room or an apartment. While the war against the official synagogue involves a specific effort and a bit of organizing on the part of the authorities, the problem of how to deal with the private *minyanim* is a simple one to resolve. By its very nature the *minyan* is illegal, and no house of prayer can be maintained unless it is organized under the rules of the *dvadtsatka*. In the cities and small towns where the synagogues have been closed, or in large cities where old Jews cannot walk long distances on Saturday or festivals to the existing synagogues, some Jews try to organize a *minyan;* but this is fraught with great danger. Housing conditions being what they are in the Soviet Union, with several families living in the same apartment, any Jew who desires to start a *minyan* must make certain that all the neighbors, Jews or non-Jews, will agree to the undertaking. On occasion they have to be bribed. And the *minyan* is in constant danger of being closed, usually as a result of the work of an informer. The person in whose apartment or room such a *minyan* is held, lives in constant fear of a raid by the authorities. They will disperse the *minyan*, confiscate the one and only Scroll of the Law and the few prayer books, and arrest him for criminal behaviour.

With the approach of the High Holidays, *minyanim* appear here and there, mainly in the cities where thousands of Jews live and where there is not even one synagogue. This is the time when the authorities get busy and instigate a sudden combing operation of suspected houses in order to frighten the old Jews. Then during the holidays, when fearful worshipers gather, the authorities will occasionally enter the room where the *minyan* is being held, stop the service, and disperse the Jews.

The story of Shechter the circumciser

The fourth stick wielded against the Jewish faith is directed at "the barbaric ceremonials and rituals of the reactionary Jewish religion," particularly circumcision. The war waged against circumcision is subtle and somewhat complex. It does not call for a flourish of feature articles and news items in the papers, possibly because the subject touches upon sex, which is not publicly discussed in pseudo-Victorian Soviet society. Nevertheless, in the atheistic booklets which attack the Jewish religion, the readers are informed about circumcision and are told that it is "rooted in the rites of savage and primitive tribes." But the main battle against circumcision is more indirect. The campaign is waged not only against the ritual itself but also against those who carry it out.

This is the way it is done. When a Jew, usually aged, is caught performing a circumcision, he is asked: Comrade, is it true that on such and such a date, at this and that place, you performed a surgical operation on an eight-day-old Soviet citizen, whose name is so-and-so? When this is admitted, the interrogation continues: And where is your surgical diploma? Where did you study medicine? Who licensed you to perform surgical operations on people? If the circumciser claims that this surgery has been his occupation for decades, they will tell him, in no uncertain terms, that he is breaking Soviet law and that if he is caught at it again, he will be arrested and convicted of a serious crime.

At certain times, the government uses the matter of circumcision as a spearpoint to strike at the whole crumbling structure of the Jewish religion. A typical instance of this is what happened to Shechter, the circumciser of Chernovtsy.

In Chernovtsy (capital of Bukovina, which was once part of Rumania, and was annexed after the war to the Soviet Ukraine) there are today about seventy thousand Jews, comprising approximately half of the city's population. The Jewish community of Chernovtsy was once famous for its flourishing religious and secular institutions, but at the time of the Shechter incident in 1959, only two small synagogues remained; the others had been closed by the Lvov technique, the latest occurrence having taken place in 1962.

A young Jewish couple was blessed with a male child. The parents, like most local Jews, had been reared in the Jewish tradition and wanted their son to be circumcised. (No one, of course, thought of making it the festive occasion it traditionally is, a most inadvisable idea.) They turned to Shechter, one of those who clandestinely performed such ceremonies in the community. He came and circumcised the baby. Some days later, the mother was frightened when the baby bled. The father tried to locate Shechter, but he was not in town that day, having gone somewhere else to perform another circumcision. The panicky parents called an ambulance to take the child to a clinic. He was treated by a young Jewish doctor, who bandaged the wound and calmed the parents. He said it was nothing serious. They took the baby home and the whole incident would have been forgotten had it not been for the non-Jewish ambulance driver, who reported the incident to the authorities.

The authorities decided to deal seriously with the matter. They arrested the father and, through him, found out about Shechter. He did not deny having performed the ceremony and was arrested. Two months later, posters were put up in the town inviting the public to come to the

Philharmonic Hall in Chernovtsy for an "evening of Jewish culture" connected with some atheistic activity. Few of those present were able to guess what kind of "Jewish culture" they would witness. The Jewish public, avid for anything having to do with Judaism, hoped that, following the stereotyped lecture on atheism, they would be treated to some Yiddish songs or a reading from Sholem Aleichem.

Instead, there appeared on the stage all those involved in the Shechter incident. First, the father told the audience that under the influence of tradition he had placed the baby in the hands of the circumciser; that after the barbaric ritual had been performed under unspeakably unsanitary conditions, the cut had bled again; and that thanks to the achievements of modern medicine in the Soviet hospital, the child's life was saved. The father told the audience that this had cured him for good. He appreciated now what a mistake he had made and said that he would never repeat it. Then came the Jewish doctor who told his version of the story. He explained how dreadful the incident was from a medical point of view, how it negated the achievements of Soviet science, and violated the most elementary principles of sanitation and hygiene. Then Shechter, the "star of the show," appeared on the scene, a broken man.

He told the people that he had performed these barbaric rites for decades, that this was his livelihood and he could do no other constructive work. However, he did not appreciate until this incident how vile his profession had been. But now, after it had all been explained to him, he was convinced that the operations he had performed on these babies were not only illicit but also opposed to advanced Soviet medicine. He promised the assembled audience that he would never again go back to this occupation and he appealed to all the young parents present not to be led astray by primitive religious symbolism and not to place their children in the polluted hands of circumcisers.

Finally, to inject a bit of variety into this "evening of Jewish culture," the organizers introduced a pair of "expatriates" from Israel (the authorities hold in readiness "local color teams" of Israeli "expatriates" who speak occasionally over the radio, television, or at lectures, to tell "the whole truth about Israel"). They related that they had lived a year in Israel and recounted the "facts of life" there. They talked about the terrible heat, the debilitating unemployment, the life of fearful exploitation in the *kib-*

butz, the rule of reactionary rabbis, about the country being one vast armed camp, and so on. This ended the "evening of Jewish culture." One can imagine how the hundreds of Jews felt as they filed out of the hall.

But that was not enough. The authorities felt that the wider Jewish public as well as the non-Jewish Bukovinian Ukrainians with their centuries-old known tradition of anti-Semitism, should share equally in the benefits of the "evening of Jewish culture." The full story of the Shechter incident appeared in the Chernovtsy *Radianskaia Bukovina,* complete with pictures of the father, the doctor, and Shechter.

This is what happened in the Chernovtsky community, where the Jewish population has been cut off from its traditional moorings only since the end of the Second World War. But among the Jews living in the heart of the Soviet Union, who have been divorced from their past for three generations, there are very few circumcisers left, and it is no surprise that large numbers of Jews there are not circumcised at all.

Once, a naked and lovely two-year-old baby attached himself to me at a beach on the Black Sea. After a while his grandfather came to take him away. He apologized and asked if the child was annoying me. Then his eyes fell on a Hebrew paper lying near me, and he was astounded. He would not leave me until he had heard as much as possible about Israel. He played with the baby on his knees; then with tears in his eyes, he said: "Look at my grandchild, a Jewish child. He has not been circumcised. What can we do; we have no circumciser in our town and my son does not want to risk going to the big city to find a circumciser illegally." He murmured again and again: "My grandchild is not circumcised, my grandchild is not circumcised."

The measures taken to separate the Jews from their traditional ties also affect the rites which mark a turning point in the life of a Jew (bar mitzvah, Jewish marriage, and burial), and the observance of Jewish festivals.

If circumcision is the most significant Jewish rite, the next is the admission of the Jewish boy to religious maturity when he becomes a bar mitzvah. Because this rite, in which a boy is called to the pulpit to recite the blessings over the Torah, is inextricably tied to the synagogue (unlike circumcision which can be performed clandestinely), parents wishing to celebrate their son's attainment to the

status of bar mitzvah must take the risk of a public performance in a synagogue. And, indeed, I never saw a boy
called to the reading of the Law on my numerous visits to
the great synagogues of Moscow and Leningrad. Yet these
cities contain hundreds of thousands of Jews. No one except the Soviet authorities would dare maintain that there
are not at least a few hundred or a few dozen parents out
of these hundreds of thousands of Jews, who do not wish,
with all their heart, to see their thirteen-year-old boy
called to recite the blessings over the Torah. The ceremony is not only replete with religious significance but it
has a tremendous value in terms of Jewish sentiment and
the sense of attachment to the Jewish heritage. It is a fact,
though, that none of them dares bring his son to the synagogue for a bar mitzvah celebration. The reason for this is
as simple as it is clear: the synagogue is accessible to everyone, including informers of every kind. The parents are
justified in fearing that the boy's appearance in the synagogue will be entered sooner or later in his school record.
This record would state that he had "taken part on this-
and-this day in a reactionary Jewish religious ritual in the
synagogue." This would serve only to worsen his already
delicate status as a Jew in the school. Why, the parents ask
themselves, should they purposely handicap their son and
place additional obstacles in the path of his progress and
studies? And so they heave a sigh and give up the idea of
celebrating his bar mitzvah.

The same is true in the case of marriage. Religious marriage is not recognized by Soviet law. Only civil marriage
is binding. Nevertheless, there are quite a few parents who
would want their children to be married by a rabbi as
well. But they are deterred by a feeling that this might
hurt the young couple who have just completed their education and are only now beginning to venture into Soviet
life and society. Why damage their prospects? And so they
give up the idea of a ceremony. A little more daring is evident, nevertheless, where marriage is concerned, and one
sometimes sees a wedding performed by a rabbi. But it is
all done surreptitiously and hurriedly; and the percentage
of Jews who have a Jewish wedding ceremony is very
small indeed.

No more consecrated ground

The same difficulties apply to burial. Here the break between Jews and their traditional rites is not so rapid. This is natural, for the dying are in most cases old and devout people. More important, their being buried in a Jewish cemetery will not interfere with their "career." That is why their families feel safer in maintaining the traditional burial customs.

The government, on the other hand, obstructs Jewish burial in various and peculiar ways. As long as there was enough room in the old Jewish cemeteries, people were allowed to bury their dead there. But when these became full, it became increasingly difficult to secure new ground and, in many cases, the authorities now oblige the Jews to bury their dead in the public cemeteries. It so happens that the old cemeteries are found in the heart of cities and they interfere with town planning and reconstruction, and with the planting of parks. Pressure is therefore brought to bear on the Jews to give up the old cemeteries. They are allotted a specified time to transfer the dead to new grounds, and the old grounds are set aside for other purposes.

The case of the Vilna cemeteries is typical. The oldest cemetery of the Vilna Jews, where the great Gaon of Vilna was buried, was confiscated by order of the government and made into a city stadium. Before this was done, the Jews were allowed to transfer the tomb of the Gaon of Vilna and those of other prominent Jews. The Jews also possessed another burial ground which, before Vilna was annexed to the Soviet Union, had been considered "new." This was the Rezhitsa cemetery. It was in a central location and became filled to capacity during the Soviet regime. The Jews were then ordered to move to a new burial ground some miles away from town (the same cemetery to which the Gaon of Vilna and the collective tombs of the victims of the Holocaust had been moved), which they accordingly did. Before long the authorities wanted this cemetery abandoned as well, to make place for a residential district.

I visited the famous Jewish cemetery of Berdichev on a winter day. It was deserted and I had a hard time locating the non-Jewish watchman who lived in a shack at the far end. I asked him to show me the tomb of the great Rabbi Levi Yitzchak of Berdichev. It took a lot of explaining before he understood what I meant, and then he pointed in the general direction. The cemetery was a shambles. Gravestones were scattered all over the place. The tomb over the grave of Rabbi Levi Yitzchak lay in ruins, and the Jews of the community have since gone to a great deal of trouble to place on the grave a bare concrete slab on which is inscribed the name of the great rabbi. The work of destruction had been perpetrated by the Ukrainian Nazis who used the gravestones in the construction of sidewalks and for border markers.

The condition of hundreds of Jewish cemeteries in the small towns which were abandoned by the Jews is far worse. Destruction takes place more rapidly. There is no one to care for them, and those that have not already been razed will be before long.

There is still another reason why the Soviet authorities oppose the opening of new cemeteries to replace those that are filled up in cities which have a Jewish community. In many cases, the Jewish cemeteries have been turned into social meeting places. They are one of the few remaining places, besides the synagogues and the "Jewish concerts," where Jews can meet as Jews. Thousands visit the cemeteries at Riga and Vilna, Kishinev and Minsk, Moscow and Leningrad, and other places. Anyone who has not been present at such a scene has not witnessed the full tragedy of a community which, splintered and scattered, seeks desperately for some way to come together and uses even its dead as a means whereby it can unify itself. Such people flock not only to funerals but to the graves of their ancestors and dear ones. Sunday—which is not a workday —is the usual visiting day for entire families: oldsters, senior members, sometimes even younger people and children. This affords them an opportunity to meet other families and to talk of this and that, and feel as Jews among Jews.

(I must point out that in matters pertaining to circumcision, bar mitzvah, marriage and burial, there is a difference that exists between the Jewish communities of European Russia and those of Caucasia and Central Asia. We will deal later with the more intensive Jewish life prevalent among Georgian Jews, the Mountain Jews, and the Jews of Bukovina.)

Why the Jews of Riga do not have matzot

The Soviet department which deals with matters pertaining to Judaism is obviously resentful of Jewish festivals and their religious, symbolic, and national significance. The festival of Passover, which epitomizes deliverance from bondage and the struggle of the Jewish people for its national and religious freedom, cannot easily be expunged even after these many decades of communist rule. The Seder, which is probably the most beautiful family celebration in the Jewish tradition, still has not lost its impact on the consciousness of hundreds of thousands of Jews in the Soviet Union. The realities of Soviet life seem, in a sense, to facilitate its observance. Nobody is required to go to a synagogue to celebrate the Seder. It is enough to gather the family for a festive evening meal, to drink some wine—and if matzot are available, so much the better. In honor of that evening the mother, grandmother, or an old aunt will prepare gefilte fish and a tasty soup. One of the older generation will relate how the Seder was celebrated in days gone by. Someone will get out a guitar, another will sing some old Yiddish songs. Hearts will warm up a bit—and right there a wonderful evening of Jewish awareness takes place for every member of the family. Despite the living conditions in the cities of the Soviet Union, with the crowding of several families, Jewish and gentile, into one apartment, it is still possible to explain such an evening to the neighbors as a family dinner party.

Sedar festivities of this sort are celebrated by tens of thousands of Jews in the Soviet Union. This is without a doubt known to the authorities, and the means they have chosen to interfere with these celebrations is the ban on the baking of matzot. The first to be affected are the orthodox Jews. Their lives are made a hell. They are forced to exhaust and humiliate themselves as they try to procure matzot. Further, other Jews are told that this festival and its Seder night are not to the government's liking. Significantly, the anti-matzot drive actually started in Khrushchev's time. In Stalin's days the authorities never thought to do anything along these lines. But in 1958, the heads of religious communities began to sense that the authorities were obstructing them in the baking of matzot before the holiday. The baking of matzot, it must be remembered, entails the acquisition of a permit from the proper authorities in order to purchase flour. After the permit is acquired, there are two possible ways the matzot can be prepared. In most communities the flour is handed over to the local government bakery, which then bakes the matzot. But matzot are also made in private bakeries, adjoining the synagogue proper, for some synagogues own bakeries whose sole purpose it is to bake matzot for Passover. The heads of the synagogues used to begin petitioning the authorities several months before Passover for a permit for their quota of flour. But, as stated, they have noticed in recent years that the authorities are given to delaying tactics, and do not issue the permit. In the end, Passover comes and the Jews, year after year, are deprived of matzot. These deceitful tactics, which smack of traditional anti-Semitism, vary from place to place and from town to town, but they are, without a doubt, encouraged by the government.

Some of these delaying tactics are worth noting, as they shed light on the attitude of the government toward the "Jewish elders." A fairly good bakery adjoins the synagogue of Riga, capital of Latvia. It is the pride of the synagogue leaders and is pointed out as one of the notable achievements of their community. A few months before Passover of 1959, they applied for a permit to secure their quota of flour. Much to their surprise, the officials requested that they bring a certificate from the Sanitation Department of the city stating that the bakery was maintained in good order and conformed to stipulated hygienic and sanitary standards. The Jews rushed to the Sanitation Department and were told that a control commission would be sent to look into the matter. The commission came around after some time, checked things over and told the Jews that they would send the municipality a written report. After a while, the Jews, who were becoming rather anxious, inquired about the report. They received a variety of answers: first, that it had not yet been written; then, that it had been written but was being debated. Days and weeks passed. Finally, the Jews were advised that the municipality had decided, after examining the report, that certain changes and improvements needed to be made in the bakery and its equipment, and that the permit could not be issued until these were carried out. The Jews quickly collected money from the various members of the communty, made the required changes within days, and hurried to advise the municipality that the improvements had been made. They asked to be given the permit but were told that another commission would have to be sent to determine whether or not the stipulated changes had in fact been made. The Jews begged and pleaded with the commission to expedite its work. To this the officials answered: "What is this, don't you have time? And why do you bother us constantly? We have other important and pressing matters on our hands." The Jews explained that the Passover was approaching and, if they did not begin baking matzot immediately, it would be too late. The answer was: "And what if it is too late? Would that be a calamity?" In the end, weeks went by and the commission did not come. Passover was just ahead and the Jews were desperate. They tried to meet with those who had the authority to grant the permit and to tell them what had happened at the Department of Sanitation; but they came up against a stone wall: "There is no permit, and therefore no flour."

Passover came and went, and the Jews of Riga had no matzot.

One might retort that this sort of confusion occurs in bureaucratic governments the world over and that Israel itself can provide ample evidence of official stupidity and callousness. But the fact of the matter is that in that same year the government created a variety of difficulties over the baking of matzot in many other communities as well. The same difficulties occurred in Riga the following Passover, and again the baking of matzot was prevented.

While the leaders of the community in Riga were busy running to the government departments, those of Kiev went through a similar painful experience. As was their custom, the Jewish elders of Kiev applied to the licensing authority for flour permits months before Passover. They began to realize that the procrastination they were being subjected to was not the same as in previous years. Fearing the worst, they tried to send a delegation of elders to the Ukrainian Supreme Soviet. They had to wait a long time before they were received by an official. From there they were sent back to the *upolnomochennyi* of the Department of Religions. They had to wait a long while in the anteroom of this Ukrainian official. When they were finally admitted, they noticed on his desk a large Russian

Bible, published, apparently, several years back by the Russian Orthodox Church. When they had expressed their wishes, the *upolnomochennyi* asked them: "Excuse me, gentlemen, what is the hurry? There are still a few weeks to go before your Passover." The Jews explained that they first had to get the flour, then bake the matzot, and then pack and distribute them, all before the holiday. The *upolnomochennyi* opened the Bible and told them: "But I do not understand one thing. It is written here that the unleavened bread must be baked on the eve of Passover, as it would not be kosher otherwise. How can I lead you into doing something that is contrary to the ritual requirements? Come over on the eve of Passover, and we shall discuss it." They understood that the man had made up his mind to prevent the baking of matzot. The Jews of Kiev did not have matzot that year, nor any year thereafter.

That same year the synagogue leaders of the Jewish community of Chernovtsy in Bukovina collected large sums necessary for the preparation of matzot. The amounts were considerable because the authorities in Chernovtsy, even before 1959, imposed an oven tax on the Jews in addition to the regular tax on the bakery. This was to compensate for the fact that "they interfered with the regular routine of government baking for the general population, in order to bake a special ritual bread which is not a requisite food." The Jews claim that such oven taxes found their way into the pockets of the people in the Department of Religions, as they got no receipt for them nor was there anything in writing concerning the tax. That year, the officials of the Department of Religious demanded an exorbitant tax which the religious community could not meet. The Jews of Chernovtsy did not have matzot that year, nor in the years that followed.

The communities of Moscow and Leningrad, and various other communities, were not permitted that year to bake matzot for one reason or another. These occurrences indicate that an order was given by a central authority to prevent the baking of matzot. The manner of executing this order was left to local officials, and this accounts for the different means by which it was carried out. (It is worth noting again that such restrictions against Passover and matzot were not used in the centers populated by Oriental Jews, in the Caucasus and Central Asia. We shall return to this point later.)

What did the Jews do in towns where the baking of

matzot was forbidden? They baked clandestinely and illegally; they asked the Oriental Jews of the Caucasus and Central Asia to help them; and they appealed to their brethren living in the West, beyond the borders of the Soviet Union. Some Jews secured flour privately and paid considerable sums for it, of course. Others were able to manage with this or that bakery, or used primitive ovens which they set up in their homes. A number of these Jews then sold matzot at very high prices (this is not surprising if one considers the risks involved). The authorities arrested some of these Jews and made the most of it, either by giving the matter wide publicity in poisonous feature articles or, as a means of furthering their war against profiteers, by putting them on trial for economic crimes. In the towns of Caucasia and Central Asia, where Oriental and Ashkenazi Jews lived in mixed communities, the former provided the latter with a small supply of matzot, but they had to do this in semi-clandestine fashion.

The restrictions on the baking of matzot became known outside the Soviet Union, and caused a furor in world Jewry. Some of the large Western Jewish communities, especially those in the United States and England, organized shipments of matzot to the Jewish communities of Russia. The Soviet authorities did not care for this at all. They found a hundred and one ways to interfere with the deliveries: by customs taxes, by delaying clearance—and by letters signed by Jews and addressed to the senders of the matzot, saying that they did not need gifts and bequests, that they had all they needed, and so on.*

The government's war against the institutions and symbols of the Jewish faith does not stop at matzot and Passover. It is waged against other areas as well. Sukkoth, for example, during which the Four Species—the palm frond (*lulav*), citron (*etrog*), myrtle and willow—are used, greatly annoys the authorities, for the Four Species remind the Jews of another country, where palms and citrus trees grow. This country, with its distant, warm landscapes,

---

* By the spring of 1965 there were indications of a partial lifting of the ban of matzot. This gradual reversal of the policy of the eight previous years continued into 1966 and 1967 when the few remaining synagogues in Moscow, Leningrad and other major cities were permitted to organize the baking and sale of matzot, but baking still was not permitted in State bakeries nor sale in State stores.—*Publisher's note*

arouses forbidden feelings and yearnings in the hearts of the Jews.

If a citron or palm frond somehow finds its way to the old rabbi of a community, it is regarded as so precious an object that the rabbi himself keeps careful watch over it to prevent its being damaged while it is touched by hosts of people during the festival. It is deeply moving to see the awe and reverence with which the old Jews handle a palm frond which has been cut from a tree thousands of miles away and which, by the time it gets to the rabbi, is dessicated and has lost its color and shape. To witness the elder of the community, swathed in his prayer shawl, shake the dried and withered frond reverently before the worshipers, is to realize that there is no more fitting symbol for the fate of the Jews of the Soviet Union.

A drop of wine from Jerusalem

On Sukkot I happened to be in the synagogue of the Mountain Jews of Baku, capital of Azerbaijan. After praying together with some two hundred Jews, I followed the crowd into the *sukkah* which had been erected in the synagogue courtyard. The *hacham* was a venerable old man who had not lost his spirit. He was a very clever man indeed.

In the *sukkah* the *hacham* showed me a small bottle of Israeli wine which he had somehow managed to obtain. The bottle was labeled "Carmel Oriental." He was very happy, for he could now make the blessing over wine from the Holy Land. I asked how he expected all the members of his congregation to share in the *kiddush* with such a tiny quantity of wine. The old man told me not to worry about it. He asked the congregants to form a line, then instructed them to fill their glasses or goblets with the homemade wine each had brought along. Then he posted himself at the entrance to the *sukkah,* and in his hand was the tiny bottle from Israel. As each worshiper passed before him, the *hacham* dropped a few drops of the "wine from Jersaleum" into his glass. When the little bottle was empty, all the congregants joined in the benediction over glasses that had been consecrated by drops of wine from the Holy Land.

Not only does the government attack religious symbols and festivals, it also tries to deny religious Jews the sacred objects necessary for prayer, such as prayer books, Bibles, various religious books, prayer shawls, and phylacteries, without which prayer is not complete or cannot be performed. The approach is simple: since such objects naturally deteriorate in the course of time, they can be made extinct merely by preventing them from being remade or imported.

The Bible, according to the authorities, is "religious, Zionist, and reactionary propaganda." It has not been reprinted in the Soviet Union since the days of the revolution. The prayer book, which is full of "Zionist and anti-Soviet propaganda," also cannot be printed in the Soviet Union.

The late Rabbi Schliefer, who officiated as the rabbi of the religious community of Moscow, managed in 1956, after much difficulty, to receive permission to publish a few thousand copies of the Shalom Prayer Book which were soon sold out and are now very hard to obtain. Today, Jews have no way of acquiring a prayer book unless a Jewish tourist or visitor from the West, who might be visiting the synagogue, yields to their entreaties and leaves them his own. Is it any wonder that an entire "industry" has mushroomed around the few existing prayer books? It is, of course, forbidden to make phylacteries, which the authorities refer to as "primitive ritual objects." The making of prayer shawls is also forbidden. You see Jews in synagogues wrapping themselves in faded, tattered shawls which are in various stages of disintegration. A small number of Jews manage to obtain prayer shawls as gifts from relatives or tourists. But the authorities look unkindly upon this, and at times they force the recipient to return them to their relatives with a note, saying: "We do not need gifts; we have everything we need."

The Jewish calendar is another source of irritation to the authorities. It is regarded by them as a medium of Jewish identification, because through it Jews come to know when the festivals occur, what the weekly Torah and *Haftorah* portions are, when to say *Yizkor* (memorial service), and so on. The leaders of the two large Jewish communities of Moscow and Leningrad engage in a campaign every year for a permit to issue a calendar. This must be arranged ahead of time, for it also involves acquiring a permit for paper. Getting the basic permit, however, is merely the first step. One must then find a scribe or a good calligrapher who will write the entire calendar by hand, since Hebrew type is not available to these communities. This is then photographed, page by page, by a Jewish photographer, and only then can the photographed pages be bound into small booklets.

In this instance, as in the case of matzot, the authorities find ways to make things difficult. At times, the Jews are likely to wait for weeks on end for the calendar permit, or for the paper permit. On occasion, when the calendar is already printed, bound, and ready for distribution, the synagogue *gabbaim* are forbidden to distribute and sell it. Sometimes the calendar is deliberately delayed at one stage or another, and its appearance is permitted only a long time after the Jewish New Year. A calendar that appears many months after the New Year is of little value. On the whole, hardly any of the religious communities set out to publish a calendar ahead of time in semi-official fashion, as few have the means and the necessary equipment for a project of this kind. Despite this, with the advent of the High Holidays some Jews in scattered places draw up private calendars for their own use. There are Jews who, gifted with a fine handwriting, prepare a few calendars and give them away to their friends, or even operate a "business" in handwritten calendars. Some of these calendars are quite beautiful, and are a clear indication of the hard work and love invested in them.

Yom Kippur of the shadow people

Because the synagogue is the last and only organized Jewish institution still extant in the Soviet Union, its importance is far greater than that which is normally attributed to synagogues elsewhere. It is therefore not possible to equate the synagogues in the Soviet Union with those in the Western Diaspora, and certainly not with those in Israel, where the synagogue is only one among a totality of religious, national, cultural, and social institutions.

The buildings housing synagogues in the Soviet Union are quite insignificant when compared with synagogues elsewhere. Most of them are located in basements, wooden shacks, and tumble-down houses. The exceptions are those found in Caucasia and Central Asia, and the large synagogues of Moscow and Leningrad, whose imposing structures were erected by wealthy Jews in czarist times. The Soviet authorities appreciate the fact that Moscow and Leningrad are show places for the outside world, for tourists, diplomats, and newspapermen; that is why they maintain a relative degree of tolerance toward these synagogues. But far more depressing than the miserable appearance of the buildings is the appearance of the regular worshipers. Most of them are the elderly and the very aged, mainly pensioners, whose clothes are not always clean and whose appearance arouses compassion.

The Jews themselves will tell a visitor from overseas that the synagogue swarms with informers planted there by the government, and many will point to one another as informers. It is not unlikely that the authorities oblige Jews to inform on each other in order to sustain a climate of permanent tension and nervousness within the confines of the synagogue and to maintain constant supervision over what goes on there. Despite it all, this lamentable synagogue, the last and only focus of Jewish life, can suddenly grow and assume unusual proportions, and take on a task that goes far beyond the bounds of the miserable wooden shack attended by a few dozen old Jews.

The High Holidays have always been, and are still, the powerful life-giving source which draws observant and nonobservant Jews to the synagogue. This occurs wherever Jews live. The Jewish New Year, the sounding of the ram's horn, the *Kol Nidrei* prayer, the fast of the Day of Atonement, the memorial service for the deceased—all of these have become so deeply engraved in the heart of Jews, that one can hardly find a Jew, even a nonobservant Jew, who will ignore them.

But the High Holidays in the Soviet Union carry an additional significance which is not found among Jews elsewhere. The Jew in New York, London, Paris, or Buenos Aires has a hundred and one opportunities to identify himself as a Jew during the year, whether in the limited social milieu where he lives, or in the clubs, voluntary associations, fund drives, and other social and cultural events. The Jews of Moscow and Leningrad have no such opportunity. Furthermore, the Jews of the Soviet Union stand closer today, spiritually and psychologically, to the Holocaust, the war, and the terror of Stalin. There is not a family which does not have a father or brother, a son or a relative who was killed in the ghetto, or in the ranks of the partisans or the Red Army, or in the camps in Siberia. It is not surprising that they are moved by a powerful urge to commemorate, at least once or twice a year, in public and among their own, their near and dear ones.

There are a few rare occasions during the year which seem to favor what might be called "safety in numbers." Specific dates in the Jewish calendar, such as the New Year, Yom Kippur, the Seder night, and so on, are familiar to hundreds of thousands of Jews even if they do not own a Jewish calendar. The "Jewish grapevine" works most efficiently at such times. The date becomes known through conversation. And it is enough for one member of a family to know it, for it is then passed on rapidly by word of mouth to relatives, friends, and acquaintances. Every Jew knows that on a specific day thousands of Jews will converge on the synagogue. He is not afraid of being conspicuous. He can always explain his presence as the natural curiosity of an ordinary citizen who wishes to see how thousands of people are attracted by some event.

The synagogue of Kiev is a sad looking two-story structure. During the week a few dozen old Jews pray in its basement. On the Sabbath the large auditorium is opened; it can scarcely accommodate a few hundred worshipers. On an ordinary Sabbath about two hundred Jews worship there.

I happened to be there on Yom Kippur. When I arrived, the path leading to the synagogue was already thick with crowds of Jews. I shouldered my way inside with great difficulty. Thousands of people, possibly tens of thousands, stood jammed together near the entrance and in the alley. It was very cold. The people wore black or gray overcoats. They arrived singly or in pairs, but not in groups. As I watched them closely, I noticed that the people in the street did not speak to one another. It must be remembered that there is only one synagogue in Kiev, a city with a population that includes about two hundred thousand Jews. The Jews there do not live in any one specific neighborhood or quarter. These people had come from every part of the city. There were Jews who did not know one another and who were not inclined to say much to one another—for who knew to whom one might be talking? They all felt certain that there were informers in the crowd. So why jabber and take risks?

As I examined them more closely, I noticed that, unlike

those who can be seen in the synagogue on weekdays and Sabbaths, there were many middle-aged and young people among them, even adolescents and children. The Jews who stood outside did not pray. Likewise, many of those inside the building did not participate in the service. Most of them did not have prayer books, and even if they had, hardly any would have been able to read the prayers. They stood in the street, silent, moving very slowly toward the synagogue, peering in for a moment, glancing at the Ark and the Scroll of the Law, and listening to the half-audible supplications of the cantor.

Then, somehow, the word *"Yizkor"* was heard—and the crowd was suddenly hushed and motionless.

I could see everyone retreating into himself for one long, lonely moment. I saw tears and heard choked sobs. I sensed that these thousands of people were now identifying themselves with one another and that they felt, if only for a very short time, that they stood among their own and shared a common destiny. During the hours of Yom Kippur those Jews did not try to discover whether they were a "nation," a "religion," or a "sect."

Simchat Torah: the greatest of festivals

The month-long period of the High Holidays ends with the festival of Simchat Torah. Unlike the Jewish New Year and Yom Kipper, which are solemn and grave, Simchat Torah is a gay festival, perhaps the gayest of Jewish holidays. This is the time when Jews dance joyously with the Scroll of the Law, when one may imbibe wine or liquor so as to sing all the better. And the songs are not the usual melancholy supplications, but jolly hasidic tunes, or Jewish variations on non-Jewish secular and folk songs. This festival, more than any other, has endeared itself to the Jews of the Soviet Union. They have invested it with most of their desires, yearnings, longings, and feelings of identification. It is the only festival which can be compared to a "popular concert," in which children may also participate. It brings some measure of happiness—a thing so often lacking during the year. It is also an occasion for dancing what is akin to a Jewish snake dance. Thus Simchat Torah has become the greatest of the Jewish festivals in the Soviet Union, one with a character all its own.

The things that take place on the night of Simchat Torah in the synagogues of the Soviet Union shed a powerful light on Jewish life in Russia.

This is what I heard from the head of an Israeli family who was present in the great synagogue of Moscow on the night of Simchat Torah:

"We dressed our children in their holiday clothes and gave them the traditional colored flag topped by an apple, with a candle in the apple. The whole family went to the Moscow synagogue. When we got there, it was already hemmed in by thousands of people who filled the street from end to end. Everyone made way for us, as our children were the only ones who carried flags, and you could hear Jews whispering to one another, *'Amolige kinder'* (children of the past).

"The interior of the synagogue seemed to be luminous with a light which came not only from the chandeliers but also from thousands of shining eyes and from the bright face of the crowd, which now did not comprise only the aged.

"I glanced around and saw young people here and there. I noticed the dark, smiling, curious eyes of a charming girl, who came close to pulpit. (On Simchat Torah the traditional separation of the sexes inside the synagogue is overlooked, and the women mingle with the men.) There were new faces all around. Had I met any of those people on the street, I would never have associated them—on account of their age, dress, and expression—with a synagogue or a Jewish holiday. They were the kind of people one meets at the Bolshoi, in Gorki Park, at an exhibition in the Pushkin Museum, in the Lenin Stadium, or at a lecture in Dom Kulturi.

"Where were they from? What were they doing here? Was it merely the curiosity of the young that drove them to come and see how their fathers and ancestors had celebrated their festivals? Or were they drawn by a longing for an unknown past?

"The Torah processionals began. The old rabbi and the *gabbaim* of the synagogue took out dozens of Torah Scrolls from the Ark, well-cared-for ancient rolls of parchment that were wrapped in colored velvet embroidered in golden Hebrew letters. The Scrolls were crowned with filigreed decorations, jeweled flowers, and bells. The old, bent Jews, in dark, faded, and worn-out clothes, seemed to be swallowed up in the colorful procession, and it was as though the splendid and ornamental Scrolls marched on unsupported.

"The old rabbi and the *gabbaim* were followed by a few Israeli children carrying miniature Scrolls of the Law and flags. A little five-year-old girl was lifted up by the young people and carried on their shoulders. They joined the procession of the Scrolls. We saw smiling faces everywhere, a rare and wonderful sight in this old and sad synagogue.

"When the first processional was completed, the cantor, accompanied by some of the regular worshipers, began to sing some happy songs. The microphone near the cantor was grabbed by a number of people who boldly sang into it Jewish folk songs and hasidic tunes. Many of the people in the crowd joined in. The processions continued at a faster and gayer pace. The Scrolls were no longer carried by old people or by the regular worshipers. The snaking 'rondo' of the Scrolls swirled through the packed crowd, reaching almost outside the walls of the synagogue and the open area before the synagogue, where thousands more stood crowded together.

"Then some people started dancing. A circle was formed. Everybody danced, old men and women, boys and girls. The circle widened as a second, third, and fourth circle formed within. Then dozens of people were dancing, their arms linked as they moved to the tune of *'Vetaher Libenu.'* Someone started to sing 'David King of Israel lives on forever,' and the dance immediately changed to the more fervent pace of a *hora*.

"As we watched, the dance grew in warmth and ecstasy; the old, worn, and heavy-footed dropped out, and their places in the circle were taken by the young. In the end the circle was made up almost entirely of young people. The dancers, who appeared to be mostly university students, were not adept at the *hora*, but they soon grasped the basic nature of the dance and the words of the song."

I have asked myself: Who were these young people who danced with such great enthusiasm? Was this an isolated event in their lives, a casual occurrence? Are they like the many young Russians who fill the great churches on the eve of Christmas to listen with curiosity to the choir of old women?

I am told that the same thing happens in the synagogue of Leningrad on the night of Simchat Torah, but on a more massive scale. Perhaps this is because the Leningrad synagogue is larger than the one in Moscow, or because a more Western atmosphere prevails in Leningrad. The fact remains that a still larger number of students and Jewish youth assemble there, and the building, the area outside, and the street are filled with thousands of people. And when one hears of similar events occurring in other towns, one begins to wonder whether it is possible that the intense interest the young people show in that evening is not just casual but has very deep roots.

This is how my friend, who described the Simchat Torah celebration in Moscow, put it: "It is difficult to talk to them. When the evening is over, they scatter into the night. And you don't see them, or the likes of them, until the following year. . . ."

The High Holidays are over and Simchat Torah has passed. Once again the synagogue sinks into the grayness of the Russian winter. Once again a few oldsters gather there on weekdays and Sabbaths. Once again arguments, disputes, and schisms arise. Once again they must deliver reports to the authorities. But deep in their hearts, these synagogue Jews know that they, old and degraded as they are, are the ones who guard the embers of the ancient Jewish tradition, which blazes into flame for a brief moment a few times a year.

Reb Dovid mingles with diplomats

Now I want to tell a story about one of these guardians of the embers who once was given the opportunity to demonstrate his inner strength, quite unconsciously, before the "great and mighty."

Every country's Independence Day is by far the most important day of the year for its embassies. For a few hours the embassy becomes the focal point of the host country's attention. Public opinion, the press, radio, and television keep it in the limelight. While this is the general rule everywhere in the world, it is emphasized even more with regard to the embassies of non-communist countries in Moscow, whose activities are quite limited throughout the year. Few Soviet visitors come to these embassies, and those who do come are closely watched. And the embassies are not able to disseminate any information about their respective countries. But with the advent of each country's Independence Day the situation changes. The embassy is transformed overnight, Cinderella-like, into a resplendent princess. Its building, which stood desolate through the year with a bored Russian guard posted at each of its doors, now becomes a center of attraction. Traffic police direct the stream of long, foreign, diplomatic cars. Black Soviet cars—Chaika, Zim, and Zis—dash up and stop with a screeching of brakes, and out come leaders of the Soviet Union, statesmen, ministers, and high-ranking military officials, their chests covered with medals. On occasion Russian Orthodox priests will also arrive, heavily bearded and wearing golden crosses encrusted with pearls and diamonds. Newspapermen, television and radio technicians, and their paraphernalia crowd the entrance. All of these attract a large crowd of curious onlookers who gather in the street and in the area near the embassy to listen to the announcements of the traffic policeman: "The car of the Ambassador of Ghana is called to the entrance"; "the car of the Ambassador of the United States is called to the entrance"; and so on.

The embassy building is decorated with flags and is bright with colored lights. Inside there is great excitement. The ambassador and his aides rush from one guest to another, shake hands, smile, and point out the embassy's valuables and its treasures of national art. And at the end of a very long and exhausting evening, after the hundreds of guests have all left, the diplomatic personnel sit around the large hall, now empty and strewn with leftover sandwiches and half-filled champagne glasses, remove their tight shoes, and proceed to take stock of themselves by answering the question: Who came and who didn't?

It must be noted that this taking stock is a matter of great importance in Soviet Russia, at least insofar as the embassy is concerned. It represents a sort of barometer of the Soviet Union's attitude to the embassy in question. And it can be done in accordance with precise criteria: How many members of the Presidium attended? And which members? How many ministers? And which ministers (there are "very important," "ordinary," and "unimportant" ministers)? How many marshals, generals, admirals? How many leaders of society, the arts, and sciences? All this assumes significance and is the subject of a long and detailed report to the mother-country.

In this respect the Israeli Embassy is the same as all the others in Moscow. But there is also a difference.

Dozens of elegant cars call there on Israel's Independence Day; a huge cocktail party is held; there is feverish excitement within the embassy. But certain unusual features characterize the event. The crowd which surrounds the building does not consist of only the curious. Anyone who observes closely can see that a considerable number of Jews are present, their eyes shining. A tear glistens; here and there a man can be seen taking out a handkerchief and surreptitiously wiping his eyes; here and there one onlooker will say in a half-whisper to another of his acquaintance: *"Gut yontev"* (happy holiday).

And inside the embassy, among the hundreds of guests, there are a number of Russian Jews who were invited and dared, or were given permission, to come. There is a well-known Jewish artist, a famous violinist or pianist; and here, sure enough, is the rabbi of Moscow, tall and white-bearded, dressed in black, accompanied by his small, thin wife. The two of them circulate among ambassadors, military attachés from every country in the world, and Soviet army officers. They are surrounded with every sign of affection and love by the Israeli Embassy personnel. They also attract some tourists from Israel who, like myself, happen to be in Moscow on Independence Day. This is their opportunity to get close to the Moscow rabbi and exchange a few words with him.

Then another Jew comes into the embassy. This is Reb Dovid, one of the elders of the tumble-down little synagogue located in a remote suburb of Moscow. He did not arrive in a Zis or a Chaika, or even in a taxi like the rabbi of the great synagogue. His eighty-year-old feet dragged him in and out of several buses and subway stations, and here he is. He had of course been invited to the Independence Day celebration—and he dared to come.

Reb Dovid is dressed in some kind of shabby frock coat, shiny with wear. There is a gray scarf around his neck and a cap on his head. His beard and thick eyebrows are white as snow and gleam against the dark background of his clothes. His black eyes are bright with life and take in everything around him. This is his first and, probably, his last visit to the embassy. He wanders around and peers at the oil paintings of Israel that hang on the walls, and he asks one of the Israeli secretaries: "Ah, is this Zion, and is that a view of the Carmel? Is this the way Tel Aviv looks?

Is Lake Kinneret really that blue?" He draws close to the bound Hebrew books that are on display and kisses a silver-embossed Bible which rests on a black velvet stand in a corner. He feels quite at home in the embassy. He pays no attention to the Norwegian ambassador to his right or to the Russian admiral to his left. He came here to find Israel—and he has found it.

When the time comes for the evening prayer, Reb Dovid turns to the Israeli secretary who took him around and asks: "Nu, is there a *minyan?* Let's pray *Ma'ariv.*" The young secretary, somewhat taken aback, rushes to the ambassador with Reb Dovid's request. In a few minutes a *minyan* is formed around him which includes the rabbi of Moscow, the ambassador, and some of the members of the embassy staff. Even a famous singer of the Moscow Opera joins in as though from a distance and seemingly out of curiosity.

Reb Dovid opens the service in a clear voice, and as they come to the Eighteen Benedictions a hush permeates the hall. Ten Jews, led by Reb Dovid, pray silently, their bodies swaying forward and back. Ambassadors, diplomats, Soviet officers stand around reverently. And only with the conclusion of the brief service does the tumult of the cocktail party rise again from the crowd.

When Reb Dovid has finished praying, he leaves the building. He has a long way to travel and it will take him two hours to return to his tiny room. But he has found what he sought. He has fulfilled his greatest desire and has done what he most wanted.

4

Place in Society

The demographic situation

In January 1959, the Soviet Union took a population census. Before this, the authorities engaged in an extensive campaign to induce the people to answer the numerous and complicated questions of the census takers. The background of this census must be understood. It was the first census to be taken since the death of Stalin, and the fear which had become an inseparable part of the life of the people was still deeply rooted. In the days of Stalin the average citizen's one and only reaction to the questions posed by government census takers and investigators was: Avoid getting involved as far as possible. Every question was suspect and every unsolicited answer could turn out sooner or later to be a trap. One may go so far as to say that this fear is very deep among the Russian people, and that its roots go as far back as the time of the czars and the era of feudal serfdom.

The authorities, nevertheless, made a supreme effort in 1959 to overcome this fear. They explained to the population through the radio, press, and television that the census takers would not ask for identity cards or other papers to verify the answers, that the answers would be kept secret, that they would never be used against the persons answering, and so on. This effort had the desired effect, and even if the fear and the hesitation never disappeared completely, one may safely assume that most of the answers were in accord with the facts. When the census was completed the statisticians began to process the tremendous amount of material and publish it in sections (probably under party direction and supervision). The full report was published in 1962–63, in sixteen volumes.

Jewish data appear mainly in two sections of the census, under the headings "Nationality" and "Mother Tongue."

The census shows that 2,267,814 citizens registered as Jews (under "Nationality"), making the Jewish nationality the eleventh largest in the Soviet Union. When we undertake to analyze this figure we must bear in mind that the general fear of answering questions applies more particularly to Jews, many of whom did not want to identify themselves as such during the last years of Stalin's life. One may also assume that many Jews dissociated themselves from their people during the first twenty years after the onset of the Soviet regime. It was easier then to change the family name, so that thousands of Rabinoviches registered as Ivanovs (though their nationality remained Jewish on their identity cards). It must also be remembered that in the great turmoil of the Second World War tens of thousands of Jews "lost" their identity cards and acquired new ones, and as a result of endless wanderings as refugees many were able to change their nationality. In Nazi-occupied territory many Jews succeeded in obtaining non-Jewish papers, and thus cheated death. And many held on to these papers even after the war.

In 1959, when the government census takers promised that they would not ask for any papers to verify answers, many Jews gave false answers regarding their nationality status. They thus removed themselves from the Jewish nation insofar as the census was concerned, despite the fact that according to their identity cards they are Jews and will remain Jews, for it is much more difficult now to change the family name; in fact, it is virtually impossible.

This touches upon a problem that is crucial to our understanding of not only the response of Jews to the question "What is your nationality?" but also their reaction to anything at all that has to do with Jewish affairs. This is the problem of the total atomization of the Jews as a people and the great loneliness felt by each individual Jew as he faces questions of this sort. It is in essence the sociopsychological problem of the shadow people that we discussed above. Because there is no social or cultural Jewish body, and because the synagogue and the religious commu-

nity incorporate only a small minority of Jews, most Jews
have no opportunity to seek guidance. There is no place at
all where ten or twenty Jews can get together to look into,
discuss, or decide what to do about such a question as:
"How is one to respond to a census taker's question regarding national affinity or the mother tongue?" They cannot even find anyone to advise them on simpler issues,
such as: "How are we to behave as Jews toward Jewish
tourists from the United States or Israel?"; or "How do we
answer letters coming from relatives living outside the Soviet Union?"; or indeed any question that affects them as
Jewish nationals.

In the absence of any overall advisory body, it is possible to say that we have before us a few million individual
Jews, each of whom bears the Jewish burden on his own
shoulders. We do not have here a nationality, a tribe, or a
group, however they may be defined, but a host of individual Jews who have no organizational link between them,
save the name of the nationality that is stamped on their
identity cards.

An appreciation of this point is crucial to an evaluation
of the way these individual Jews react to every one of
their problems. These reactions are not identical; they are
at times spontaneous; but they are always the reactions of
isolated human beings.

The family: the sole Jewish institution

There is, understandably, one exception to this general
picture—the family. In a normal society, the family is
merely one of many groups or institutions which a man
can consult whenever necessary. But in the Soviet Union
the Jewish family has become the only place where a Jew
can find a refuge of some sort and where he can seek advice
regarding his Jewishness and nationality. Here the father,
mother, and children can, and often must, get together to
decide how to answer the census taker, how to receive the
relative from the United States, or whether it is worth
going to a "Jewish concert." Here they will weigh matters,
and set their longings and feelings against the difficulties
of reality. Here they will come to a common understanding and a final decision. I venture to think that when Jews,

as individuals or as families, had to decide what to answer the census taker, some of them, for a variety of reasons, responded that they were not Jews but Russians. And the reasons were quite serious. For it must be remembered that the majority of Jews in the Union speak Russian fluently. It is indeed the mother tongue not only of most of the Jews of the Russian Republic but also of the other republics. Moreover, in the large cities of the Russian Republic in Europe and Siberia, it is easy for Jews to be taken for Russians. This is particularly true of the great cities, such as Moscow and Leningrad, which are more cosmopolitan and less homogeneous than other cities, and in which one can disappear among the millions and hide one's Jewish origin. It is also true of the new cities in Siberia where the people are for the most part recent arrivals. We ought not to forget that the Jews are widely scattered within the various cities. There is no specifically Jewish quarter in any city of the Soviet Union (except in the case of the Oriental Jews of Central Asia and the Caucasus, whom we shall discuss later); nor is there any section in which one can observe a heavy concentration of Jews. There is nothing in Moscow that can remind one of Golders Green in London or of Brooklyn in New York. The dispersion of Russian Jews is total, and this greatly facilitates their disappearance.

Thus far we have been speaking mainly of the Russian Republic. The situation is different, however, in the other national republics. It is possible for a person to hide his Jewishness in Kiev, the capital of the Ukraine, and say he is Russian; but it is difficult to believe that a Jew, even one with a family name that is not typically Jewish, would tell a census taker that he is a Ukrainian. A blood-stained history separates the Jew from the Ukrainian, and the smattering of Ukrainian language and culture that they have in common is not enough to bridge that separation and would hardly induce a Jew to call himself a Ukrainian. If this is true with respect to Kiev, it is all the more true with respect to the small towns in th Ukraine. In places like Berdichev, Zhitomir, Korosten, and dozens of other small towns, the Jewish population is completely exposed, in all its smallness, against the Ukrainian majority, without there being any buffer population of Russians or others to stand between them. The Ukrainian majority is on one side and the Jewish minority is on the other—and nothing more. There is hardly a single Jew who is not known to his neighbors and the census takers, and who would dare to claim that he is Ukrainian. This is no less true with regard to Estonia, Lithuania, Latvia, Moldavia, and so on. These are small republics. In most of them the Jews live in the capital cities. They are known and identifiable. Their language is Russian (or Yiddish). They speak the dominant national language, but it is really not their own. There are not many Jews who would dare identify themselves as Latvians, Lithuanians, or Moldavians.

We shall deal later with the problem of intermarriage in the Soviet Union; here we will only note that many Jews, men and women, who married non-Jews, registered themselves according to the nationality of the gentile partner, and thereby concealed their Jewishness.

The Jews are dispersed unequally throughout all the fifteen Soviet republics. If we take the population census as our basis, the following picture can be formed:

JEWISH POPULATION ACCORDING TO THE REPUBLICS

Name of Republic	Number of Jews according to the 1959 Census	Estimated number of Jews
Russian Republic	875,307	1,400,000
Ukrainian Republic	840,314	1,100,000
Belorussian Republic	150,084	300,000
Moldavian Republic	95,107	130,000
Uzbek Republic	93,344	130,000
Georgian Republic	55,582	120,000
Azerbaijan Republic	40,204	110,000
Latvian Republic	36,592	40,000
Kazakh Republic	28,048	40,000
Lithuanian Republic	24,672	35,000
Tajik Republic	12,415	18,000
Kirghiz Republic	8,610	10,000
Estonian Republic	5,437	8,000
Turkmen Republic	4,078	5,000
Armenian Republic	1,024	1,000
Total number of Jews in the Soviet Union	2,267,814	3,447,000

By adding to the total number of Jews in the Soviet Union, as recorded in the census, an additional one-fourth or one-third of the official figure so as to include those Jews who are registered as Jews on their identity cards, but who concealed their origin from the cenus takers, and by supplementing this with a figure that represents the natural increase of the Jewish population between 1959 and 1965, we arrive at a total of three and a half million Jews who now live in the Soviet Union.

The Jewish population in the Soviet Union is basically urban and is concentrated in large and medium-sized cities. This is essentially true of Jews everywhere, but there are specific motives and reasons for it in the Soviet Union.

The situation was different before the establishment of the Soviet regime. Though few Jews lived in farm villages during the czarist period, there were no large masses of Jews in the big cities. The czarist regime prohibited Jews from living in the capital and in a number of other large cities, and Jews who wished to live in those areas were required to have special permits. The Jewish population of Russia, the Ukraine, and Bukovina was centered mainly in the Jewish Pale in western Russia, and most Jews lived in small towns, where they created a unique Jewish *shtetl* culture. Millions of Jews emigrated from those towns to England, France, and the United States. It was in those small towns that Zionism sprang up and its leaders were born.

By the end of the czarist period, however, the Jewish small town and the Jewish Pale were already crumbling. Jews managed, one way or another, to migrate to Kiev and Odessa, to Kharkov and Minsk, to Moscow and Leningrad, as well as to Baku and Irkutsk. The process was greatly accelerated by the First World War and the resulting streams of refugees. The civil war in Russia and the waves of pogroms served as an additional impetus that forced hundreds of thousands of Jews to abandon the small towns and seek the large cities.

During the early years of the Soviet regime, those cities were thrown wide open and tens of thousands of Jews found their way to them. The *shtetl* was dealt a final blow by the Nazis during the Second World War. The Jewish sections of those towns were wiped out and their occupants murdered.

After the war, when hundreds of thousands of Jewish refugees returned to the Ukraine and Belorussia, those of them who had once lived in the small towns had nowhere to go. Most did not want to go back to the graves of their brethren. The few who did return found a hostile gentile population which refused to absorb them. The Jewish *shtetl*, after agonizing for a long time, had died cruelly in the Holocaust. Today the Jews are concentrated mainly in small and medium-sized provincial towns, in the regional capitals, or in the large cities. The process of Jewish concentration in the large cities, which began in recent years, continues to this day.

Fully 95 per cent of the Jews of Russia live in urban areas, and the number continues to increase. About one-half of Russian Jewry is now concentrated in the large cities of the Soviet Union: Moscow, Leningrad, Kiev, Odessa, Kharkov, Minsk, Riga, Vilna, Chernovtsy, Kishinev, Tbilisi, Baku, and Tashkent.

What of the remaining 5 per cent who live in the villages? During the czarist period the Jews who lived in villages were for the most part not farmers but innkeepers, artisans, and small merchants. In the early years of the Soviet regime some attempts were made to direct Jews to agriculture. A few dozen Jewish settlements, and later a number of Jewish *kolkhozy*, were founded, mainly in Crimea and the southern Ukraine (the Birobidzhan experiment will be discussed later). But this modest beginning was utterly destroyed by the German invaders. The small number of Jews who still live in Soviet villages are mostly agronomists, veterinarians, accountants, and the like.

Another demographic process is taking place as a result of the slow but persistent shifting of the important Jewish centers of gravity eastward to the new regions of the Soviet Union and to Siberia. This began even before the Second World War with the young Jews who were seeking a fresh start in the east. It was indirectly accelerated by the thousands of Jews who were among the millions of forced labor workers sent eastward by Stalin. It was given a tremendous impetus by the flow of hundreds of thousands of Jewish war refugees from the Soviet Union and Poland to eastern European Russia, Central Asia, and Siberia. Most of the refugees moved back to western Russia at the end of the war. Some of them went beyond the borders of the Soviet Union into Poland (and from there many emigrated to Israel). Nevertheless, a large number remained in their new homes in the east.

The trend to the east still continues, though it is gradual and slow. Individual Jews leave European Russia and move on to the new urban centers of Asiatic Russia. In Siberia, where new cities constantly spring up and existing cities continue to grow at a fantastic pace, young Jews find more room and better opportunities to succeed in their technical and scientific professions, and have a better chance of being absorbed into a newer, more varied, and relatively younger population which is less encumbered with prejudice than the "old motherland" in the west.

Jewish troubadours in Khabarovsk

I visited Khabarovsk, the large and growing city on the Amur River in eastern Siberia. I had heard that a few thousand Jews lived there but that they did not have a "religious Jewish community." To my great surprise, on the day I arrived I saw posters announcing that a "Jewish concert" would be held that evening in a hall belonging to the officers' club of the local military command.

I quickly purchased a ticket and that evening found myself in a hall that was packed mostly with young Jews, some of them in military dress. The entertainers were a middle-aged married couple from Riga who, like the medieval troubadours, wandered from town to town, giving concerts of Yiddish folk songs. Neither their voices nor their choice of songs was of the best. But the crowd of young people greeted them with an enthusiasm that mounted with every song. As I watched the audience, I noticed again something that had struck me at other "Jewish concerts" in the Soviet Union: young people tended to stay close to an older acquaintance or relative who would whisper the translation of the words of the songs into their ears.

After the concert I went backstage to see the singers. They told me that on the following day they would appear in Novosakhalinsk, the chief town of Sakhalin Island in the Pacific Ocean. I expressed surprise that such a God-forsaken place would want a "Jewish concert." They said that the invitation to appear had come from the Jews who lived there, most of them young people, scientists and technicians, who were eager to hear a Jewish word and tune.

The half million Yiddish-speaking Jews

The 1959 census offers still another measuring rod by which we can look into the state of Jews in the Soviet Union—that of "mother tongue." It is logical to expect that the nationality of anyone responding to the questions of the census taker would coincide with his mother tongue; that is, most of the Russian nationals would regard Russian as their mother tongue; and so on. But this identification of nationality and mother tongue does not correspond in the case of some nationalities, and this lack of correspondence is indicative of the degree to which various nationals have been Russified, as well as of the extent of their resistance to the influence of the Russian language.

There is no doubt that a relatively large number of people, particularly the young intellectuals of the "new" nations, such as the Kazakhs, Tajiks, Kirghiz and so on, feel conflicting loyalties when registering their mother tongue. On the one hand, there is national pride which is encouraged by the authorities, as we have seen. This compels the registering of one's national language (Kazakh, Uzbek, and so on) as the mother tongue. On the other hand, there are other factors, such as snobbishness and the desire to belong to the great Russian culture, which come into play and which induce many to claim Russian as their mother tongue. In most instances, national pride proves to be the stronger of the two, and the language of the national republic is claimed as the mother tongue out of a spirit of identification with one's culture and people. And though we find that million in Uzbekistan and Kazakhstan registered their mother tongue as Russian or Ukrainian in the census, there is no doubt that these were in fact Russians and Ukrainians who migrated and settled in Central Asia as a result of the process of colonization.

The situation of the Jews with regard to the problem of mother tongue is, once again, unique. The majority of Jews, slightly over 75 per cent, registered their mother tongue as Russian. Slightly more than 20 per cent (487,686 in number) claimed Yiddish. The remainder registered other languages.

When one considers that the Jews have no communal organization which they can consult regarding the matter of language, that every individual Jew and every family must make its own independent decisions, that there is no prevailing Jewish climate of opinion which would influence the individual Jew concerning his choice of mother tongue, and that the absence of such a climate of opinion is in contradistinction to the positive climates that prevail among all other nationalities—when one considers all this, it becomes a source of no small astonishment to see that half a million Jews registered Yiddish as their mother tongue.

There is no doubt that the majority of Jews in Russia not only speak Russian fluently but also regard it as their mother tongue in the fullest sense of the term. This is certainly true of the Jews in the Russian Republic, in most of the Ukraine, in Belorussia, and in other areas where they have been cut off from the rest of the world for three generations. For an entire generation these Jews have had no means of teaching Yiddish to their children, even had they wanted to—no school, no textbooks, nothing. The only way parents can impart the Yiddish language to their children is to teach it in the family circle, a procedure some of them no doubt follow. But this has to be done orally, as there are no textbooks available.

The situation is somewhat different in those parts of the Soviet Union which were annexed during the Second World War, such as the Baltic countries, Bukovina, and Moldavia. Most of the Jews who live there now were raised in Yiddish, and this is their true mother tongue. Yiddish is still kept alive by the parents; it is spoken in many homes (though not in the street, for the moment the Jew crosses his threshold he begins to use Russian, which he speaks fluently). Even the young people and children still hear Yiddish at home. Some of them speak it themselves, though the number of those who can read and write it is steadily decreasing because of the lack of textbooks.

The Jew who lives in these areas and who must determine, all by himself, what language to register as his mother tongue, can respond in one of three ways: he can claim Russian; he can claim the native tongue of the national republic in which he lives (Estonian, Lithuanian, Latvian, Moldavian, and so on); or he can claim Yiddish. He would not be lying if he claimed either Russian or

Yiddish, as both are equally his mother tongue. Very few claimed the national language of their republic (though they are fluent in it). They did this for the same reasons that led them not to declare their nationality as Lithuanian or Ukrainian; either because the census taker would not look kindly upon such an answer, or because the Jews really do not belong to these nationalities; they simply cannot be Latvians, Estonians, or Moldavians, nor can their mother tongue be Latvian, Estonian, or Moldavian.

Unwilling Russifiers

It is important to point out another phenomenon related to the problem of language. Because the Jews of the national republics speak Russian, they find themselves between the hammer and the anvil. In the eyes of the nationals, the Jews are regarded as strong proponents of Russification because they not only speak and write Russian but also send their children to Russian schools where the language of instruction is Russian, and thereby lend greater impetus to the Russification program of the central government. The Jews appear, therefore, to be an anti-national element breaching the walls of the separate nationalities in whose midst they live and facilitating further Russian penetration.

But let us return to the problem of language in the census and look again at the figure of half a million Jews who claimed Yiddish as their mother tongue. Where did this figure come from? The census indicates that about a hundred and fifty thousand Jews of Estonia, Latvia, Lithuania, Bukovina, and Moldavia, all of which were annexed to the Soviet Union after the war, registered Yiddish as their mother tongue. Most of the others, namely about three hundred and fifty thousand, live mainly in the prewar area of the Soviet Union. What motivated tens of thousands of Jews in Moscow and Leningrad, or thousands of Jews in the new cities of Siberia, to claim Yiddish as their mother tongue? They could just as easily have claimed Russian and still have been telling the truth. This is especially true of Moscow and Siberia, where the Jew who declares his mother tongue to be Russian does not have to be afraid of being labeled a Russifier. Moreover, when they claim Yiddish, many are actually declaring an untruth, for it can be said of only a very few homes in Moscow that their mother tongue today is Yiddish.

The distribution of a periodical such as the *Sovietish Heimland* can serve to indicate the extent of the ignorance of Yiddish in Moscow. This periodical began to appear a few years ago. It is a small publication, with a readership of only some tens of thousands, of which a mere few thousand are in Moscow. It may be assumed that the reason Yiddish-speaking Jews do not read this periodical is that they find it utterly objectionable, while the younger, non-Yiddish-speaking Jews do not read it because they cannot understand it.

Why then do so many thousands upon thousands of Russian Jews claim Yiddish as their mother tongue?

Yiddish as a symbol of identification

After the results of the census became known, I began to look into the phenomenon of the one half million Jews who had claimed Yiddish as their mother tongue. On meeting Jews, young and old, in Moscow and elsewhere, I would ask them what language they had given, and I was surprised to learn that many young people had claimed Yiddish. I would say to them: "You don't really know Yiddish, or your acquaintance with it is remote. Why did you declare it as your mother tongue?" The answer I received was: "This is my real mother tongue, and the fact that I do not know it is neither my fault nor the fault of my parents."

Assuming that there really were thousands upon thousands of such people—though for lack of proof, this is merely a conjecture—then what we have before us is a host of individuals who demonstrated, indirectly, their identification with their people and their national culture and whose response is tantamount to their having said: "If we are registered as Jewish nationals, then we are proud to register our language as Yiddish despite the fact that we don't speak it." Suffice it to say at this stage that the official disclosure itself, which admits that half a million people declared Yiddish to be their mother tongue, consti-

tutes a vital issue in the controversy between world Jewry
and the Soviet regime over the suppression of the national
rights of the Jewish people in the Soviet Union. For it is
inconceivable that half a million such citizens are not
given any opportunity, no matter how meager, to teach
this language to their children.

None of the Jews claimed Hebrew, because Hebrew was
not accepted as a mother tongue by the census takers.

The status of Hebrew in the Soviet Union is yet another
indication of the state of Jewish culture and deserves some
attention. From its very inception the Soviet regime has
dealt the Hebrew language crippling blows that have virtually killed it. Whereas the regime adopted Yiddish as the
"idiom of the Jewish masses" in order to use it as a vessel
into which it could pour "socialist content," it behaved toward Hebrew with uncompromising hostility.

Hebrew as the language of the Bible and prayer book
was considered by the government to be dead and was
simply another battle in the overall atheistic war that was
waged against the Jewish religion. But Hebrew as a modern language, with its origins in the Pale of Jewish Settlement during the czarist period, with its beginnings as a living language rooted in Russian soil, with its own schools,
newspapers, literature, poetry, and theater—Hebrew as a
living language was looked upon by the regime as a snake
whose fangs had to be pulled before it poisoned the Jewish
masses in the Soviet Union. The authorities regarded it as
a vehicle for the hated Zionist movement and as a bond
which united the reactionary, anti-Soviet Zionist youth
groups. Thus the Soviet regime mercilessly destroyed the
Hebrew press, literature, and theater, and prohibited their
very existence; and the language quickly disappeared from
the Jewish scene in Soviet Russia.

Hebrew as a modern language was almost entirely forgotten by Soviet Jewry until the Second World War. It
was preserved only in the Scrolls of the Law, in commen-
taries, in the faded and worn-out pages of the prayer
book, and in the mouths of cantors who often did not
know the meaning of the words they uttered.

The Jewish refugees who poured into Russia during the
war from Poland, Lithuania, and other lands brought with
them tens of thousands of young people for whom Hebrew was a spoken language, or at least the language that
inspired their ideological and spiritual life. The annexation

of the Baltic countries, Bukovina, and Moldavia added still more thousands of Hebrew-speaking people to the Soviet population, most them graduates of fine Hebrew schools. This situation in no way altered the government's attitude toward Hebrew; on the contrary, it served only to harden its determination to prevent this "Zionist poison" from coming back to life.

The creation of the State of Israel, however, compelled the Russian government grudgingly to acknowledge the existence of the language. The Soviet authorities have only gradually admitted the need to train some of their diplomats and experts to read and understand the language of the State of Israel. They have also found that a considerable number of Russian Jews, among them young people and adolescents, are interested in learning Hebrew. They have therefore found it necessary to recognize the language. In 1963, a Hebrew-Russian Dictionary was published in Moscow, the first to appear in two generations. It was compiled by F. L. Shapiro; then, after his death, it was adapted and edited for publication by Professor B. M. Grande. The introduction to this dictionary stresses the historical continuity between the biblical language and the living Hebrew of modern Israel.

If the state of Yiddish is comparable to a desert in which there is an occasional oasis, that of Hebrew is like an utter wasteland. Deep down below its desolate surface there may be hidden sources of water, but one must dig far down to reach them. Yet there are some Jews in the Soviet Union who are willing to search out such sources to quench their thirst for Hebrew.

Kol Ha'am, the Hebrew daily of the Communist party in Israel, is virtually the only Israeli newspaper obtainable in the public libraries of Moscow and Leningrad. If you ask politely, the librarian of the large world-press reading room in the Lenin Library of Moscow will make a copy of this paper available to you. When it comes from the stacks, the girl at the counter tells you to take good care of it. You look at it and see that it almost crumbles in your hands because it has been read so often. You realize that hundreds of hands have held it before you, and you see how the print has faded beneath the touch of so many fingers.

One sometimes sees, in this library or in the Saltykov-Shchedrin Library in Leningrad, a Jewish reader, usually middle-aged, who seems to be consuming the paper with awe and reverence. These are apparently Jews who came to Moscow or Leningrad from Lithuania or Moldavia, or as refugees from Poland, and stayed on in the Soviet Union—Jews who were educated at the Tarbut Gymnasia of Bialystok, Vilna, Chernovtsy, or Kishinev. And occasionally one also sees young people bent over the Hebrew paper, reading it with the help of a dictionary.

They are not alone, as one discovers when traveling through the country. There are others as well, some self-taught, having learned Hebrew by themselves systematically and thoroughly. From the questions they ask it is clear that some young people have tried to take one step beyond that of declaring Yiddish as their mother tongue. There is no doubt that a small number of Russian Jews, especially among the young, also want to learn the Hebrew language, and to take pride in it. Many such Jews, who have come to realize that the only way to fill the void is through Hebrew, are also aware of the tragic fact that Yiddish is not only persecuted in the Soviet Union, possibly without a chance of recovery, but is also on the decline in the large Jewish centers in the West. Any casual encounter between these Soviet Jews and young Jewish tourists from the United States, England, or Canada, proves that there is no common language between them. They realize also that Hebrew is not only the language of the State of Israel, but that it is gradually developing into a cultural tool that serves to unite and bridge the Jewish dispersion as well. This realization impels Jews in the Soviet Union, each in his own way, to learn the living Hebrew language of our day.

A young Jewish father from a provincial town, who had taught himself basic Hebrew of sorts, decided to make a bold attempt to get Hebrew textbooks for himself and his small daughter. His was an ingenious approach. He had no address in Israel to write to and no one whom he could ask for books; but he assumed that the municipal schools there, as in the Soviet Union, were numbered serially. He wrote a Hebrew letter and addressed it to:

School Principal
School No. 1 (A)
Tel Aviv, Israel

As it turned out, he was right and the letter was delivered to High School A in Tel Aviv. The principal read it with great excitement: "I [the writer's name and that of his father] and daughter mine [her Hebrew name] want learn Hebrew. We Jews want know language people. I learn myself Hebrew four year. But no books on Hebrew. We want very much send us books, some stories, books poetry, history Hebrew people. We want reading in Hebrew Sholokhov of Israel. Stories for me and daughter mine beg send stories for class C, D, E, but I beg what you need books in Russian I send you. Writing me [correct address in the Soviet Union]. I want and daughter [her name] friends with children Israel. This small part friend Soviet Union with Israel. *Shalom,* good friend. We want records and postcard 'Tour of Israel.' Goodbye." [Signature of the man and his daughter.]

This letter, with its misspelled and halting Hebrew, is testimony to the feelings of many Jews in the Soviet Union today.

Social and occupational strata in the Soviet Union

In order to understand the social stratification of the Jews and their status in Soviet society, one must utilize both the facts available in official statistics as well as observations gathered through conversations and personal experience. A brief description of Soviet society in terms of social stratification is necessary for any assessment of the Jewish situation in this context.

Soviet communist propaganda, which once spoke of a Soviet society of workers and peasants, may have sounded good in the past; but the Soviets know full well that their society today is composed of various strata and that it is a complex entity filled with internal tensions. The picture is not as simple as it appeared in early revolutionary days, a fact which is admitted. Thus the Soviets themselves speak of three basic elements of their society: the agricultural workers in the *kolkhozy* and *sovkhozy*, the industrial workers in the towns, and the intelligentsia. The latter includes members of the liberal professions, and sometimes also government officials. But even this classification is too broad and too simplified, for in reality the picture is far more complex.

Anyone attempting to develop a schematic structure of Russian society along sociological lines, might well classify its many layers in accordance with a ladder system: upper, middle, and lower. Each of these is divided in turn into an upper and lower, giving six strata:

Upper upper
Lower upper
Upper middle
Lower middle
Upper lower
Lower lower

Despite the generalizations and simplifications inherent in this system, it is possible to divide Soviet society according to the functions performed in each of these categories:

Upper upper
    Top level of the party (in the Presidium, Secretariat, Central Committee)
    Top level of the Soviet government (Council of Ministers)
    Top army level (high-ranking military officers)
    Outstanding scientists
    Outstanding writers and artists

Among the first three elite groups are the real rulers, the party people being the most important and decisive element.

Lower upper
    Top party members in the republics and large cities
    Senior government officials
    High-ranking military officers
    High level scientists, university professors
    Directors of large plants, top technicians
    Top directors of government trade
    Important writers and artists

Upper middle
    The organization (*apparat*) personnel of the Communist party
    Middle range government officials
    Middle range of the military and police command
    Directors of medium-sized industrial plants, directors of *kolkhozy* and *sovkhozy,* engineers

Doctors, teachers, lawyers (all those with seniority)
Employees in government trade services and brokerages

Lower middle
Lower civil service in the Communist party
Lower middle range of government civil service
Young doctors and engineers
Accountants
Foremen with seniority, various technicians
Lower middle level officers, sergeants in the army and the police

Upper lower
Lower government civil service
Sergeants, corporals, soldiers in the regular army and the police
Skilled workers and peasants in the *kolkhozy* and *sovkhozy*
Employees in government trades and stores
Artisans

Lower lower
Unskilled workers in industry and agriculture

It may be noted in connection with this ladder that it is, first of all, a framework, and as such far from perfect. Secondly, since advancement in Soviet society is effected through accomplishment (though instances of "belonging" and "wire pulling" [*proteksiia*] are evident at marginal top levels, the demarcation between layers is more elastic than in other societies. There is constant transition upwards, though this is qualified by the fact that thousands of people were demoted on political grounds at the beginning of the Soviet regime and in the Stalin era and suddenly found themselves on the lowest levels of Soviet society.

The Jewish elite

With this picture of Russian social stratification in mind, one can attempt to explore the position of the Jews in this scheme.

There are virtually no Jews in the top levels of government. The Central Committee of the Communist party of the Soviet Union (from which the main strength of the Presidium and top government positions are recruited), elected in the 22nd Congress in 1961, has 0.3 per cent Jews. This is about one-fourth of what the Jewish representation should have been had the Central Committee been constituted according to the proportion of nationalities in the general population, where the Jews number 1.5 per cent.

But this fact in itself does not indicate the true extent to which Jews are absent from the top level of government. It should be remembered that the number of Jews at the head of the regime in the days of the revolution was much larger, and was out of all proportion to their numbers in the population. Khrushchev once said to a French socialist delegation: "In the early days of the regime the Jews were in the front rank of revolutionaries and they may have been more revolutionary than the rest of us." The historical and sociological factors which account for this deserve a special study. It will suffice merely to point out that the Jews in czarist Russia had been urban and, compared with their Russian neighbors, intellectual; but they were socially degraded, persecuted, and full of bitterness against the regime. They naturally tended to join the extreme revolutionary movements, to which they gave their wholehearted devotion and strength. Years before the revolution, many young Jews were among the most prominent members of the underground and exiled Russian revolutionary movement.

With the seizure of power by the Soviets, and for some years thereafter, Jews began to occupy vital positions in many levels of government. The purges of the thirties affected many of these Jews. There is no doubt that Stalin did not want to be surrounded by Jews who were "too smart," "too clever," "too intellectual," and "too cosmopolitan." Despite this, however, Jews were at that time so necessary and so firmly rooted among the ruling elite, that even as late as 1939 they represented 10 per cent of the entire Central Committee of the Communist party. They were second only to the Russians (and ahead of the Ukrainians!). For reasons already explained, Stalin decided, during and immediately after the war, that the Jews were a security risk. A drastic change took place. The percentage of Jews in the Central Committee fell sharply. In 1952 it was 3 per cent and in 1956, only 2 per cent.

Khrushchev followed the policy initiated by Stalin. Kaganovich, the last Jew in the Presidium, was deposed in 1957, along with the whole "anti-party group." This purging of the Jews went on also in the lower strata of the top levels —until they sank to a position that was the reverse of the one they had occupied at the beginning of the revolution: from having the highest representation, out of all proportion to their numbers in the population, they now had the lowest.

The situation is not much different in high level government or administration, though some Jews are still in evidence there. This is true as well of the top army command, whose elite has practically no Jews; and if in a moment of need the Soviets suddenly "discover" a Jewish general, it is indeeed an unusual occurrence.

Immediately below the summit of the Soviet pyramid stand the leaders of the Communist party and those of the republics and the large cities. This is another level which Jews can no longer reach, and it is no exaggeration to say that this stratum is virtually empty of Jews.

In the national republics there is keen competition for party advancement between the young leaders who represent their individual nationalities and those who are Russifiers, particularly Ukrainian-Belorussian Russians, who were born and grew up in those republics, or were transferred there. The Jews are suspended between these two worlds and can participate in neither. Knowing this and realizing their position, the Jews no longer attempt to take even the initial step up the national ladder. They feel certain that somehow or sometime one of the rungs beneath their feet will snap and that they are likely to break their necks in the fall.

What is true of the republics is generally true of the large cities as well. Many of these cities are also capitals of national republics (Moscow, Kiev, Minsk, Tashkent, Alma-Ata, Tbilisi, Riga, and so on) where there is great competition for advancement between the various nationalities, with the Jews excluded.

There are more Jews in the senior service than in top levels of government. But it would seem—though there are no statistical data to bear this out—that they are mainly in professional positions; further, their number is smaller than their proportional share of the population. An extreme example, probably unusual but highly significant, is the status of Jews in the foreign service. Once again we must return to the genesis of the Soviet regime in order to understand this situation fully.

At that time hundreds of Jews served in the highest grades of the Soviet foreign service (the most outstanding personality was, it will be remembered, Foreign Secretary Maxim Litvinov). Stalin set out to purge this delicate and sensitive area of Jews even before he turned to other branches of the government. Today there are no Jews serving outside the Soviet Union in any of the higher or middle diplomatic grades—no ambassador, no minister, no adviser. There may be some in the lower grades, but if so, they are completely out of sight. There are Jews in the foreign service in Moscow in departments of investigation, but they have no contact with foreign diplomats.

The situation is different with regard to the two other groups at the head of Soviet society, namely, those consisting of the leading scientists and artists. The Soviet regime allows maximum liberty to men of genius in science, particularly the natural sciences, and this is true in the case of Jewish genius as well. The lists of the yearly recipients of the Lenin Prize and other great prizes for science, and of new members admitted to the various academies of science, contain a great number of people who bear typically Jewish names. Jews figure in nuclear science, astronomy, chemistry, higher mathematics, biology, and allied branches to a far greater extent than their proportion in the population. In these areas the Soviet regime requires the highest intellectual talent, and it does not care whether this talent belongs to someone who is registered as being of Jewish nationality.

A story which sounds like a joke, but which some claim is true, is told about one of the first encounters between some great Soviet and American atomic scientists. The heads of the two groups were introduced to one another as Professor Winkler of the Soviet Union and Professor Winkler of the United States—both were Jews.

The area of science includes a high proportion of Jews at all levels; and indeed it is the only area of the upper upper stratum which is really open to them.

There are not many Jews in the upper levels of literature or the plastic arts. The area of the arts which is most accessible to Jews is music. Some of the best known and greatest Soviet musicians are Jewish (incidentally, most of them are performers, not composers). The prominence of Jews in music is perhaps due to the non-national and universal nature of this art form, whereas literature, painting, and sculpture are anchored to the scenery, nature, and history of particular nationalities and republics. This wealth of setting and background material is in the possession of creative people of all nationalities—except Jews, who of necessity must use characterless, hackneyed expressions, such as "Soviet" scenery, "Soviet" nature, or a "Soviet" individual. These are meaningless compared to such realities as the colors of a Russian landscape, the rugged Georgian scenery, an Armenian type, a historic figure from Ukrainian lore, and so on.

The Jews have a larger share in the middle and lower levels of the world of art—again mainly in music, but also in the theater and cinema. Some of the best Soviet movie and stage directors are Jews.

As regards the universities, there are still a good many Jewish professors and heads of departments, mainly in the branches of the natural sciences. But they are an aging remnant of the past and their number is quickly decreasing. This is particularly evident in the universities of the national republics. There, Jews are replaced by nationals in an effort to fill the teaching positions with an ever increasing number of "national professors."

One has the impression that the percentage of Jews who are directors of large industrial plants is also decreasing, though there are still many who are in economic planning and in Soviet financial and trade organizations.

Lieutenant Feldman: "One of yours"

There are, of course, Jews in the middle and lower middle echelons of the party organization, but their numbers are few. This does not mean that Jews do not belong to the Communist party. But they are aware that, for them, the curve of promotion and status flattens early; therefore they do not attempt to enter the party organization. And even when they do, it is only to ensure themselves the necessary "credit" in other avenues of advancement. There are Jews in the middle and lower middle ranks of the Red Army. But the impression is that there are few in the conventional units and more in the highly specialized units—particularly professionals whose work lies in the area between that of the scientist and the combat soldier.

In the spring of 1960, shortly after the Soviets brought down the American U-2 aircraft, the spy plane was placed on exhibit in Gorki Park, which is the largest and loveliest park in Moscow. On display were fragments of the plane, many optical and acoustical instruments, the pilot's flight gear, personal papers, spy equipment, and weapons.

This exhibition was well organized and was a center of attraction for months. Hundreds of thousands of civilians saw it, and thousands of school children were brought there by their teachers. Every foreign visitor to Moscow was taken there by Intourist guides. An odd atmosphere prevailed: part circus, part spy movie, part scientific exhibition, and part propaganda against the "enemies of the Soviet Union" and for the "greater wariness of citizens against spies who lurk in every corner."

I visited the exhibition and was particularly interested in the reactions of the school children. I sensed no rabid hatred in them for the "imperialist spy," but a deep curiosity and interest in the technical aspect of the plane's construction and operation. There was a sense of pride that "we" succeeded in downing the "apparatus" and a slight feeling of contempt for the unlucky pilot.

Among the visitors were some professors from the Weizmann Institute in Israel who had come to the University of Moscow for an international convention of biochemists. The Soviet foreign service official who received important guests at the exhibition heard that these were well-known professors from a scientific institute in Israel. "Ah, from Israel," he said. "You will probably be interested to hear that the officer commanding the rocket battery which brought down the U-2 was one of yours (*odin iz vashikh*)—Lieutenant Feldman." This Russian official had forgotten that in theory there can be no connection between an Israeli professor and a rocket officer of the Soviet Union, and he unconsciously linked them together because both were Jews. One may assume that there are no few such Feldmans in the special units of the Russian Army.

We have dealt with various areas of Soviet life in which comparatively few Jews are engaged. We come now to those occupations in which there are many Jews: engineers, doctors, teachers, lawyers, accountants, and the like. It is possible to say without any exaggeration that one out of every three or four Jews in the Soviet Union is a doctor, engineer, or teacher. And since there are over one million Jewish wage earners, the number of doctors, engineers, and the like, runs into hundrds of thousands of Jews.

Of these, the largest groups are those comprising engineers and doctors. Tens of thousands of Jews have graduated from the higher technical schools and universities in all the branches of modern engineering: architecture, construction, industrial engineering, chemical and pharmaceutical engineering, electronic and mining engineering, optical and mechanical engineering, and so on. The same holds true with regard to all the branches of medicine. Incidentally, there are many Jewish woman doctors in every field of medicine. There is scarcely an industrial plant, and certainly no hospital, without its professional Jews. They do not necessarily occupy the top positions, but are mainly among the professional rank and file.

There are tens of thousands of Jewish teachers as well, but their status is peculiar, particularly in the national republics. Here again is a situation which has been met before. The majority-nationals of the republics regard the Jewish teacher as a foreign element and a Russifier. They prefer to keep the vital work of educating their young in the hands of their own people. This fact tends to reduce the percentage of Jews in the teaching profession.

There are also thousands upon thousands of Jewish accountants whose status, because of the make-up of Russia's economy and trade, is both sensitive and precarious, as will be explained.

Many Jews are found in the supply system as workers in various government stores, as employees in restaurants and hotels, and in the middle and lower grades of the government transportation network.

There are hardly any Jews in the lower echelons of the Soviet regular army and police, or in managerial positions in the *kolkhozy* and *sokhozy*.

Quite a few Jewish artisans are still to be found in the many small co-operatives: shoemakers, tailors, and so on. But the younger generation of Jews are doing their utmost, with their parents' help, to enter the more dignified professions, such as medicine or engineering. In transportation the Jews are mostly taxi and truck drivers, and there are not many in the railways or in shipping nor in the skilled industrial or building trades. There are even fewer in the unskilled occupations. Finally, among the many millions of peasants and agricultural workers, there are virtually no Jews at all.

The pendulum returns

To sum up the matter, there is one important sociological difference between the status of the Jews in czarist times and today. In Czarist times, Jews lived, geographically, ethnically, and culturally, in a society that was almost entirely sealed off from the Russian world around them. They constituted for the most part a vast middle class of merchants and middlemen. Below this middle class came strata of artisans and laborers (but not peasants). Above it were Jews who tried to break through the narrow gateway to the liberal professions (doctors, engineers, and so on). A small number, by dint of great wealth or conversion, attempted to reach the peak of society, and almost invariably failed.

The Soviet revolution opened the land to the Jews in a geographical sense. At that time there was also a vacuum in administration and government, which had to be filled. As a result of modernization and industrialization, a high degree of professional talent was needed and absorbed into the new system. Jews grasped these opportunities and contributed in full to the socio-economic revolution which transformed both the Soviet Union and themselves. They penetrated the highest ranks of Soviet government and local rule. But at an early stage of the regime, attempts were already underway to make the Jews "productive." Organizations were founded whose purpose it was to transfer large numbers of them to agriculture, to found Jewish *kolkhozy* and to settle as many Jews as possible on the land.

Now, three generations after the revolution, the Jews of Russia are utterly splintered. They are dispersed and scattered throughout the land and their culture has been virtually destroyed. But from the standpoint of their social stratification, it is as if the sociological pendulum has returned to the middle of the ladder.

The attempt of Jews to settle on the land failed. Once again they occupy an important middleman position in government trade of every kind. The greatest change is, of course, the major share they now have in Soviet technology, though again on a middle rung of the social ladder.

Typical of this trend—which is summed up in the admonition that "Jews should not elbow their way in to the head of the line"—is the status of Jews in the Soviet universities. The percentage of Jews in Russian universities and institutions of higher learning is greater than their percentage in the population. But if one examines these statistics in the light of the situation that existed in the early days of the regime, one will realize that their number is steadily decreasing. Two reasons account for this: first, the obstacles they must overcome in entering a university; second, the increasing number of other nationals seeking admission.

Is there some kind of official *numerous clausus* for Jews? Certainly not. The use of this term would be angrily countered by Soviet officials and would be called anti-Soviet propaganda. There is, indeed, no semblance of any law or regulation, written or oral, regarding the permissible percentage of Jews in a given university. Nor is any such law or regulation likely to be adopted.

The fact remains, however, that time and again one comes across the same story of the actual experience of Jewish parents and students, the gist of which runs as follows: "Our Misha wanted to enter the faculty of physics in our town. His school marks in this subject were excellent and he is generally a gifted boy. He presented all the papers and certificates required by the university authorities and was then asked to bring further certificates and go through all sorts of formalities. Then there were days of procrastination while we spent a lot of time in university waiting rooms trying to reach all sorts of administrative officials. Finally, Misha was advised that there was no room in the faculty of physics that year and he could not be admitted. Other students who finished their studies at the same time and with lower marks than his, were admitted. They did not have to go through all the formalities that were requested of Misha. But he wanted to enter the university at all costs. So we decided, with him, that he should change to chemistry. He actually preferred physics and wanted to specialize in it. But what could we do? We did not want to waste another year. His marks in chemistry were also very good and he presented his application and required forms at the proper time. He became more and more nervous during the period of waiting. An answer finally came, saying that because his marks in chemistry were not 5 (excellent) but only 4 (very good), while he had gotten excellent marks in physics, the university authorities strongly advised him to study physics. A year passed and we did not weaken in our resolve to get him a higher education of some sort. We consulted friends and asked around, then learned that there was a chance of his being admitted to a veterinary school. We hurried there, taking the papers which proved that Misha also had good marks in biological subjects. After a few anxious months we were happy to hear that Misha was admitted. He is in his second year there now. The course is not easy, but we are all very glad that he will at least graduate, though he wanted so much to become a physicist."

This story might be attributed to the sensitivity of the parents. One might say that there may really have been no place in the faculty of physics, that the admission standards for the faculty of chemistry are so high because of the many students who wish to enter, that there is actually no proof of a *numerus clausus* in this story or any indication of anti-Semitism, that the university authorities refused to admit the boy on reasonable grounds and the Jewish parents blamed them without cause. Further, the matter ended well; the boy will graduate and have a fine profession. And one might argue, too, that non-Jewish parents probably have similar experiences.

But one hears such stories over and over again, with many variations, from Jewish parents and their sons. And when one suggests that they might be exaggerating, they respond angrily: "No. The matter is not so simple as it appears. They push us aside, they put obstacles in our way, because we are Jews." Only very slowly does one begin to suspect that an unwritten State policy of preventing Jews from entering the universities really exists.

Jewish parents and children, knowing of the difficulties they are likely to encounter, sometimes try to find university officials who can be induced with appropriate "gifts" to expedite and facilitate the admission procedure, or a kindly professor who might be more charitable, or faculties that have more openings than they have candidates to fill them. There are those, too, who travel very far from home in search of universities which it might be easier to enter.

This is all on an individual basis, of course. No one

openly casts a slur on officials or professors, or maintains that they harbor anti-Semitic feelings. It would be inconceivable for a number of parents or their children to attempt to organize and work together. Each family tries its best separately to overcome the obstacles and either achieves its goal, or fails, knowing full well that at the root of the situation is the word *"evrei"* on the registration card.

This situation, like others we have described, is more marked and is more acutely felt in the national republics: in the Ukraine, Belorussia, Lithuania, Latvia, and in the Central Asian republics. The nationals compete with young Jews for the prize of higher education which leads to advancement in society and life. Professors and certainly students, as well as university officials, regard the Jews as unfair competition, because "these Jew bastards get such high marks and grab the places belonging to our sons." Hence, without any actual direction from the authorities, the stage is set to make it as difficult as possible for Jewish youth to gain admittance to academic institutions. The extent of the difficulties depends on the particular university and sometimes on the particular professor.

The story is told that when Khrushchev (or the then Minister of Culture, Madame Furtseva) was once asked by visitors from the West what accounted for this situation, the answer was: "The Jews may or may not encounter unusual difficulty in being admitted to the universities. It would do no harm if there were one Jewish *shakhter* (miner) for each Jewish student."

This is precisely the root of the Jewish tragedy in the Soviet Union. Khrushchev, or his Minister of Culture, did not accuse the Jewish people in general, nor any group representing the Jewish people, of being non-productive. No such group exists. The statement was directed to every Jewish father and mother individually: "Take your Grisha (or Sasha), who received a grade of 5-5-5 in his studies, and make a *shakhter* of him. You, the father, might be an engineer, and you, the mother, a doctor; but you had better take that step so as not to set your neighbors against you —against you as members of the Jewish nationality."

"They cut off my chance"

Jews and Armenians are two peoples in the Soviet Union who have preserved a strong sense of humor. There is no doubt that these two persecuted peoples have developed their own special kind of humor as a protective shield against the bitterness of their daily lives. Whoever in the Soviet Union tells a sharp, spicy joke, something that is almost always done in a closed circle, quietly, with tongue in cheek, usually attributes the story to Armenians or Jews.

Here is a story I once heard about the "special treatment" accorded Jewish students in the Soviet Union. Misha Rabinovich and Ivan Popov have reached the final stage of their examinations for entrance to the university. They sit and wait in the anteroom of the old-time Russian professor, who is about to decide which of them is to receive the coveted prize. Popov is called in first, and when he comes out half an hour later, he tells Rabinovich: "Don't waste your time. I already have it." Rabinovich asks: "What do you mean? I haven't even been examined yet. I'll go in." He does so, and the Russian professor tells him: "Comrade Rabinovich, let's forego the examination, because I have decided to recommend Popov." Rabinovich is stunned. "But why? You haven't even examined me." The professor says: "This Popov is a real genius. I have been teaching for thirty years and have never seen anyone with such a phenomenal memory. This fellow remembers, to the last detail, everything that happened to him since he was two years old." Rabinovich counters: "Just a minute. I also have an extraordinary memory. I remember everything that happened to me since I was eight days old." The surprised professor asks: "Really? What happened when you were eight days old?" Rabinovich answers: "That's when they cut off my chance to enter the university. . . ."

Jews tell many jokes about the hardships they encounter trying to enter the professions and how the authorities prefer non-Jews wherever possible. Take this one for example: The head of the Soviet Union comes back from a visit to the United States, calls his aide, and tells him:

"We have to do some effective propaganda about this Jewish business. At a press conference in the U.S.A., on television, in the White House, they kept asking me: 'What about the Jews? Why do you close the synagogues? Why are there no schools? Why, why? These Jews completely spoiled my whole trip.' The aide asks: "And what do you suggest, Comrade Chief of the Government?" He answers: "I suggest we immediately build a splendid synogogue at government expense on the Kremlin grounds, near the ancient churches, then open it to Jewish worshipers. When diplomats, newspapermen, and tourists come from the United States and from the West, we will take them on a tour of this synagogue and shut the mouths of the Jews once and for all." Says the aide: "A brilliant idea, Comrade Chief of the Government." He is told to go ahead and see to it that the palatial building is ready within six months. "It will be done, Comrade Chief of the Government," says the aide. And he gets to work. Six months later the chief looks out of his office window and sees a symptuous synagogue, complete with golden *Magen David* decorations, standing on the Kremlin grounds. He calls his aide, congratulates him over the job he's done, and asks: "Is it filled with Jewish worshipers?" "No," says the aide. "We are looking for a rabbi, then they will be able to pray." A few weeks later the chief sees that the synagogue doors are still closed. He asks his aide: "What happened? Why?" The embarrassed aide answers: "We are still looking for a rabbi throughout the country, but we haven't found a proper candidate." "Why? We have many rabbis in this country." "Yes," says the aide, "but the trouble is that all the rabbis we found were Jews."

Intermarriage

A people which is not a people and a society which is not a society in the Soviet Union has no way of preventing its sons and daughters from abandoning it through intermarriage. There is no law, regulation, or custom that might influence an isolated Russian Jewish family to marry its children within the fold of the Jewish nation or religion; there are no means of collective persuasion through the utilization of the influence of the Jewish milieu, for such a milieu does not exist.

Intermarriage is not a new problem to the Jews of the Soviet Union. During the first generation after the revolution, when all barriers were broken and there was less unwillingness on the part of gentiles to absorb Jews who burst en masse into the new society, Jews began to intermarry without any difficulties or restrictions. They hoped that the different national origins of marriage partners would be considered insignificant in the new and enlightened socialist society. The regime placed no obstacles in their way. Only civil marriage was recognized by the authorities and at the ceremony of registration neither the religion nor the nationality of the parties was ever questioned; they were merely Soviet citizens who had decided to marry. This made intermarriage quite simple. Though no statistics exist, there is no doubt that thousands of Jews intermarried during that period.

Then came the tragedies. The Nazis conquered the areas in which most of the Jews were concentrated. To this day Jews tell of the agonizing problems faced by those mixed couples. Should they reveal to the occupying authorities that one of them was Jewish? If they kept silent, they might be denounced anyway by neighbors or spies, which would make matters even worse. And what of the children? Should they inform the Germans that one of their parents was Jewish? And what about the Jewish family name and the Jewish looks of the father or mother, which might give away the secret? These were the life and death decisions which mixed couples had to make. It is said that there were many quarrels between them, and often the non-Jewish partner reported the other and thus decided his or her fate. Intermarriage was greatly reduced during and immediately after the war, and the horror of that experience has not yet been forgotten by the Jews who lived through it and whose children are now of marriageable age. Today, as in the past, there is no social or legal pressure to prevent young Jews from intermarrying. On the contrary, there are many factors that operate in favor of intermarriage, particularly the opportunity that mixed couples have to register their children under the nationality of the non-Jewish parent. An additional factor is the apparent desirability of Jewish husbands, who are much sought after by gentile girls because "they neither drink nor beat" (*ne piut i ne biut*). The Jewish husband usually brings his pay home and does not squander it on the way. And by his very nature, possibly because he has married one who is outside the fold, he is less violent and aggressive than others. The Jewish girl is no less in demand. There is something exotic about her to gentile eyes. She is considered "warmer," "Mediterranean," "gipsy-like," and is thought to make a better mother. These stereotyped beliefs, no truer in reality than any other, account for the strong attraction of Jewish bridegrooms and brides.

Three forces operate today against the tendency toward intermarriage. One such force consists of the Jewish parents—not necessarily the elderly, but those who well remember the tragedies and catastrophies that resulted during the war from the mixed marriages of their friends and relatives. These people associate intermarriage with a possible future calamity. They cannot define this calamity: another world war, an economic crisis, a revolution, or something of the sort. But they are certain that if any sort of crisis were to occur, the first to suffer would be the mixed couples. Such parents, though they are modern and neither religious nor nationalistic, will make any sacrifice and go to any length to find Jewish mates for their children. They rush around madly, moving from town to town, sometimes getting themselves seriously into debt, so that their Misha or Sonia will remain within the fold.

A second such force is the love and nostalgia of the young people for their parents and grandparents. They know that by intermarrying they will cause the family great pain, and many take this into consideration. And, finally, there is the new feeling of nationalism which has awakened in many young Jews and which acts as a barrier against intermarriage.

In spite of everything, however, intermarriage remains a serious problem. It may be assumed (again, without statistics) that tens of thousands of young Jews have intermarried and are still doing so today. These intermarriages are bringing about an erosion which is likely in the course of time to transform Russian Jewry into an arid desert.

The parallel economy

In order to understand the position of Russian Jews in the Soviet economy, it will be necessary to describe briefly what I will call the parallel economy of the Soviet Union. Soviet Russia has had this parallel economy from the very beginning of communist rule. The Communist revolution was born in a period of economic chaos and during a serious shortage of consumer goods that grew out of the First World War and the civil war that followed. The situation was such that the demand, which amounted to an absolute hunger for goods, was always greater than what the new Soviet agriculture and industry could supply. The Soviet regime brought to this chronic economic sickness a tough and dogmatic ideology which prevented private enterprise from raising its head. This ideology entirely disregarded the economic principles of the free market, attempted to impose its own rules upon the market, and diverted the main resources of the country, which were poor to begin with, into heavy industry.

It is not surprising that millions of hungry citizens looked for cracks and breaches in this new and unfamiliar structure and sought any means, legal or illegal, to fill, even at black market prices, their empty bellies.

In my childhood my parents used to tell me endless stories about the situation in Russia in the early twenties. They told me of the hunger, the black market, the long lines for a bit of food or coal, and the hundred and one ways Father found to feed his family. Many years later, when I read Boris Pasternak's description of the period in *Doctor Zhivago,* I recalled my parents' tales.

In 1921, when Lenin realized that the official Soviet economy was going to collapse and that the people would not tolerate a state of constant hunger and shortage, he tried to find a way out by sanctioning the parallel economy and the private initiative which had hitherto existed underground. This became the "new economic policy"— N.E.P. Some years later Stalin abrogated the N.E.P. and imposed powerful punitive sanctions on private agriculture and on private enterprise in the towns. But even in the darkest days of Stalin's regime the parallel economy did not disappear. And afterward, in Khrushchev's time and later, it came to represent an integral element of the Soviet economic scene.

A distinction must be made between what I call the parallel economy and what is understood in the West as the black market. The parallel economy has a wider scope, runs deeper, and covers much more ground than any black market in Western society. In fact, the Soviet parallel economy is the most concrete expression of private enterprise. It is motivated by a personal desire to acquire a little more money and a little more pleasure. At the same time, it helps lubricate the heavy and cumbersome machinery of the Soviet economy.

The parallel economy is in evidence in every vital branch of the Soviet economy, in industry, agriculture, and trade.

Every industrial plant, large or small, is dependent for its planning, budgeting, building materials, raw materials, and markets on certain bureaucratic administrative forces which operate from a distance and are far removed from the plant's day-to-day problems. A plant manager who tries to master the multiplicity of problems which have to be faced in order to maintain the production schedule dictated from above, or possibly even exceed the quota and win distinction and promotion, must not only fill out hundreds of forms in order to secure authorizations from his superiors, but must also maintain a special employee who is himself a product of this system. This person, the *tolchak* (pusher), is a kind of intermediary, agent, organizer, and manipulator all rolled into one. He knows all the important people in the various offices at headquarters. He can arrange for a file or authorization to get priority and be moved ahead. He knows all the people in charge of the supply of raw materials and through inducements, presents, and bribes, he obtains the materials which the plant needs. What is most important, he gets them on time. He is acquainted with the other plants in the neighborhood and with the other *tolchaki* and can arrange exchange deals with them to benefit his plant. For example, should his plant, which manufactures nails, require timber to build a much needed extension, then the *tolchak* runs over to his colleague at the nearby sawmill and exchanges a few tons of nails, badly needed at the sawmill, for the required quantity of timber. This seemingly primitive barter system is the special fuel which keeps the wheels of many a plant moving.

It is hardly correct to say that the manager and his *tolchak* are breaking the law and are moved by personal greed. It is quite likely that both have at heart the improvement of the plant and the fulfillment of the quotas called for; but because of the limitations of the prevailing system they find it necessary to employ certain tactics which might be frowned upon by the authorities. This situation, in various shades and endless variations, is an instance of the parallel economy.

A particularly significant example of private enterprise in agriculture is evidenced by the tremendous amount of production going on in the small private plot of land near the home of each *kolkhoznik*. At present the regime tolerates these plots and has even created special means to absorb their produce—the *kolkhoznyi rynok* (*kolkhoz* market) which flourishes in every town. These are essentially gray markets, which sell private produce at prices that are often many times higher than those quoted in government stores. This produce, incidentally, is usually of fine quality and is worth the price paid for it.

Anyone who has not seen the small, peasants' plots on the *kolkhozy*—beautifully tended by the father of the family, the mother, the grandmother, and the children, who pour into them all of their spare time and energy—has never in his life seen genuine private enterprise. To someone passing by the *kolkhoz* market in Moscow, it will seem as if endless streams of old women are pouring in from the villages. They come wearing high boots or felt shoes, with colored kerchiefs on their heads; and they carry jars full of excellent cream and fresh rounds of homemade cheese.

Georgian tomatoes and pocket money

Those who get the most out of the market are peasants from the far south, chiefly the Caucasus.

It is worthwhile for the mustached Georgian father and his two tall, broad-shouldered sons to set out on a fine spring day, at four o'clock, before dawn, from their house on a *kolkhoz* about sixty miles from Tbilisi. Leaving the village, each carries a bag which contains 44 pounds of beautiful red tomatoes grown in the private vegetable patch near their house. They board a TU-104 jet after checking their three bags (every passenger is allowed 44 pounds of personal baggage). Our three friends fly to Moscow at a speed of about 650 miles per hour and land at nine o'clock that same morning at the Moscow airport. They hire a cab and by ten o'clock they are in the *kolkhoz* market of the busy capital. Opening their bags, they set their tomatoes in rows and wait for customers. Housekeepers, mostly of the privileged classes, prefer these lovely tomatoes and buy them at four or five times their prevailing price in the government shops.

By four in the afternoon, our Georgians have disposed of all the tomatoes. They go shopping in GUM, the large department store in Red Square, and in Detskii Mir, the large children's store in the heart of Moscow, where they buy gifts for their wives and toys for their children. Then they spend a few hours at the Aragvy, a fine Georgian restaurant, where they enjoy good Georgian wine and hand out coins to the musicians who play sentimental Georgian tunes for them. Thus the busy day ends gaily. The next day they go back to Tbilisi and from there to their village. The money they bring back will be invested in their private farm. They repeat this routine a number of times during the season.

These "jet tomatoes" are yet another element of the parallel economy.

The intrusion of the government into all branches of the economy has resulted in the establishment of a dual pattern of behavior on the part of workers. One is the official pattern. The other, the "not-so-official pattern," is referred to in the vernacular as the "left side" (*na levo*), in contrast to the "right side" (*na pravo*). In Russian, as in other languages, the term "right" denotes conformity to law.

There are, for example, many ways of getting a taxi *na levo* in a large city. Anyone who has lived in Moscow for a while knows the meaning of the special wink that links a driver and his potential passenger. The driver will look at you, decide that you are "all right" then suggest that he stop the meter if you are willing to agree with him on a mutually satisfactory price for the ride. At times one can get hold of a cab which is really not a cab at all: official cars will often park in central parts of Moscow after taking their passengers to government offices, to scientific institutes, and the like. These cars are driven by chauffeurs. Knowing that his boss has gone in for a meeting that will last for hours, the chauffeur takes a chance, drives around in town, and thus makes a little profit on the "left side."

The *na levo* can even be ludicrous at times. One day I stood near the Intourist hotel in Irkutsk, waiting impatiently for a cab to take me to the airport a few dozen miles away. For some reason the cab did not arrive on time. I was joined by three other passengers, one of them an army officer, who were also trying to make that flight. Time was passing and we knew that the plane would not wait for us. We became increasingly impatient. We went out to the street, hoping to stop any vehicle that might get us to the airport. We ended up standing in the middle of the road and waving at every passing car. Suddenly a city bus stopped alongside us with a grinding of brakes and the driver asked what was the trouble. We explained. The driver looked around, then said: "Quick, hop in." He drove us quickly to the airport. He told us rather casually that he had been on his way to the municipal garage. We each gave him a few rubles and everyone profited.

It should be stressed again that such "left side" practices ought not to be regarded as actual black market operations, but rather as procedures akin to some of the more or less commonly accepted practices in the West, such as cheating on one's income tax, which is something of a national sport in many countries and is indulged in by virtually everybody in one way or another. Most of these Soviet practices are a by-product of the regime's policy, which gives rise to a variety of attempts at circumvention by the "little man."

Tipping, for example, is strongly discouraged by the authorities, who regard it as a capitalistic bourgeois custom which degrades both giver and taker. In reality, however, a tip given by an experienced hand will achieve the same miraculous results in Moscow as in Rome, in Leningrad as in Paris.

As the tourist prepares to leave his hotel room and is packing his bags, a few of the girls who cleaned the room during his stay in the hotel appear suddenly and help him look under the bed where he might have left his slippers, or in the bathroom where he might have left the toothpaste. He naturally thanks them for their past courtesies and present consideration—and gives each of them a tip, which is received with the same air of gratitude as in any Western city.

When one comes with his friends to a quality restaurant and the bearded doorman tells him that there is not a single empty table, he should not give up hope; a nice tip will get him a table. And a tip will prompt the porter at the train station to help the traveler find his seat and make him comfortable.

If anyone thinks this custom is reserved only for foreigners, he is quite mistaken. The tip, too, is part and parcel of the parallel economy, though it is not in any way to be regarded as bribery.

There is a real black market, of course, as well as real bribery and corruption of every sort. There is a supply and a demand for "black" dollars, as any tourist will realize after strolling through one of the central squares in Moscow or any other large city. There is a supply and demand for "black" clothes, music, records, and books from the Western world. This black market is operated along the same lines as are black markets everywhere in the world. Its wires extend to the underground and it has connections higher up. Its people know who is likely to have the required goods or cash; they know who needs what and who is ready to pay. Bribery occurs at various levels of the government structure, and there are also cases of actual theft and fraud.

It is difficult to draw the line between what we have been calling the parallel economy and actual criminal activity. The reason for this is that the government wages a relentless war against all these practices indiscriminately. However, despite the sanctions imposed from time to time against the parallel economy, I feel certain that the authorities realize that specific phases of it are the result of the clash between policy and reality. As long as the present policy prevails, there will be no escape from the parallel economy with all that it involves, and no preventive administrative measures will help.

Before discussing the Jewish aspect of this situation, it is important to note the special role played by the *bukhgalter* (accountant) in the Soviet economy.

The precarious position of the bukhgalter

The *bukhgalter* is a pivotal figure in the Soviet economy. Responsible officials or mangers of every shop, restaurant and cooperative, possibly even of every ice cream stand, and certainly of every industrial plant or agricultural unit, must submit to their superiors a mountain of reports which contain itemized accounts of quantities and prices, income and expenses, sales turnover and stock, and so on. Each of these concerns, therefore, employs a *bukhgalter*. He is the expert on Soviet red tape and paper work.

If a particular plant has to resort to the parallel economy; if anyone in any position of authority participates in any side activity; if figures have to be juggled in order for the plant and its manager to excel in carrying out the "plan"; if the acquisition of "black" raw materials or the "leakage" of finished goods must be concealed—in short, if there is any deviation at all from normal procedure, then the *bukhgalter* must be "in the know." He is in such a pivotal, sensitive, and delicate situation in the network, that nothing can be accomplished in the plant without his knowledge (except, of course, in cases of outright embezzlement).

The *bukhgalter*, therefore, knows all the secrets of the organization. He knows which of his superiors is involved in what the authorities call "economic infractions" and which of the employees are cooperating with them in these infractions. Indeed, in most cases he becomes a partner to the conspiracy, at times an active partner. Often he has no choice, for the initiator of the scheme might well be his superior, who will tell him plainly: "You either cooperate with us or I discharge you and hand you over to the authorities." He is caught between the hammer of the corrupt manager and the anvil of the security forces. His job is both dangerous and thankless. Anyone involved in cheating and fraud knows that he is at the mercy of the *bukhgalter*. The managers despise him and the workers hate him.

This brings us to the Jews. It has already been noted that they are mostly urban people and that they play a significant role as middlemen in all sorts of government trade and in the organization of supplies. In addition, because they are able to adapt themselves to varying situations and peoples, and because other opportunities are often closed to them, many Jews occupy the position of *bukhgalter*.

When the government decides to punish economic infractions, as it did a few years ago, it strikes at the Jews in particular. Not that Jews are specifically victimized as a group; it is only individual Jews who are involved. But the effects are felt by the Jews as a whole. They are in no position to ward off the blows, for they have no organization through which they can defend themselves. Campaigns get under way against corruption and theft in Soviet institutions and plants; trials are staged; and the minutes of the trials are given wide prominence in the press and radio. Severe sentences are handed down, usually the death penalty; and when these sentences are given wide publicity through all the available media—then every Russian Jew trembles. Whenever those who are sentenced or pilloried have names such as Abraham Izakovich Iakubovskii (which usually head the list) and are accused of being the instigators of crimes or the enticers of criminals and thieves, then all sons of Abraham, Isaac, and Jacob fear. And when one comes to realize that 60 per cent of those sentenced to death in recent years for economic crimes were Jews—fifty times their percentage of the population —one is forced to suspect that there was a guiding hand from above.

People of every walk of life are involved in the parallel economy—Russians, Lithuanians, Ukrainians, Georgians, Moldavians, Uzbeks, and Jews. But when Jewish names head the list of economic criminals while those of other nationals trail behind, the impression is created that the non-Jews were only naive and honest people who played a minor role in the economic conspiracy and whose only fault was to let themselves be drawn into the "Jewish net." All of this occurs in an atmosphere in which nothing positive or praiseworthy is ever attributed to the Jews in the Soviet Union. The only conclusion that can be drawn from this is that the Jews are being made the scapegoat for the government's economic entanglements.

The absurdity and deceitfulness of giving such prominence to Jewish economic criminals becomes all the more blatant when one examines the situation that exists in the other communist centers of eastern Europe. Polish, Czech, Bulgarian, East German, and Hungarian authorities also take vigorous and vicious action against economic crimes, which sometimes assume very serious proportions. They, too, conduct trials and hand down severe sentences. And the press in those countries also joins in the holy war against theft and corruption. But in none of those lands is the Jew ever singled out as a criminal.

In the Soviet Union, where shortages and an imbalance in the supply of goods and commodities prevail, the publicity given to Jews as arch criminals has anti-Semitic undertones which speak directly to the masses and which can easily evoke prejudice. When a Soviet housewife stands in a long line to buy fresh fruit and, while waiting, reads in her newspaper a detailed account of the trial of one Rabinovich who was convicted and sentenced for stealing apples on a large scale and selling them on the black market, her normal, instinctive reaction is to lay the blame for her difficulty in getting apples on all Rabinoviches, on all Jews.

Those who institute this policy often manage to deal with several Jewish situations at one time, thus killing many birds with one stone. For example, when newspaper readers are told that the center of the black market in foreign currency was the synagogue of a certain town, that stolen dollars were found in the cover of the Torah Scroll, that the old rabbi was an accomplice of a gang of thieves; and when an affair of this sort is further associated with an Israeli tourist or a tourist with a Jewish name from another country, then the result is clear: the very meaning of the word "Jew" becomes connected with the notion of potential thieves linked with a reactionary religion and with their hateful capitalist co-religionists throughout the world.

The antennae which Jews use to gauge the atmosphere of the lands in which they live are as sensitive as scientific instruments. Almost every Soviet Jew has such antennae. Some years ago, when the economic trials began, with their publicity, denunciations, and subsequent executions, the Russian Jew started to feel the thick dust of anti-Semitism gathering around him. Even the Jew who works in science, technology, engineering, or medicine now feels that some of the mud thrown at Rabinovich, the "economic criminal," sticks to him; he feels that some of the bullets which killed Shapiro, the "deceiver of the government," whom the execution squad stood against the wall, ricocheted and struck him as well.

5

Four Portraits

Types

As a result of my repeated encounters with Russian Jews, I developed the habit of sorting them into types. I shall try to describe four types as I saw and remember them: the old Jew Reb Chaim; the citizen Iosif Naumovich; the citizeness Sonia Moiseevna; and the student Grisha.

Reb Chaim remembers and hands on the heritage

Reb Chaim is a synagogue Jew. He still remembers the pre-revolutionary era, the czarist days, the pogroms, the Jewish *shtetl*, the Jewish Pale of Settlement, the *heder* and yeshiva, the Zionist movement and the Bund (Jewish Socialist movement). Reb Chaim is the kind of Jew who will answer the question "Why is your lot in the synagogue so wretched?" with a nod of the head and the typical, fatalistic Jewish response "It has always been so." Countless generations of persecution, oppression, and cruelty lie behind this response. He can tell you not only about the Nazi atrocities but also about the Khmelnitskii massacres and the Kishinev and Petliura pogroms.

Reb Chaim is seventy or more, perhaps nearly eighty.

He was over thirty when the revolution took place. His Jewishness was at that time already so rich and strong that he simply continued to live as a believing Jew, keeping the spark alive; perhaps he did not even work out consciously what he did, or why. He is a Jew who prays daily "May our eyes behold Thy return to Zion in mercy," because this was the way his father and forefathers prayed.

This old man wears a tattered black coat and a Russian *kasket* on his head. He drags his tired feet from the office of the *upolnomochennyi* to other government offices and is interrogated by the officials and asked to account for all his actions. He struggles mightily, as his father and forefathers did before him, to get from the authorities a permit to print a calendar, to bake matzot, to acquire a prayer book as a gift from Jewish tourists from America or England, or to obtain a microphone for the area in front of the synagogue. Reb Chaim is inured to the rude and insulting responses of the authorities, as were his ancestors. He will return, beg, and beseech until perhaps the God of Abraham, Isaac, and Jacob comes to his aid.

He needs no lessons in Jewish history, for he is an integral part of it. At times, when he blesses the Hanukkah candles, he feels that some of the blood of the Maccabees courses through his calcified veins; when he dances during Simchat Torah, past generations of Hasidim dance with him; and when he hums an old, melancholy Jewish tune, or a passage of the Psalms, it seems to him that King David accompanies him on his lyre. He does not even need any description of Zion and Jerusalem, nor does he have to be shown pictures of Mount Moriah, the walls of the Temple, the Judean vineyards, Mount Carmel and Tabor—for they have been engraved in his mind from childhood, along with the legends which his teacher in the little town told him in the *heder* sixty years before.

Day after day he prays for the fertility of distant fields. In the snowy Moscow winter he prays for rain to fall on the orchards of Sharon, and in the Moscow summer, for dew on the wheat of Samaria. When he opens the door of his poor abode on the Seder night, the Prophet Elijah comes in dressed in his white robe and greets him with a festive *"Sholem aleichem."* On Shavuot, the Festival of the Giving of the Law, he identifies himself with the revelation and with the thousands of his brethren who stood at the foot of Mount Sinai. On the night of *Kol Nidrei* at the onset of the Day of Atonement, he sees himself as a son and a brother of the forced converts of Spain, who prayed to the God of Israel from the basements of Granada and Seville. When he intones "I believe with firm faith in the coming of the Messiah," Reb Chaim imagines himself on the same path as those who mounted the scaffold to sanctify the name of God—that long, uninterrupted path leading from those who were martyred by the Romans to those who marched to the gas chambers of Maidanek, Treblinka, and Auschwitz.

In the dark of night, in his little room, he takes his grandson Sasha or Yasha on his knee and tells him, secretly, of the heritage of heroism and wisdom, kings and revolutionaries, philosophers and scholars, and of the Book of books, which his people bequeathed to the world.

He will also tell him that he, Reb Chaim, knows with absolute certainty that his people are still fully alive, that they have large and powerful communities throughout the world; and, above all, that young Jews have risen in the ancient land of their forefathers and rebuilt its ruins; that they plough the soil with tractors and harvest with combines "just as in the *kolkhozy*"; that young pilots fly planes "just like our TU-104" and steer ships over the wide seas "like our Admiral Nachimov"; that they build new towns in the wilderness "like in our virgin soil in Kazakhstan and Siberia." He will also tell him that these Jews write and speak the ancient-new tongue "which our forefathers wrote and spoke." And when the grandson asks what this language looks like, he will show him a tattered prayer book or a worn Bible.

And if the boy brings out an Israeli stamp from his album, or if he shows his grandfather a coin which is part of his collection and on which there appears a palm branch or an olive twig, the old man will say: "Yes, my child, this is the land of your ancestors, where your relatives and brethren now live. Never forget it, because I, my father, and my grandfather carried it in our hearts all our days."

The fate of Iosif Naumovich

Iosif Naumovich is now fifty years old. He was given the name Iosif by his grandfather. He was an infant at the time of the revolution. He has only a vague recollection of those early years. But he remembers this: when he was a boy he learned to hate the little town in which he grew up, and the heritage of his father and grandfather, and their language. He also learned to despise the synagogue which stood near his home, and the old rabbi, and the congregation of devoted Jews. With all his youthful energy, he embraced the new society which opened its gates wide to him and gave him every opportunity to study, to enlarge his horizons, to acquire a profession.

Iosif wanted to, and indeed did, see himself as an equal among equals in the new egalitarian society, and as one of its builders. He put all his strength and enthusiasm into his profession as an engineer, intent on helping the growth of the Soviet state. In the thirties, during the great purges, Iosif felt that the regime was for some reason more suspicious of him than of other citizens, and that there was an attempt on its part to identify him as a Jew, a label he wanted to rid himself of.

Iosif Naumovich was one of the first to volunteer for the fighting units during the Second World War. He fought, was badly wounded at the front, and was hospitalized. Before recovering, he volunteered again for the front, was wounded again, and received a number of medals. While serving in the Red Army, Iosif Naumovich the Jew felt that many of his comrades-in-arms were treating him not as an equal but as a foreigner, and that some of them were often disinclined to believe that he really was fighting for the motherland.

This was the Jew who advanced with the Red Army into liberated territory and saw his small, native town razed to the ground, who ran to find his parents and relatives and discovered them in a large common grave, who heard how the Nazis, actively assisted by local murderers, had wiped out his entire large family, who cried for vengeance, and in so doing felt that this vengeance should be wreaked not only on the enemies of his native land, the

Soviet Union, but also on the enemies of the Jewish people.

Iosif Naumovich was one of those who opened the gates of Auschwitz and stood terror-struck before the cremation chambers, and who listened to the survivors as they related what had taken place there. He was the Jew who arrived in Warsaw with his regiment, and walked through the ruins of the ghetto, and saw the surviving Jewish guerillas come out of their bunkers, and listened as they told him how the Jewish underground had fought. He was the Jew who came as a conqueror to Berlin, driving a tank or plunging his bayonet with raging fury into the last Nazis who were defending the city.

In conquered Germany, Iosif Naumovich met Jews from other parts of the world. There was Joe, the Jewish American soldier, who claimed that his parents came from the little town in which Iosif was born. He also met a Jewish soldier from Palestine, who wore a *Magen David* on his sleeve and the badge of the Jewish Brigade. This one even hugged him and told him that they were related.

Iosif Naumovich, who was appointed sub-commandant of a base in Germany, helped scores of Jewish refugees to look for the remnants of their families and to gather in camps before setting out toward the Mediterranean, toward the land which, they claimed, was to become their only land.

The Jew Iosif returned from the army to his town. He tried to regain his place in his profession and in life, and was dumbfounded to hear, both openly and by implication, that he had not actually fought at the front, but was a cheat who had bought his medals at the market in Samarkand. He was branded as a "cosmopolitan." He felt that he was being discriminated against in his job and realized that the avenues of promotion were closed to him.

During Stalin's last years he saw some of his best friends arrested and dragged away, never to return, on charges of "Jewish nationalism," of "conspiracies with Zionism," or because they had taken an active part in developing communist Yiddish culture in the Soviet Union.

Iosif Naumovich withdrew into himself. He stifled his anger and silenced his humiliation. He carried on his everyday life and his work silently, with bowed head, in order to survive the terrible days of Stalinist terror, in order to protect his wife and children. This is the man who said at home: "We should not be too conspicuous as Jews. We should not be seen or heard too much. We should not succeed or fail too much. And, above all, let us not get involved with the authorities."

Now the time of Stalin has gone and the days of the liberal thaw have come. The threat of terror no longer hangs over Iosif's head. At first glance the wounds seem to have healed. Iosif carries on his work, earns a living wage, spends his holidays at the seashore, goes skiing in the winter. He attends concerts, plays chess, enjoys watching television in the evening. His older children have acquired professions and are establishing themselves. But deep down he knows that everything has gone wrong, that the great dreams of his adolescence and youth have been utterly destroyed. He was not absorbed into the society in which he lives. He was "foreign" and "different," and will remain so. He realizes that his father and forefathers were probably right, and that the little town and its culture and traditions were not so awful, after all. Sometimes when he sees a poster announcing that a Yiddish concert is to be held in a little theater at the far end of town, an indefinable urge sends him rushing to get a ticket. While he is there, surrounded by other Jews and listening to Yiddish folk songs after decades of deliberate forgetfulness, there is a choking in his throat He, the soldier, the engineer, the Russian Jew who had hardened his heart for so many years and thought he had forgotten everything, suddenly bursts into tears. The next day he returns to the draftsman's desk (or the laboratory, clinic, or plant) and carries on his gray existence.

This Jew prays in his heart that his young son will not have to go through experiences like his own, and that he will manage, some way, somehow, to become integrated into Soviet life and society. His heart almost stops beating when his son comes to him one day and asks: "Father, why did the boys in school call me a dirty Jew?" He bites his lip, controls himself, and answers: "Never mind, it is just a meaningless word; don't pay any attention; everything will be all right. I'll go to the teacher and speak to her. It's nothing. Forget about it. The main thing is that you study hard, attend to your lessons, and all will be well."

Sonia Moiseevna: a "Yiddishe mama"

During the twenties, Sonia, who was then a young Jewess, was prepared to toss away the kerchief of the *"Yiddishe mama,"* as well as the future which awaited her in her parents' home and in her small Jewish town: bearing children, being a good housewife, and building a home for her family.

She looked upon these aims as ridiculous and provincial in contrast with the challenges offered her by the new regime: to learn a man's profession, such as engineering or economics, and earn an equal position at work and in society; to go out among the people as a teacher or doctor; to remove the barriers between herself and men, Jews and non-Jews. All of these drew her like a magnet.

She spent some fairly turbulent years among other enthusiastic students, studying medicine, and then she fell in love with a young Jewish engineer. She did not choose him to please her old parents, against whom she had rebelled, nor out of national or religious motives, from which she wanted to be free. But: "He was more refined, he treated me more gently, he drank less." This is how she remembers him today. They never considered being married by a rabbi, nor did they have a Jewish wedding. After their marriage, they got a room in a four-room apartment in a large city in central Russia. Sonia began her career as a young doctor in a suburban clinic. Her husband worked in the arms industry. Soviet society demanded all their time and strength, which they gave generously.

But nature also had its demands, and during the thirties they had two children, a boy and a girl. They could not allow themselves more. Work took all of the young mother's time. And raising the children in their one-room apartment became increasingly difficult.

Late one night there were knocks on their door. Armed policemen burst into the room and took her husband away to prison. Sonia was stunned; she shielded her children, who trembled with fear. She suddenly remembered those horrible moments of her childhood in a small Ukrainian town, when her mother had protected her and her little brother, while drunken Cossacks burst into the house with whips in their hands. After some months of rushing around brokenhearted, Sonia found that her husband was in a forced labor camp in northern Siberia. She volunteered to serve as a doctor in the villages nearest the camp. She packed some belongings, took her children, and set out on her journey. She saw her husband at fixed times, though a lot depended on the mood of the camp commandants and guards. She lived in a little wooden hut in the Siberian village and existed only to bring up her children, to take care of the sick, and to visit her husband.

When the war broke out her husband was released from the camp. Because he was an engineer and a weapons expert, he was immediately put into a combat engineer unit. During the first year of the war, he was killed in the bitter fighting in Belorussia.

Sonia herself was conscripted as a doctor and, in the years that followed, she served in several military hospitals. Her children were being cared for by the State. She was by then in her late thirties.

In the last year of the war, Sonia attended a badly wounded soldier from the German front. Slowly, under her devoted care, he recovered. She came to know him. He was a Jew, a physics teacher from a provincial Ukrainian town, where he had lived with his wife and son until the war. He did not know what had happened to them. When he was well enough to stand on his feet, he rushed off to look for his family. He returned to Sonia after some months, broken, bereft of his family. They began to start their lives anew; he gladly adopted her children. They wanted another child very much and their only son was born two years later.

They went to live in Moscow where Sonia and her husband found jobs, she as a doctor and he as a physicist in a large research laboratory.

Toward the end of the forties and in the early fifties, Sonia and her husband began to feel as though a cloud had descended on them. At work, Sonia would suddenly hear people muttering that she was not just a doctor like the others, but a "Jewish lady doctor" who was in contact with other "Jewish doctors." At his own job, her husband was not given access to certain secret material because, it was hinted, he was too "cosmopolitan." He was demoted and permitted to work only at routine jobs; finally, he was dismissed from the research institute. Stalin's last year was a nightmare for them. Friends and acquaintances were arrested and jailed; the family lived more and more apart from everyone else.

Some years after Stalin's death Sonia's husband again moved into research physics and made rapid progress. He succeeded, and gained international recognition in his speciality. Sonia worked part time at her profession although she no longer needed the salary. The family moved into a housing development reserved for scientists. Her husband acquired a car and driver; their living conditions improved greatly.

And then, when she had found peace at last and had more time to look back and assess her life, she tried, in a way which appeared strange to her at first, to reproduce within her own family some of the old customs she had seen in her mother's home.

One Friday evening she lit candles and explained to her children what this had meant to their grandmother. Once she prepared gefilte fish and brought it to the table with great fanfare. One Passover she went with her family to some relatives, who, she had heard, were having a Seder.

At such moments her life turns full circle and she becomes again a *"Yiddishe mama."* Actually, she has nothing to hold on to, save a nostalgia for the past and a few memories of her parents' home. But it seems to her that she makes up for this void by her deep love for her little family, a love mingled with sadness. And she thinks: "This love and this sadness are also Jewish; perhaps they are my heritage."

Grisha in the Pioneers Camp

There was much activity in the All-Soviet Pioneers Camp near Yalta. Several thousand happy youngsters were there from every part of the Soviet Union—sloe-eyed and smiling Kazakhs, tall and blond Estonians, broad-built Russians, and dark-eyed Armenians.

Grisha had come with the pioneers from his town, Leningrad. And after cold and gray Leningrad, these had been wonderful days indeed. The sun, the bathing in the warm waters of the Black Sea, the games and the entertainment at night—he felt himself a companion and brother to all the others, who were as gay and suntanned as himself. It was like being a member of a large and powerful family of nations, and of a beautiful and wonderful land. He lived in constant delight. Now, among the cultural events that were being prepared for the closing day of the camp, was an evening devoted to the peoples of the Soviet Union.

The head counselor of the camp, a young and jolly Ukrainian who could play the accordion and guitar, asked for volunteers who could represent their peoples in dance, song, music, and recitation from their national literature. On the bulletin board of the camp hung a paper which was divided into columns, each headed with the name of a people: Russian, Ukrainian, Turkman, Kirghiz, and so on. He asked everyone who wanted to participate, and who felt that he could contribute to the program, to write his name in the appropriate column.

Grisha, who played Russian folk songs well on his harmonica, quickly put his name down among the Russians. He was a native of Leningrad, and he considered himself a Russian. He knew no language other than Russian. True, at home and from friends he had heard that he was a Jew, but he had never asked what that meant. He was not even interested, busy as he was with his studies and sports.

The next day the counselor divided the volunteers into groups according to the list. There were groups composed of Georgians, Latvians, Belorussians, and so on. The Russian group was the largest and the counselor came to it last. He began calling the names of the boys who had volunteered for it, but left out Grisha's and those of two other boys.

Grisha thought that the counselor had made a mistake. But when he finished reading the list, the counselor said: "actually, Grisha Davidovich, Victor Samuilovich, and Sasha Leibovich have also entered their names as Russians, and we shall be very glad to have them participate; but I think they are Jews, so we will ask them to add some variety to the evening and sing us Jewish songs."

Grisha and the two other boys, who came from Rostov, and whom he did not know, were astounded and shamefaced.

"But we don't know any Jewish songs," said Grisha after a long moment, with everyone looking at him.

The second Jewish boy said: "Comrade counselor, I don't think there are any Jewish songs."

The third boy remained silent.

"All right," the counselor said. "If not songs, maybe one of you knows some Jewish dances."

The three boys did not answer.

"What, no dances either?" the counselor asked in surprise. "Well, maybe one of you can tell us an interesting Jewish story."

There was no reply. The counselor realized that he had gotten himself involved in an unpleasant situation, and he said: "Never mind, it's not important. You may join the Russian group and everyone will contribute his share. Forget it."

But Grisha did not forget.

When he returned home, he told his parents of his experiences in camp and mentioned the incident. He asked his parents: "Are there Jewish songs? If there are, can you sing them?"

The parents were somewhat taken aback and told him that they also did not remember any Jewish songs. "Do you know any Jewish stories?" the boy insisted. No, they did not. "Why do you have to bother about all this?" they said. "You have plenty of schoolwork and you must do well in your studies."

The boy didn't ask any more questions just then, but his curiosity was not appeased. What did he have in common with the boys from Rostov? Why were they called Jews when they could speak only Russian, sing only in Russian, and looked completely like other Russians? Such questions and others of the same sort began to bother him.

Grisha asked some of his friends in school, whom he identified as Jews by their names, what they thought of the matter. Some did not even want to discuss it. One told him: "Leave me alone. I am not a Jew and do not want to hear anything about it. I am a Russian and so are my parents. When I grow up, I'll do everything in my power to change my family name to a Russian one, and I won't be bothered with such nonsense anymore."

But there were other boys, curious and confused like himself, who were ready to discuss the subject because it troubled them a great deal. There was one boy among them who knew a great deal more than the rest. He told them that his old uncle had said that the Jews were a very ancient people who had come out of Egypt a few thousand years ago and had founded a state of their own in Palestine; they had had great kings and priests who served the God of the Jews in temples. Their language was called

Hebrew. They had had writers and poets who wrote a great and important book called the Bible. The boy told them that these Jews had fought the Assyrians, Babylonians, Greeks, and Romans for their freedom, and that about two thousand years ago the Romans had destroyed the Jewish state, after which the Jews were scattered throughout the world. Since then they had lived in almost every country. Some of the greatest men and scientists of all time were Jews. Those Jews, the uncle had said, carried with them, wherever they went, their fathers' customs and the books of the Law and the Bible which they brought from their land. They had many holidays symbolizing the great events of their history. His uncle had also told him that some decades ago the Jews had begun to return to their land and to rebuild their nation. Finally, after fighting a war of liberation, they had founded their own state, called Israel. The language spoken there was Hebrew, the same as that in which the Bible was written.

Grisha listened intently to these stories, but he could not quite understand what it all had to do with him. Why should he care about some Jews who had founded a certain state called Israel in the eastern Mediterranean, or that there were other people called Jews in Western capitalistic countries? What was all that Jewish business to him, a young Soviet citizen who wished only to complete his studies with distinction, to learn aeronautical engineering and be a cosmonaut?

Some time later Grisha came to realize that this "Jewish business" was registered and stamped on his papers, and that this somehow made him different from his non-Jewish friends. By the time he was nearly old enough to enter a university, he was already infected with some of the nervousness and tension of his parents, who feared that he would not be accepted because of his Jewishness. They no longer hid from him the handicap of being a Jew. His father told him about the sufferings of the Jews, about the Holocaust and the Nazis. But he had very little to say that was positive about Jews and Judaism, so that all Grisha heard from him were stories about troubles and persecutions.

He began reading what the Soviet papers wrote concerning the State of Israel, where so many Jews lived. He learned that it was a horrible country; that the climate was hellish; that it was riddled with constant unemployment and hunger; worse, that the country was in fact an armed camp; that even the girls were called to the army; and that this army, for aggressive imperialistic reasons, from time to time attacked the peace-loving Arabs who lived in neighboring Egypt, Syria, and Lebanon.

Grisha read more and more, including essays and articles on Jewish subjects. Again and again he came across accounts about people with names similar to his own who were being accused of theft and corruption. He read about synagogues which served as centers of black marketeering and reaction. Not once in all his reading did he find a single good thing connected with the name "Jew." And he began to doubt the truth of what he was reading.

He asked himself why he should believe that only he had sprung from an utterly evil heritage and why it was that he knew so many fine and splendid facts about the Russians and their past? Why was the Georgian, his friend, so proud of everything connected with Georgia? And why was his other friend, the Ukrainian, so in love with everything connected with the Ukraine? And why should he, Grisha, believe that he alone, because he was somehow connected with the label "Jew," belong to a reactionary, evil, and vile people? He asked himself: "How is it that two million people in Israel, who, according to the papers, are all suffering from sunstroke and unemployment, can attack their neighbors with tanks and new planes—neighbors who outnumber them tenfold and more?" There was something illogical about it all, something possibly untrue.

From here it was only one step to the thought that perhaps the reverse was true. Perhaps the Jews in the synagogues were not all cheats. Perhaps his people had a past no less glorious than that of other nations. Perhaps one should believe the exact opposite of what is written in the Soviet press about Jews and Judaism.

Traveling from Moscow to Minsk, I sat opposite a young man. In the course of our conversation I discovered that he was a Jew, an agricultural engineer who had just finished his studies and got a job in a *kolkhoz*. He spoke of the great difficulties he had experienced in getting into the university on account of his being a Jew, of how much he missed not having Jewish friends at the *kolkhoz* and nearby, and so on. While talking, he saw the Hebrew paper I held and started leafing through it. It turned out that this was the first time he had ever seen an Israeli newspaper. As he handled the pages, he asked whether it was very difficult to read from right to left. I told him that this was our language and that it was quite natural for us. He answered, smiling: "Well, actually it is not so hard, because that is how I read *Pravda* every day, from right to left."

Skepticism about Jewish matters is only one step removed from cynicism concerning the truthfulness of the regime's propaganda. Indeed, the young Soviet Jew is one jump ahead of his non-Jewish friends in cynicism and sarcasm. But many segments of the present young generation of Russians, particularly technologists and intellectuals in the large cities, are becoming increasingly indifferent to communist ideology and have begun to see the world through the eyes of sober individualists.

Grisha also went through this stage, and then began looking for a positive approach to his identification with the Jewish people. He talked with several of his Jewish student friends in the university in order to get more information from them about Jews. Some had met Jewish tourists from the West or from Israel. Some had heard fuller accounts about Jews and Judaism from their families. Some had listened to foreign broadcasts. One had read the book *Exodus*, which he had received as a gift from an American tourist. From all these fragments Grisha reconstructed a picture—vague, indistinct, superficial, and full of gaps and question marks—concerning the past and present of the Jewish people.

When a friend suggested that he come along to the synagogue, Grisha gladly agreed. His interest was a mixture of the natural curiosity of youth to see something new, and a strange desire to be among Jews and to see all around him a living denial of the propaganda, the literature, and atheistic brochures which he had been fed.

Everything in the synagogue was foreign and strange: the pale old Jews swathed in their prayer shawls, the Ark decorated with ornaments and Stars of David, the Hebrew inscriptions on the walls of the building, the Scrolls of the Law in their velvet covers, the unfamiliar prayer book.

It was a holiday and the place was crowded. The heat was almost unbearable. Only his sharp longing to try and identify himself with these people kept Grisha there.

He listened carefully to the Jewish liturgy. There was no musical instrument in the synagogue, only the cantor and a few old Jews who made up the choir. Gradually, the melancholy tune began to insinuate itself into his heart. The melody was quite different from anything he had ever heard. Yet he felt as though he had always known it. Then he reminded himself that these were the songs he should have known at the Pioneers Camp in Yalta years before. The tunes were beautiful, and his ancestors had sung them for many generations. The Scrolls of the Law, the prayer shawls, and the customs had a history of thousands of years. The blood of the people who wrote the books and scrolls, who composed the tunes, flowed in his veins; he was their heir. He was elated because he had convinced himself that he belonged to something ancient and great, that he was part of a mysterious stream, the springs of which were far away in time and space.

Then he saw that the people around him had made a narrow path through which the rabbi, who was holding a Scroll of the Law, passed. He saw Jews bowing toward the Scroll, and kissing, yes, actually kissing it. The rabbi came near him and Grisha felt an overwhelming desire to kiss the Scroll. But a sudden shyness brought him back to reality. How could he, a modern and progressive Jewish student, who belonged to a communist, atheist, and progressive society, kiss an ancient parchment in front of everybody? He saw a few young faces here and there in the crowd, people who might speak about it at the university, where he would become a laughingstock. At the last moment he held himself back from kissing the Torah as it passed him by, consoling himself with the thought that he might do so some other time.

He left the synagogue with the feeling that he would return. He said nothing of his experience to his parents and very little to his friends. He continued to work hard at his studies, and was ready to receive his diploma and enter his chosen profession. But secretly, without arousing attention, he continued to gather facts about his people. He read what there was by Yiddish writers in Russian translation and pictured in his mind the small Jewish towns of past generations. He went again to synagogue with a few friends on the High Holidays.

During his last year at the university he often met with two Jews from the United States who were there for post-graduate study as exchange students. He became friendly with them and heard a lot about their country and their feelings as Jews. One of them had visited Israel quite often during his holidays and had worked in *kibbutzim*. He talked eagerly about the small country and its people.

Gradually Grisha built a new inner yardstick by which to evaluate himself as a member of the Jewish people; at times he even felt proud of being a Jew.

6

From West and East

The remaining one-fourth of Soviet Jewry

I have indicated a number of times that my description of
the current situation of Soviet Jewry refers to a majority
of the Jews of the Soviet Union, but certainly not to all of
them. This majority—about three-quarters of the total—
includes most of those in the Russian Republic, the
Ukraine, and Belorussia. They have two common denominators: their Western origin, and the fact that they were
born or have lived within the borders of the Soviet Union
since the revolution—which means that for three generations they have been cut off, completely or partially, from
the rest of world Jewry.

To determine the whereabouts of the remaining one-
fourth of Russian Jewry, and how it differs from this majority, we must make a geographic rather than a social, oc-
cupational, economic, or age-group division. We will then
find that these Jews live in two geographical areas, western
and eastern Russia, and that the common denominators
we have mentioned do not apply to them. More precisely,
those who live in western Russia are of European origin
and have lived less than three generations inside the Soviet
Union, while those in eastern Russia have lived there since
the revolution and before, but are not of European origin.

The Jews of the western borderlands

During and after the Second World War, the Soviet Union annexed large areas and populations into its western borders. Some of these areas either had been part of the Russian empire at one time, or had been coveted by Russia. Thus the three Baltic countries, Estonia, Latvia, and Lithuania, which had been sovereign nations between the two world wars, now became Soviet republics; large areas of the eastern part of Poland were added to the Ukraine and Belorussia; and parts of Czechoslovakia and northern Rumania became Carpatho-Russia, Bukovina, and Moldavia. As a result of these annexations, the purpose of which was the strengthening of Russia's western defense perimeter, many more peoples and languages were added to those already present in the Soviet Union.

Large numbers of Jews had lived in these annexed areas before the Second World War. During the war, some of these Jews escaped from the Nazis and wandered with other waves of refugees deep into Russia, or enlisted in the Red Army. After the war, very little was left of the once great centers of Jewry in eastern Europe.

After these areas were annexed, scattered remnants of Jews began to return to their former homes. Some came from the east—Siberia, Central Asia, and other remote parts of the Soviet Union. Others, survivors of the Polish death camps, came from the west. Some were Jewish partisans who came out of hiding in the forests; others were demobilized soldiers of the Red Army. They returned in the hope of finding their surviving relatives.

They went through frightful years among the physical and spiritual shambles of their homes, surrounded for the most part by people who had taken their places during their absence and could not understand how these Jews had managed to survive when by all accounts the Jewish people had been completely exterminated.

Some Jews could not bear living in the shadow of broken homes and bloody memories. A number tried to get out through various "repatriation" agreements; and because many had formerly been Polish citizens, they were able to return to Poland, and from there to go to Palestine. Others were not so successful. Of these, some went to the large urban centers of the Soviet Union, or to the Soviet republics in Central Asia and Siberia, hoping to make a new start.

But there were also those who, despite the memories, remained where they were and began to build a new life. Now, almost a generation after the war, three to four hundred thousand Jews live in the rebuilt Jewish communities of Tallin, Riga, Vilna, Lvov, Chernovtsy, Kishinev, and the like. All of these Jews have one thing in common: they are "new people" and "new Jews" in the Soviet Union, and they are undergoing almost the same psychological and sociological pressures as those experienced by Soviet citizens, especially Soviet Jews, in the twenties and thirties. The Jews of Bukovina and Lithuania do not have to be seventy years old to remember what Judaism is. Any Jew in these areas who is now thirty or forty years old still remembers well the *heder* and the rabbi of his little town, or the kindergarten, the school, and the Jewish gymnasium in his city. He may have been a student in one of the famous yeshivas of Lithuania, a member of the Zionist youth movement in Latvia, a pious follower of one of the hasidic rabbis of Galicia, or a student in one of the Jewish seminaries in Moldavia. These people, almost without exception, grew up with Yiddish or Hebrew or both as their mother tongue. The synagogue, the Jewish tradition, the Zionist movement were once integral parts of their lives. They lost them only a short time ago—and the wound has not yet healed. This fact has even found expression in the official census of 1959. While the number of Jews registering Yiddish as their mother tongue was approximately 20 per cent throughout the Soviet Union, it was 50 per cent in the republics of Moldavia and Latvia, and more than 70 per cent in Lithuania! Had it been permitted to declare Hebrew as one of the languages recognized by the census, thousands most certainly would have claimed it.

There is still another tragic feature concerning the Jews of Bukovina, Moldavia, Latvia, Lithuania, and elsewhere who happened to live within Soviet borders during and after the war. Almost without exception, they have close relatives and childhood friends who now live outside the Soviet Union, especially in Israel. The fact that they themselves remained "here" while the others are now "there" increases the hurt, for they consider themselves victims of the cruel absurdities of war. By mere luck one brother had wandered east to Central Asia, while another remained among the partisans; one sister happened to marry a Polish Jew and thus was able to go to Palestine, while another stayed in the Soviet Union; quite accidentally a son who had survived a German concentration camp was liberated by the American or British Army and crossed over to Palestine as an illegal immigrant, while the father was liberated from another camp by the Red Army and wandered back east to his hometown, looking for his son—and remains trapped there to this day.

There are as many variations to these stories as there are Jewish families throughout the annexed areas.

These two factors—the memory of the great vitality of Judaism in the not too distant past, and the anguished separation from close relatives and friends in the present—create a state of feverish tension among the Jews in these areas, and a powerful desire to escape their fate. It is the sort of tension that gives rise to rosy dreams which are baseless, to hopes for miracles that will somehow improve their lot, and, in the end, to depression, hopelessness, and utter despair.

An Israeli comes to Vilna

I visited Vilna a few years ago, shortly after it was opened to tourists. I inquired at the hotel concerning the whereabouts of a synagogue and was told that in that entire city, which once had been one of the great centers of Jewry and had been known as the Jerusalem of Lithuania, only one synagogue remained. The others either had been destroyed by the Germans together with the ghetto, or had been closed by order of the authorities.

But I was not the first Israeli to visit Vilna since it was opened to tourists. I was preceded by my friend, one of the official delegates of my country, who came there with his wife and son on the eve of the Jewish New Year. This is his story:

"When I came with my family to the synagogue, I found it filled to capacity by hundreds of men and women, while hundreds of others who could not get in crowded the yard and the street outside. The head of the community and the beadles led me and my son to the eastern wall, the place of honor in the synagogue. My wife was led to the women's gallery. I was not surprised to see the place so crowded on the High Holidays, as I had seen the same thing before. Nor was I surprised that my visit had been expected. The Jewish grapevine works well. If an employee at the airport or a waiter at the hotel hears of the arrival of the first Israeli in Vilna, many others will know about it that very same day. What did surprise me in Vilna were the many children and young people among the worshipers. They had come with their parents, and their presence gave the synagogue a different appearance, brighter, more colorful, and healthier than that usually seen elsewhere. Even before the prayers, the people began crowding around me—first a few, then more and more, until there were hundreds of them, all inquiring about their relatives in Israel and other lands, or sending regards to their parents, brothers, and children.

" 'Do you know the Goldberg family in Tel Aviv?'

" 'Give Abraham Shapiro in Jerusalem the warmest regards from his brother.'

" 'My father, Nathan Cohen, lives in Brooklyn. Maybe you know him?'

"It was not easy to explain to these Jews that there are a good many Goldbergs in Tel Aviv and quite a few Cohens in Brooklyn. I stood helplessly before them, able only to say: 'I'll try to remember; yes, I'll try to tell him. . . .'

"When the service started the people reluctantly went back to their places. But the children could not be restrained; they swarmed around my son. It was the first time they had seen a boy from Israel with a *Magen David* in his lapel, a lovely little prayer shawl, a blue-and-white cap on his head, and a new prayer book in his hand. The beadles tried to move the children away but were unsuccessful. A group of a dozen or so stayed close to him throughout the service.

"I sensed that hundreds of eyes were staring at us, that our presence was lending a special festive air to the service, that the cantor was singing with more than normal intensity, that the worshipers seemed to be lingering over their prayers so that the sight of an Israeli boy surrounded by Jewish children of Vilna might last a little longer.

"An even more dramatic scene took place in the women's gallery. My wife is a native of Kovno, the second largest city and the former capital of Lithuania. Her parents and sisters had been killed by the Germans during the war and she was sent to a forced labor camp in Hamburg and then to Bergen-Belsen. In 1947 she arrived in Palestine aboard a blockade runner.

"We had thought it likely that she would meet friends or relatives in Vilna, since many of the city's survivors had returned after the war. Soon after she sat down, a woman approached, stared at her in amazement, and then said with great excitement: 'Excuse me, isn't your name Hannale?'

" 'Yes,' said my wife, 'it is. How do you know?'

"The woman burst into tears. 'I was your dressmaker. I made dresses for you and your sisters when you were small.'

"The two hugged each other.

"The dressmaker told everyone that the guest of honor was 'our little Hannale.' Minutes later, two of my wife's best frends came up to her. She had not known that they had survived, and until that moment they had believed that she had perished with her family.

"When the prayers were over the *gabbaim* asked the congregation to let me and my family go quietly and without disturbance back to our hotel. The older people understood; they remembered the bitter aftermath of the spontaneous demonstration in honor of Golda Meir in Moscow in 1948. After hundreds of handshakes they took leave of us and we went out into the street, deeply moved.

"But the children had no intention of leaving us alone.

"From the synagogue to the hotel, a distance of almost a mile, we went in procession through the main streets of Vilna: two well-dressed strangers and a boy, preceded and followed by dozens and dozens of Jewish boys. As we went along, many of them turned to me, in Russian or in Yiddish, with the childish request: '*Diadia* (uncle), take us to *Eretz*.' They used the Hebrew word '*Eretz*,' an abbreviation of '*Eretz Yisrael*,' which had been in common use among the Zionist youth movements during the twenties and thirties in Lithuania, Poland, Rumania, and other eastern European countries. Thus, in the very heart of the Soviet regime, the parents had handed down to the children one of the symbols and concepts of their youth."

This was the experience of my friend.

I was not fortunate enough to have gone through such an experience. I did not visit Vilna during the High Holidays, and my presence there did not draw so much attention. But I could sense some of the same atmosphere described by my friend.

In 1960, an Israeli artist, the pianist Frederick Portnoi, was invited by the Russian government to tour the Soviet Union for a series of concerts. Posters announcing the concerts appeared in the streets of Moscow, Leningrad, Minsk, and Riga, and stated explicitly and in bold type that the artist was from Israel.

Two concerts were held in Riga on two successive evenings. It was not easy for me to get a ticket, even with the help of the hotel, for the moment the advertisements appeared the box offices were stormed by Jews. There was even a black market in tickets many days before the concert. But after much trouble I finally managed to obtain one. The concert hall was beautiful, paneled with embossed and engraved wood in the old style of the Hanseatic cities. It was filled to capacity. Most of the people in the audience were Jews. They were dressed in their best clothes. The atmosphere was unusually festive. "This is a holiday for us," Jews told me before the performance. I felt once more how eager they were for any chance to identify themselves as Jews, or even to sit for a few hours in a hall among hundreds of their own.

The concert consisted mainly of pieces by Chopin, the Israeli artist's forte, and every piece was accorded loud applause. But toward the middle of the concert, the pianist played a composition by Paul Ben Chaim, who was identified in the printed program as an Israeli composer. The music was modern and unfamiliar to Soviet audiences. It had no particular Jewish or Israeli motifs, but one could see clearly in the people's expressions that they were trying to detect in this Israeli creation something special, some echo of a far-off yet nearby land, some kind of collective greeting sent to them by a composer and a pianist, both of whom were Israelis.

When the music ended, there was thunderous applause which went on and on, out of all proportion to the intrinsic merits of the music. The wild acclaim was without a doubt a response to the entity called "Israel." Only through the sanctioned and innocent means of their applause could the people find an appropriate means of expressing their feelings toward Israel.

I am told the same thing happened the next evening:

the same festive and deeply moved crowd, the great sympathy shown the artist, and once more the same tumultuous applause. And again, in Leningrad, where the pianist gave one performance, hundreds stood during the concert in a packed hall. Students who couldn't find seats went up on the platform and sat at the pianist's feet. After the concert, the audience applauded until the hall management put out the lights. Only then did the crowd slowly disperse.

The Jews of the Asian borderlands

During the eighteenth and nineteenth centuries the czars sent military expeditions to the Caucasus and Central Asia. After many years of violent fighting, the czar's armies subdued Caucasia and a number of Central Asian lands. These were annexed to the great Russian empire. As a result, Russia absorbed nations, peoples, and tribes which were totally foreign to her in language and civilization. Among these were Armenians and Georgians, who had a very rich and ancient history, older by far than that of their conquerors, and who had accepted Christianity long before it had been adopted by the Russians. They had their own culture, poetry, painting, and architecture at a time when the Russians were still at a very primitive stage of development.

The peoples of Central Asia, who for thousands of years had been part of the civilizations and empires of the ancient Near East (Babylonians, Persians, Parthians, Sassanids, Moslems), were also swallowed up by the Russian empire. Millions of Moslems were incorporated into the territory of the Russians, along with cities which had a long and brilliant history, such as Bukhara, Khiva, and Samarkand. Jews had lived in these conquered areas for hundreds of years. They, too, were added to the Russian empire—and later to the Soviet Union.

Today they number about a quarter of a million and comprise three distinct groups: the Georgian Jews, the Mountain Jews, and the Bukharan Jews. They differ considerably from the millions of Ashkenazi Jews who live in Russia, the Ukraine, Belorussia, Lithuania, and other parts of European Russia, and are descendants of Jews who migrated to Russia from western Europe over a period of many centuries. Their ancestors were the Judeans exiled by Rome, who made their way eastward during the final years of the Roman empire and the Middle Ages, wandering slowly, in the wake of incessant persecutions, from the lands of the Franks to those of the Germanic tribes and from there to the wide living space of the Slavs—first to Poland, then to Russia and the Ukraine. In the nineteenth century, a few million Jews lived in the Pale of Settlement in the western part of the Russian empire. They had brought with them their own unique and rich civilization, which included a comprehensive religious system, consolidated by generations of rabbis, legislators, and scholars, as well as an array of educational institutions. They had also brought with them from medieval Germany a fluent and rich dialect, Yiddish, in addition to Hebrew, their sacred tongue, which they had always preserved. These Jews possessed characteristics which are typical of all creatures that are subjected to constant persecution: suspicion, cunning, curiosity, nervousness, and alertness.

It must also be noted that during their centuries of wandering through central and northern Europe, they absorbed many of the ethnic, anthropological, cultural, and sociological traits of the people among whom they lived.

The history of the Jewish tribes of Georgia, Daghestan, and Bukhara is of an altogether different nature. They are the descendants of ancient Jewish exiles who left Palestine before and after the destruction of the First Temple, as well as after the destruction of the Second Temple. They moved east into the Assyrian, Babylonian, and Persian empires and made their way to the outlying regions of those vast territories. In time they settled in the remote and exotic lands of Armenia in the Caucasus, on the eastern and northern shores of the Black Sea, on the shores of the Caspian, and in the countries lying along the famed "Silk Road" which led from Persia and Turkey to the Far East through Central Asia.

These Jews, whom we shall refer to as Orientals (but not Sephardis, for they have nothing in common with the exiles from Spain), have lived for many centuries in the climates, landscapes, and cultures of the Near East. Their ancestors both witnessed and were victims of the rise and fall of the empires of the Babylonians, Medes, Persians, Hellenists, and Parthians. They were living in Armenia and Georgia when those lands adopted Christianity in the early centuries of the Christian era. They witnessed the great conquests of Islam in Central Asia and were decimated, as were millions of other people, by the roving hordes of Genghis Khan and those who succeeded him. They also witnessed the remarkable phenomenon of the "Jewish Kingdom" of the Khazars. They lived in Samarkand, the capital of the great empire of Tamerlane, and were an integral part of the setting of the famed emirates of Bukhara, Khiva, and Kokand.

These Jews, like their brethren in Europe, adopted the languages and dialects of the people among whom they lived. In similar fashion, they also developed a language of their own, Tati, a form of Persian written in Hebrew characters. In addition, they spoke various Georgian, Uzbek, Tajik, Turkish, and Persian dialects.

They were more deeply influenced by their environment and by the peoples and cultures that surrounded them than were the Jews of European Russia. The European Jews lived in compact communities which at times comprised hundreds of thousands of Jews; they were thus able to insulate themselves against outside influences and create their own culture. The Jews of Central Asia, on the other hand, were widely dispersed and amounted to no more than a few tens of thousands in each of their three centers: Georgia, Daghestan, and Bukhara.

It is therefore not surprising that in their manner of living, as well as in their dress and customs, they resemble so much the people in whose midst they live. The wonder is that they managed to survive at all and maintain their individuality, religion, and tradition in the Caucasus and in the steppes of Central Asia, cut off as they were not only from the stream of Jewish life in Europe but also from the large Jewish communities, closer at hand, in Iraq and Persia.

An analysis of the factors that protected and preserved these Jews in the past will help to explain their present peculiar status as Jews under the Soviet regime.

First, and probably most important, is the fact that they have lived so long in Caucasia and the ancient towns of inner Asia that they have become, as it were, part of the scenery. Since, as is generally agreed, they have lived in these areas for as long as two thousand years, they cannot be regarded as nomads, refugees, or newly arrived immigrants.

Second, the attitude of the native population toward

these Jews is markedly different from the usual pattern. The peoples among whom they live regard them as a normal, acceptable, and ancient part of their lands.

A third factor has to do with the attitude toward the Jews and the Jewish faith on the part of the dominant religions of these countries. For the last few centuries the Georgian Christian Church, one of the oldest in the world, and the Moslem leaders in Daghestan and Bukhara, have been absolutely free of the fanaticism and blind hatred of Jews which characterized the Catholic Church in Poland and the Russian Orthodox Church in the Ukraine and Russia. And if, as did happen, there was a certain amount of persecution of Jews by the Moslems and Christians of Caucasia and Asia, this was counterbalanced by a tolerance toward Judaism and its symbols. Further, the stigma of being the "crucifiers of God and the Messiah," which marked the cruel treatment of the Jews by the Christian Church in Europe, was never used against the Oriental Jews.

These Jews have also, to a marked extent, performed normal and basic functions in the societies in which they lived: as indispensable artisans in the mountain villages of the Caucasus, as rug merchants in Persia, and as wine merchants in Georgia. Because of the similarity of their appearance customs, dress, and language to those of the peoples among whom they lived, and also because of their small numbers, they were less conspicuous than their Ashkenazi brothers.

Though deprived of both the great scholarship and the mystic hasidic fervor of the Ashkenazi Jews, these Oriental Jews kept their faith and institutions with unusual obstinacy and perseverance. Their sages, unlike the great rabbis of Poland, Lithuania, and Russia, did not delve too deeply into the Talmud; but they preserved their people's religious and spiritual heritage and handed it down intact from generation to generation.

The conquests of the czars resulted in closer and more comprehensive ties between the Oriental and the Ashkenazi Jews in the empire. The first tie was of a religious nature: Ashkenazi Jews sent religious objects and prayer books eastward. This was followed by national and secular ties. As the Zonist movement grew among Russian Jews at the end of the nineteenth and early twentieth centuries, emissaries went to Caucasia and Central Asia to plant the seeds of the new movemnt. These fell on fertile soil, for a

Zionism of a naive messianic type had always been pre-served by Oriental Jews. They welcomed with enthusiasm the teachers, newspapers, modern Hebrew literature, and other media of the new Zionist movement. (There is a well-known painting of Herzl seated at one of the early Zionist Congresses with a delegation of stocky Caucasian Jews, dressed in all their splendor, wearing their jaunty fur *kolpaki,* their chests crisscrossed with ammunition belts in traditional Caucasian fashion.)

These Oriental Jews, with their unique national-religious background, were among the first to send the best of their sons to settle in Palestine and rebuilt the land.

Modern Hebrew schools, branches of the Zionist move-ment, and Zionist youth organizations were founded in Bukhara, Tiflis (later called Tbilisi), Tashkent, Baku, and in dozens of other places.

In the eartly twenties, when the Soviet regime became firmly established in Caucasia and Central Asia, the So-viets began to close down the secular-national Jewish insti-tutions. In typical fashion, they also began to oppress the religious institutions and the synagogues. The contacts with Ashkenazi Jewry and the short period of national re-vival which had followed came to an end. The Oriental Jews returned to their previous isolation.

Since that time they have undergone considerable social and economic change. With the advent of modern technol-ogy, fresh opportunities for study and professional training have opened up in Caucasia and Central Asia. New hori-zons have appeared as a result of economic expansion, in-dustrialization, and the establishment of modern means of communication. Commerce, workshops, and handiwork are no longer the main occupations of these Jews, who are now able to perform new social and economic functions in their republics.

Contacts with Ashkenazi Jews were renewed during the Second World War. Thousands of Jewish refugees came to Uzbekistan, Tajikistan, Azerbaijan, Georgia, and Daghes-tan, from Poland, Lithuania, European Russia, Belorussia, and the Ukraine, and were helped considerably by the local Jews. Most of the refugees returned to the western regions of the Soviet Union after the war. Some, however, remained in the large cities of Caucasia and Central Asia. The present Jewish population in these areas is a mixture of long-established Oriental Jews and more recently ar-rived Ashkenazi Jews.

The family as a protective wall

The situation, as we have outlined it, of the majority of Jews in the Soviet Union is totally different from that of the Oriental Jews. The latter have these factors in common: the transmission of the Jewish heritage within the family circle, the special position of religion and the synagogues, and the preservation of and pride in a Jewish messianic consciousness.

There developed and is being preserved among these Jews the large family grouping made up of three or four generations living in one house or in adjoining houses. These family groupings are clearly patriarchal, and there is even common ownership of a sort. This family structure continues to serve as a protective wall for its members and is the medium by which their way of life is handed down.

Despite the great changes the Oriental Jews have undergone, they have managed to preserve the homogeneity and unity of the family group and its functions. This is typical of the peoples among whom these Jews live. The large family unit is far more common among the Georgian, Daghestan, and Uzbek peoples, than among groups living in the large cities of Russia and the Ukraine.

The grandfather in such large patriarchal families is not just a pensioner and a dependent old man, but the revered chief of the clan; and the father is the head of the family, one who must be obeyed. The mother attends diligently to her household and brings up the children. The home thus comprises three generations.

It is customary for some ten or twenty people to sit down together to an ordinary meal—something unknown and unheard of among Russian Ashkenazi Jews. On a Sabbath or holiday eve the entire family gathers at the grandfather's house—sons and daughters, sons- and daughters-in-law, grandchildren and great-grandchildren, uncles and aunts with their children and grandchildren.

It is no surprise, therefore, that a family structure of this sort serves as a potent means for linking the generations and for training the young.

We have already pointed out that among Oriental Jews the tradition has been handed down unchanged through the generations. When their religious institutions, such as the rabbinate, the religious colleges and schools, began to be closed down by the Soviet authorities, and when those that remained open had their activities seriously curtailed, the tradition found refuge in the midst of the large family. To this very day the Oriental family protects its individual members against the corrosive influences of the outside world by assuming collective responsibility for the religious rituals that govern the life of a Jew from birth until death.

We have seen how the number of circumcised Ashkenazi Jews has decreased over the years, how circumcision has to be performed underground, as it were, and the extent to which the circumcisers are oppressed. In the case of Oriental Jews, this situation is entirely different. It is inconceivable for a Georgian, a Mountain, or a Bukharan Jew not to circumcise his son. This is true even in instances where the father is an active member of the Communist party and an avowed atheist. The boy simply must be circumcised—for the family would not accept an uncircumcised male child; it would eject both father and son from its midst. Thus, all male Oriental Jews are circumcised.

It is interesting to note that the same Soviet regime which persecutes the Ashkenazi circumcisers so severely does not interfere with this rite in the case of Oriental Jews, for it knows full well that these people would rather be killed than transgress this commandment. I would even go so far as to say that if Oriental Jews should ever be forcibly prevented from circumcising their sons, they would stop bearing children.

As for the ceremony of bar mitzvah, we have already indicated the extent to which this ritual is dying out among Ashkenazi Jews in the Soviet Union. But quite a different picture presents itself in a synagogue of Oriental Jews. I visited the synagogues in Tashkent, Bukhara, Samarkand, Tbilisi, Kutaisi, Baku, and other settlements in Caucasia and Central Asia, and there was hardly a Sabbath without a bar mitzvah celebration. The boy, in festive garb, nervously ascends the pulpit with his proud father, recites the blessings in Hebrew, with the Sephardi pronunciation, while the congregation—which includes his entire family, of course—responds with "Amen." The mother is in the women's gallery, wearing her colorful Sabbath dress, her eyes bright with joyous tears. Normal as all this is among Jews everywhere it has an added significance in a small Caucasian town. For Oriental Jews also do not have any Hebrew schools or other institutions where even the most elementary sort of religious training can be openly undertaken in organized fashion. And if these Jewish boys know how to recite the blessings, it is an indication that they have been trained somewhere; and, without a doubt, the place where they were trained was the home, and the people who trained them were members of their family. This is not to say that serious systematic Jewish studies are conducted by the family or that there are well-educated Hebrew students among today's Oriental Jews. Quite the contrary. All that the elders and parents can do is transmit the basic elements of the tradition—nothing else. Given the present circumstances, this is no small accomplishment. But in the long run, the remarkable source of strength represented by the Oriental Jewish family is doomed to dry up and disappear unless it is buttressed by organized and systematic Jewish studies.

Marriages and funerals

The Ashkenazi wedding ceremony has almost disappeared from the Soviet scene.

I once witnessed a wedding in a small synagogue in a suburb of Moscow. Twenty old people were present. The bride and bridegroom came separately in their drab, gray, everyday clothes, so as not to be too conspicuous as they entered the synagogue. The bridegroom looked very embarrassed and it was evident that he was only submitting to the ceremony in order to please the bride and her parents. The ritual was conducted in quick fashion by the old rabbi. Afterwards someone brought out a bottle of wine and filled a few glasses. Someone else produced some salted fish from beneath his coat. The Jews quickly raised their glasses, said, "L'chaim" (to life), and began hurrying away, as though saying to one another, "Let's get it over with and not run into trouble."

Among Oriental Jews an altogether different scene takes place. There is no doubt that the partners register as required by law, but they also go to the hacham and are married in accordance with the religious tradition. Weddings are very festive and the entire family takes part. If for some reason one of the partners does not wish a public ceremony, the religious ceremony would take place anyway. To do otherwise would be incomprehensible to the family; the young couple would be rejected; they would not be considered man and wife.

We have indicated the extent to which Ashkenazi Jews must struggle to secure new burial grounds or to prevent existing cemeteries, which "interfere with building and planning," from being destroyed. Oriental Jews are saved this ordeal. They still own cemeteries which are hundreds of years old, in whose soil generations of Jews lie buried. No one would think of destroying these ancient cemeteries, for they are regarded almost as historical and archeological sites and are looked upon as integral parts of the local scenery. By and large, the Oriental people are not militant atheists, nor do they want to destroy any reminders of their past. On the contrary, they take pride in and try to preserve every old gravestone and palace, every ancient monastery, church or mosque, all of which they regard as integral to their history.

Whereas Ashkenazi Jews bury many of their dead in mixed cemeteries, the Oriental Jews without exception bury them in their own special cemeteries. It is unthinkable for a Bukharan, Georgian, or Mountain Jew to be buried in his home town in non-Jewish ground. This would never be sanctioned by the family. The dead, too, belong to the family: the burial, the mourner's prayer, the seven days of mourning, and the thirty days of mourning are fully observed and help to unite the family all the more and to ensure the continuity of the generations.

Why the Oriental Jews have matzot

Oriental Jews have no difficulty baking matzot. They bake their matzot openly, for all the world to see, though it must be added that conditions and customs are such that the housewives use their own ovens to bake for the entire family, and this eliminates the need for permits from bureaucrats and involvement in red tape. But this private baking is carried on without fear of interference by officials, who know full well that, as in all matters concerning religion and tradition, the Oriental Jews will act in accordance with the dictates of their faith no matter what the consequences.

The ghettos that characterized European Jewry through the centuries are no longer in existence. But in a number of towns in Georgia, Daghestan, and Uzbekistan, where Oriental Jews have lived for generations, one can still see characteristically Jewish quarters. The truth of the matter is that the segregation of dwelling places according to tribal and national division is far more common today in the Caucasus and Central Asia than in European Russia.

The Jewish families that live in these quarters have continued to preserve and maintain their synagogues. The Oriental Jewish synagogue is a far more vital and organic institution than its counterpart in western Russia. Even on a weekday one senses immediately that the atmosphere inside an Oriental synagogue is normal and calm and reminiscent of a synagogue in Tel Aviv or Brooklyn. Oriental Jews of all ages come and go; there is none of the oppressive atmosphere of fear and tension that pervades the Ashkenazi synagogue. A Jewish tourist from abroad is welcomed warmly and openly. He is not led immediately by the *gabbaim* toward the Ark; nor is he isolated in order to prevent him from coming into contact with the congregants, as prescribed by the authorities.

On Sabbaths and festivals the synagogues are crowded not only with men but also with women and children. Each resounds with the normal hubbub of a healthy congregation. Everyone knows everybody else. Children play together and laugh aloud. Parents chat about everyday matters. The atmosphere is that of a large family gathering.

The Ashkenazi Jews support their own synagogues and receive no help from the authorities. Because most of the congregants are elderly pensioners, and younger people are afraid to contribute for fear of rousing suspicion, most Ashkenazi synagogues are very poorly maintained.

In the east the situation is quite different. Every working Jew who is a regular congregant contributes ungrudgingly. The *gabbaim* of the synagogue can depend on a generous and openhanded community. All those called to the reading of the Torah are expected to offer a donation. The summons to the Torah is a sign of recognition; the *hacham* or the *gabbai* expects those so honored to contribute without hesitation.

Alongside the Oriental synagogues one can sometimes see other religious institutions which have not been in existence for a long time in Ashkenazi communities, such as the ritual bathhouse and the kosher slaughterhouse. Again, it is the families who insist on having these institutions and who maintain them.

The threat of closing the synagogue is not used here to the same degree as it is further to the west. The authorities realize that if they close down a synagogue in some city or little town in the Ukraine or in Belorussia, a few dozen old Jews will lament loudly, some hundreds will wipe away surreptitious tears, while a thousand others will grieve in their hearts—and that will be the end of the matter. But the closing of an Oriental Jewish synagogue would entail the use of force and brutality which would result in resounding repercussions. Because the authorities are aware of this and are at the present time quite eager to avoid public scandals, they permit these synagogues to continue functioning, hoping that the absence of a new generation of leaders and the lack of systematic Jewish education will cause these institutions to die of themselves in due time.

The Kutaisi Jews who barred the roadway with their bodies

Even during the dark years of Stalinism, Oriental Jews reacted untypically, and with great courage and pride, to the closing of their synagogues.

Kutaisi is the second largest city in the Georgian Republic, with a population of some hundred thousand, of which about 10 per cent are Jews who live in their own quarter along the river that bisects the city. There are three synagogues in that quarter, which is unusual even among Oriental Jewish communities. The largest of these synagogues is on the border between the Jewish quarter and the other sections of the city.

On my visit to this community I heard the story of how its Jews fought to protect that synagogue. During the last years of Stalin, when the persecution of Jews was particularly intense, the local Kutaisi authorities decided to display their initiative. The *hacham* and his *gabbaim* were ordered to close the synagogue by a certain date and to hand over the keys to the authorities. The building would be taken over to serve as a club for the local Komsomol.

The Jews were stunned. At first, they tried to get the decree revoked by asking their many Georgian friends to intercede with the authorities in their behalf. They sent delegations to the heads of the city; they pleaded and begged; they tried to buy the synagogue's continued existence with money; they announced that they had raised the money needed to build the club and would contribute it to the municipal authorities. It was all to no avail. The authorities were adamant and insisted that the building be vacated on the specified date. All the Scrolls would have to be taken out and the keys surrendered. The storm of protest grew and absorbed the entire Jewish community of the city.

When the day came and the Jews learned that on a certain hour trucks and men would come to carry out the orders and bring in the club furniture, they rushed from every part of their quarter, surrounded the synagogue, and filled the street. As the trucks approached, the Jews, old and young alike, lay down across the width of the road and called to the drivers that only over their bodies would they get to the synagogue. After much threatening and shouting, the authorities realized that they would have to resort to force to remove the Jews. They retreated; and after conferring, they decided that the affair was not worth a fight, and they left the Jews alone.

It would be absurd to claim that the authorities were helpless. The Soviet regime has enough power to close a synagogue in a Georgian town, and if it had decided to use force it could have arrested, imprisoned, exiled, or even killed the rebellious Jews. And since this event took place in the days of Stalin, no one in the Soviet Union would have dared to say a word.

The point of the story is that the Jews knew what the authorities were capable of and what price they might have to pay for their daring; and that they were ready, in protecting the synagogue with their own bodies, to pay that price. And they won. To this very day the Jews of Kutaisi and the Jews of other Georgian communities remember this act of courage with great pride.

Many of the cities of Central Asia and Caucasia now have Ashkenazi Jews as well. The two Jewish communities maintain separate synagogues in Tashkent, Baku, Tbilisi, and some other cities. The differences between the two synagogues are significant. The Oriental synagogue is a vibrant, organic, normal element of the community; the Ashkenazi synagogue, in the same town and often on the same street, is wretched in appearance, its building is dilapidated, its Jews are old, frightened, tense, and suspicious.

The three Oriental Jewish groups

There are three main groups of Oriental Jews, each significantly different from the other.

The Georgian Jews now number some sixty to seventy thousand. Most of them live in the Georgian Republic, though there are some thousands also in Azerbaijan (mainly in Baku, the capital), in Kazakhstan (chiefly in Alma-Ata, the capital), and a few in Armenia and other republics of the Soviet Union.

In outward appearance, the Georgian Jews look so much like the Georgian nationals among whom they live that it is difficult to tell them apart. Their hair is black, they are quite tall, and most of the men sport the typical Georgian mustache. The women have long hair and are regal in appearance. They are the only Oriental Jews who do not have a dialect of their own. The only language they use (besides Hebrew, their holy tongue) is the Georgian that is spoken by their non-Jewish neighbors, which is, by the way, an ancient and distinguished tongue, having nothing in common with Russian. Their family names are virtually the same as those of the non-Jews, and the name-endings, such as "-shvili" or "-adze," are identical. The specifically Jewish element in the family names ending in "-shvili" and "-adze" can sometimes be seen in the first part of the name. For instance, the common name "Hachamshvili" suggests that an ancestor of the family once served in some respected religious capacity or was a scholar.

The Georgian Jews live in the midst of one of the most highly civilized peoples of the Soviet Union. The Georgians have a history that goes back two thousand years. They are very proud of their history, especially of the fact that they were one of the first peoples to adopt Christianity. They take great pride in their royal dynasties, princes, rich literature, and great poetry, as well as in their forefathers' courageous stand during the long, hard wars against the czars. They are also proud of the fact—and they will allude to this in veiled terms—that they did not submit easily to Soviet rule and that, in the period between the downfall of the czars and the beginning of Soviet rule, they enjoyed a brief interlude of independence. In their own way the Georgians are even proud of Stalin, who was born Iosif Vissarionovich Dzhugashvili, son of a poor shoemaker of Gori, a little Georgian town. They do not love him, for during the great purges he put to death many of the leading figures of the Georgian intelligentsia. But they cannot help admiring their mustached compatriot who succeeded in bringing all the peoples of Russia under his knout.

The proud tradition of the Georgian Jews

The Georgian Jews are equally proud of their past. They claim to be the descendants of the ten tribes which were exiled from the kingdom of Israel some twenty-seven hundred years ago by the Assyrian king Shalmaneser V, and which settled on the borders of the empire at "Halah, Khabur and the River Gozan, and the cities of Media." Though there is no clear evidence in support of this tradition (as no serious study of this subject has yet been made), it seems probable that the Jewish descendants of the Assyrian exiles wandered as far as southern Caucasia, Babylonia, and Persia, and settled there. We learn of Jewish settlers in Armenia from the Jerusalem Talmud, which mentions "Rabbi Yaakov of Armenia." Josephus relates that a considerable number of Jews lived in Armenia during the days of King Tigranes (a descendant of Herod, first century C.E.). They wandered northward from Armenia and settled in Georgia. That Jews have lived in Georgia since the early Middle Ages is attested to by written documents as well as ancient gravestones.

The economy of Georgia is based on fruit-growing. Its moderate climate and fertile soil are eminently suitable for the growing of grapes. Georgian wines are famous throughout Russia and the Near East. The Jews have always played a respected and almost monopolistic role in the production and sale of wine. But they traded in other goods as well, both on a national and an international scale. Georgian Jews were much in evidence in the Turkish empire, Persia, and the Russian empire in connection with the wine trade and other forms of commerce. From earliest times, the Georgian nation absorbed its Jews without any trouble and regarded them as a small, useful, and thoroughly loyal minority.

Georgian Jews still recount the legends of the Jewish heroes who fought alongside their country's kings and princes in Georgia's incessant wars for independence.

Social and cultural contacts with other Jewish communities were maintained mainly by their merchants who traveled to Jewish centers in neighboring lands. In the Middle Ages, Georgian Jews were in touch with Jewish centers in Persia and Turkey, and this influenced their liturgy and religious ritual and provided them with biblical and religious literature. From the eighteenth century onward, they began to establish contact with Russian Jewry. Since the conquest of Georgia and its annexation to the Russian empire this contact has been steadily strengthened.

The economic condition of Georgian Jews was good—better in fact than that of other Jews within the Russian Pale of Settlement—and this enabled them to bring in rabbis, ritual slaughterers, and teachers from the West. On the eve of the Bolshevik revolution, many of the Georgian Jewish communities had flourishing Hebrew schools and nascent Zionist groups. Jewish nationalism developed quite naturally among the Jews of Georgia, for it did not clash with their ancient communal and religious affinities. By the end of the nineteenth century, Georgian Jews began to settle in Palestine.

The Soviet regime has naturally brought about drastic chances in the economic situation of the Georgian Jews. The production and sale of wine was completely taken over by the goverment and became a national monopoly of the Georgian Republic.

Thousands of Georgian Jews managed to escape to Turkey, Palestine, and Europe during the early years of the Soviet regime. Most remained behind and had to struggle for years to adapt themselves to the new situation. Their synagogues were closed, their educational institutions paralyzed, their main sources of livelihood taken from them.

Despite everything, they managed somehow to develop

effective means of preserving their identity. And they regained their former important position in the economic life of Georgia, this time within the new national framework as state officials in wine production and trade.

Georgia, like the other republics of the Soviet Union, has undergone rapid modernization and industrialization, but the wine industry has remained to this day one of the most important branches of its economy. Armenia, Crimea, Daghestan, and other areas in Central Asia also manufacture wine and liqueurs, but they cannot compete with the quality of Georgian products.

The improved standard of living in the Soviet Union has resulted in a greater demand for good wine. Consumption of these famed wines is fashionable and in good taste. Georgian wine merchants are often to be met with in trains and planes throughout the Soviet Union. They are sent by the Georgian authorities to promote the wine trade throughout the country. Most of them are Georgian Jews.

There are, of course, Georgian Jews who have made their mark in other occupations, such as technology, medicine, and the liberal professions.

With regard to their religious tradition, the proud Georgian Jews have not only succeeded in maintaining, as far as possible, the respected position of their synagogues, but are also trying to maintain, unofficially, something akin to an overall communal organization.

Most of them live today in Tbilisi, Batumi, Sukhumi, Gori, Suram, Kulashi (a little town mainly populated by Jews), and other cities and small towns. Contacts between the heads of the Tbilisi Jewish community and other local Jewish communities are much closer than those between the Ashkenazi communities in Russia. The well-established Tbilisi community often gives financial assistance to other communities in order to help them maintain their religious institutions.

The Georgian authorities, including the Department of Religions, have a more lenient and humane attitude toward the Jews than do the other national republics. The reason is that most of the Georgian ruling bodies are directed by Georgians. This small, proud nation has managed to withstand Russification more successfully than other nationalities of the Soviet Union. There are hardly any Russians in key government positions in Tbilisi. Georgia is perhaps the only republic which seems—to an outsider at least—to govern itself with little interference from Moscow.

The handling of Jewish affairs is also in Georgian hands. Influenced by a tradition of many generations, they treat Jews with a great degree of toleration.

These facts, together with the importance of the family unit, account for the great solidarity of the Georgian Jews. They are the best organized and the proudest Jews in the Soviet Union.

But it must be remembered that in the final analysis even these Jews do not have a single class in which Hebrew or Jewish religion can be taught. They have no means of training the next generation of leaders and are unable to give open expression to their almost messianic exaltation regarding the State of Israel.

"Reuma Eldar, my beloved"

As I was leaving the synagogue in Tbilisi after the New Year services, a man of about sixty asked me, in good Sephardi Hebrew, whether I knew Reuma Eldar, the well-known announcer of the *Kol Yisrael* broadcasting service. I said: "Yes, I know her."

He said: "Then will you please give her warmest regards from her loving admirer when you get back."

This expression of affection rather surprised me, so I asked how he knew her. He told me this story as we walked along:

In his youth, before the revolution, he had studied in a Hebrew school in a Georgian town. He came to love Hebrew and never forgot it. He took every opportunity to read, study, and improve his mastery of the language. Since he could not pursue formal studies, he had to do this in other ways. Here and there he found Hebrew books and newspapers, mostly in the libraries of the large cities where his work took him. He also managed somehow to learn a bit of modern spoken Hebrew. A few years earlier he had discovered that it was possible to hear daily *Kol Yisrael* programs on the medium-wavelength of a normal radio. (This is true only of southern Caucasia and part of the Black Sea coast and is a result of their proximity to Jerusalem; the broadcasts of *Kol Tsion Lagolah*—Voice of

Zion to the Diaspora—can be heard on short-wave throughout most of the Soviet Union.) So he began to listen to the Israeli broadcasts and learned to identify the news announcers by their voices—and had fallen in love with the voice of Reuma Eldar.

He continued: "My beloved wife died about a year ago. We had been happily married for many years. A few months passed. Some relatives in a distant Georgian town came to console me. A few minutes before nine in the evening I told them: 'I have already been consoled and have even found someone I love.' They were stunned. I told them jokingly: 'You will hear the voice of my beloved in a few moments.' I turned on the radio and, sure enough, heard Reuma Eldar's voice. I exclaimed: 'That's her! I have found consolation in her voice.' "

A number of lovely Georgian towns lie on the northeastern shore of the Black Sea, surrounded by magnificent mountains. Towns like Sukhumi, Batumi, and others are summer resorts which attract thousands of vacationers and tourists from Georgia and all parts of the Soviet Union.

I visited one of these towns, and on the Sabbath I entered the synagogue of the Georgian Jews. I was welcomed warmly by the *gabbaim* and was invited to the meal that traditionally follows the Afternoon Service. I agreed readily and on joining them at the synagogue later, I was surprised to encounter a group of twenty children of various ages. One of the elders, a noble-looking, whitebearded man, sat down at the well-appointed table, pronounced the benediction over the wine, and began to relate legends and homilies based on the Torah reading of that week. The children sat around the old man, their dark eyes glowing as they listened to the ancient stories of Israel's wanderings in the desert. After a while, I saw all the children get up suddenly and hurry quickly outside. A few moments later they looked through the windows, then came back. The same thing happened half an hour later. When this had been repeated a few times, I asked one of the elders to explain what was going on. He told me that an official of the Department of Religions paid surprise visits to the synagogue. If he saw many children, he had to include the fact in his report to his superiors and the youngsters were likely to suffer for it, mainly in school. But as this supervisor was an easy-going Georgian and was not too particular, the Jews had arrived at a gentleman's

agreement with him (with the help of some "presents"),
namely, that he simply "would not see" children while in-
specting the synagogue. The Jews, therefore, posted a
scout outside. When the supervisor came around, the scout
gave the signal and the children scampered out to the
yard. The man came into the synagogue for a moment and
noted that everything was in order. This happened a few
times to the mutual satisfaction of the Jews, the supervisor, and certainly the children, who regarded it as a great
sport.

When I went to the beach the next day, many of the
Jews who had seen me in the synagogue recognized me.
The news about a "tourist from Jerusalem" had spread
swiftly. A woman of about thirty came over, introduced
herself, and asked if she could talk to me. With her were
two children, a boy of about ten and a girl of five. The
boy, Alexander, blond and blue-eyed, was playing with the
Jewish Georgian children. The mother told me that she
was a native of Dvinsk in Latvia and was here for her
summer holiday. After the war she had married a Jewish
doctor who had lost his wife and children in the Holocaust. They now lived in Dvinsk and were raising a family. Recently, she told me, her son Alexander had been
through a terrible experience. Until the last few months he
had known nothing about his Jewishness. Despite his Vi-
king looks, however, the teachers and children in school
knew from his family name and the name of his father
that he was a Jew. But they never intended him any harm.
Then, shortly before the previous Christmas, she gave her
son a wafer smeared with tomato-paste. That day the boy
returned from school bruised and covered with blood. Hu-
miliated and in tears, he said that some of the boys had
told him that "your mother put Jesus' blood on the
bread"; blows followed the words. They told him he was
being paid back for the crime his people had committed
by crucifying Christ. Alexander was terribly upset; to this
day he still doesn't understand why he was attacked. The
father took care to give the boy extra love and affection
but, according to the mother, he himself had been shocked
by what had happened to his son. I asked the mother
whether she had reported the matter to the teachers.
"Yes," she said, "and they reprimanded the hooligans. But
the children absorb all these stories about Jesus and the
crucifixion and all this hatred from their homes, and not
from school. If the parents are not educated against anti-

Semitism, is it surprising that their children behave as they do?" During my conversation with the mother, I watched as the blond Jewish boy from Latvia and the raven-haired Jewish children from Georgia played and laughed together, enjoying the waves and the sun. For some reason, they suddenly seemed to symbolize for me the extraordinary fate of the Jews.

In the footsteps of the Khazars

Many diverse peoples live in the mountains and on the Caspian shore north of the Caucasus. The region is a living museum, a natural preserve of various tiny tribes which have been preserved for ages due to unusual topographic and ethnologic factors. Small tribes such as the Avars, Lezgians, Lakai, Ands, Kumyks, and many others have been exposed for many centuries to the cultural and social impact of the great empires and invaders who swept into the Caucasus from every point of the compass. They absorbed Persian, Moslem, Hunnish, Bulgarian, Mongolian, Turkish, and, of course, Russian influences. But in the mountains they managed to a surprising degree to retain their national or tribal individuality. A peculiar Jewish tribe has lived for centuries in the midst of this mosaic of peoples. They are called the Mountain Jews (*gornye evrei*) or Tati Jews. Today there are about a hundred thousand of them. They live mainly in the Autonomous Daghestan Republic, which is part of the Federated Russian Republic.

Daghestan is a Russian creation, the result of the government's experiment in uniting a few small nations into a single national-administrative entity. Most of the Jews of Daghestan proper live in the town of Derbent and in the Daghestan capital, Makhach-Kala. Both towns lie on the shores of the Caspian Sea. Communities of Mountain Jews also live in Nalchik, Grozny, and other Caucasian towns. There are also sizable Jewish communities in the Soviet Republic of Azerbaijan, especially in its capital, Baku, and in the city of Kuba.

The Mountain Jews began living in the towns only recently. In former generations they made their homes in the auls (villages in the Caucasus). Where did they come from and how did they get to the Caucasus? The origins and history of the Georgian Jews are more or less clear because they have lived among a people with an unbroken history and culture. But the record of the Mountain Jews is lost in a mist of legends and folk memories transmitted orally from generation to generation.

The older Mountain Jews, like the Jews of Georgia, will tell you that they are the descendants of the ten lost tribes and that their ancestors were Jews who had been sent into exile by Assyria, Babylonia, and Persia, and who subsequently settled along the shores of the Caspian Sea and in the Caucasus.

In any event, for many centuries, this was the land of the somewhat mysterious Khazar kingdom whose kings converted to Judaism around the eighth century C. E. It covered a wide area between the Caspian and Black Seas, broke apart during the wars with the Russian princes, and was completely destroyed by Genghis Khan in the thirteenth century.

The extent of the relationship between the descendants of the converted Khazar rulers and the present Mountain Jews can only be ascertained by a historical, ethnological, and anthropological study. In all likelihood there is Khazar blood in the veins of this tribe, and it is a fact that ancient communities of Mountain Jews were found in the mountain villages of Caucasia when these were captured by the Russians. Unlike the Georgian Jews, those Jews lived among people who had converted to Islam; further, they had a language of their own, Tati, an old Persian dialect which reveals Turkish influence. The Mountain Jews adopted it, but wrote it in Hebrew characters. Tati is used in their everyday and religious affairs, while Hebrew is the holy tongue known only to their religious leaders.

Again, unlike the Georgian Jews, they can be easily identified by their family names, which are formed in most cases from a biblical Hebrew name, followed by an ending, such as "-ov"—Davidov, Yekhezkelov, Danielov, and so on.

The Jewish communities in the villages and little towns were usually a minority of no more than a few dozen or a few hundred families. Through the centuries they lived as farmers, artisans, and tradesmen. Somehow these small mountain groups, survived and retained their Jewish heritage despite the lack of close contact with other Jewish communities and in almost complete isolation from Jewish centers outside the Caucasus.

One of the main factors contributing to their survival was the clan tradition which maintained and transmitted their religious tradition down through the generations. Village life, cultivation of the soil, riding, and fighting constitute the main characteristics of these Mountain Jews. Of all the Jews in the Soviet Union, they are the closest to nature and the most deeply influenced by their environment and their neighbors. In their personalities and sturdy physiques they resemble the Caucasian fighting people, who are famous in Russian literature. The legends they told me always featured peasants, hunters, Jewish heroes and fighters—rare subjects among other Diaspora Jews. One striking feature is the ubiquitousness of the name "Samson," as well as those of other biblical heroes and fighters.

When the Soviet regime took over, Daghestan and the Caucasus underwent great social change. The enforced collectivization of agriculture, which made individual farming and trade useless, wiped out the livelihood of most of the inhabitants of the villages. However, the spread of higher education brought new opportunities. In the last thirty or forty years, the Mountain Jews began moving from their villages to the urban centers, mainly along the shores of the Caspian. Large communities of Mountain Jews developed in Baku, Derbent, and Makhach-Kala. Jews also migrated from their villages to industrial cities such as Grozny, and to other towns outside Caucasia.

But even in their new centers the Mountain Jews have successfully preserved their family structure and their ancestral traditions.

The third stage: the ships that will sail to Jerusalem

One day I visited Derbent, some two hundred miles north of Baku on the Caspian Sea. This Persian-style city lies on the slopes of the hills which rise from the sea and is dominated by a huge fortress built by the Persian conquerors in the Middle Ages. The houses are low and set close together, the streets narrow; and only in the center of the city are modern Soviet buildings found. Of the tens of thousands of people who live there, more than a third are

Mountain Jews. The remainder are various Daghestan peoples, mostly Lezgians.

Some of the Derbent Jews are farmers with considerable experience in the growing of the famous Daghestan wine grapes. They are organized into four *kolkhozy,* the lands of which adjoin the city's residential quarters. Most of the *kolkhoz* members are Jews who live in the city; the city is, therefore, a semi-agricultural settlement. These Mountain Jews are among the few Jews in the Soviet Union whose occupation is agriculture. Most of them live in exclusively Jewish streets. Because I came there on the eve of Passover, I could easily identify their homes, which had just been painted blue in honor of the festival.

I attended the festive Evening Service. Their synagogue is not as sumptuous as those in Georgia, but it is very well kept. It was crowded with celebrants, among whom were many children. I was given a seat near the venerable *hacham,* who received me with warmth and spoke to me in impeccable, classic Hebrew. The services were conducted partly in biblical Hebrew and partly in Tati translation. After the prayers the *hacham* introduced me to one of the prominent families of his congregation and told me that I would be celebrating the Seder as a guest in that family's home.

The head of the family was a broad-shouldered vigorous man of about sixty-five who had been one of the district's leading vine dressers and had recently retired. When he heard that he would be my host, he gave me a bear hug and took me almost bodily under his wing.

The large family had already begun to gather as I approached his house, which was sheltered, Persian style, behind a high fence.

The mother had prepared the house for the Seder. A table, reserved for the men, stood in the main room, and on the carpeted floor there were colored cushions for the women. At the head of the table sat my host, with me on his left and his brother, a man of over sixty, on his right. On both sides of the table sat brothers, sons, brothers-in-law, and relatives. The male children were seated at the far end. Women and girls of all ages sat on the floor, their heads covered with colored bands and scarves.

On the gleaming white tablecloth there were round, homemade matzot, bottles of honey-colored, home-brewed wine, and a profusion of Oriental foods. I added my own share to the table, to the obvious and loud pleasure of the assembly: a bottle of Israeli wine and a package of matzot "made in Jerusalem," which I had brought from home.

The head of the family began the service and read each verse of the Haggadah first in Hebrew, then in Tati. After reading and translating the first paragraph, he honored me with the reading of the second passage, and then his brother and two or three of the family elders who knew Hebrew, with other sections. The others listened to the Tati translation; they did not have Haggadot. The three Haggadot in the hands of the elders were torn and tattered from constant use.

And so we read the entire ancient Haggadah verse by verse, and the family heard in their own language the story of the exodus from Egypt, the downfall of Pharaoh, the wanderings in the desert, and the redemption in the Land of Israel.

When the reading ended, spicy and tasty Oriental food was passed around in shining copper pots. Goblets filled with Israeli and Daghestani wine were raised. As hearts grew warmer, the people began to sing their own Passover songs. They were delighted when I joined in with Israeli Passover songs.

At the close of this wonderful and memorable evening, the elders began telling stories and legends of the life of the Mountain Jews. One of these stories made a vivid impression upon me. It related that the Mountain Jews had been exiled from Jerusalem to Caucasia many centuries ago. While the first exiles were lamenting the loss of the Temple and their expulsion, their leaders promised them that the Messiah would come sometime in the future and they would return to Jerusalem. This return would take place in three stages. During the first, which would span many centuries, the Jews would live in the mountain villages. If they maintained their religious traditions, they would reach the second stage: they would come down from the mountains and congregate in the large cities of the Caspian Sea. During the third and last stage, ships from Jerusalem would come to the shores of the Caspian and bring the exiles back to their land. (In ancient legend, the Caspian Sea seemed to be the common ocean. The fact that it is a closed sea and that Jerusalem is not a port does not disturb these people in the least.)

Turning to me the storyteller added: "The first stage has passed. We have lived for countless centuries among our gentile neighbors and have preserved our faith and traditions. The second stage began a few decades ago. Most of the Mountain Jews have come down from the mountains and now live on the seashore and in harbor towns. And now, now we are waiting and looking forward to the third and longed-for stage."

With shining eyes the celebrants raised their goblets to the "leaping" of the ships from Jerusalem to the Caspian Sea.

The ancient communities of the "Silk Road"

The Oriental Jews who live in the Soviet republics of Central Asia, particularly Uzbekistan, are collectively referred to as Bukharan Jews. The name derives from the fact that for centuries their cultural center was in the Emirate of Bukhara and in its capital, Bukhara.

There are about eighty thousand of them today. Some fifty thousand live in the Republic of Uzbekistan, with large communities in Tashkent (the capital), Samarkand, Bukhara, Kokand, Khiva, and other smaller towns. The remaining Bukharan Jews live in the Tajik Republic, mostly in its capital, Dushanbe (formerly Stalinabad); in the Turkmen Republic, mainly in its capital, Ashkhabad; and in the Kazakh and Kirghiz Republics.

While the Georgian Jews have lived for generations among Christians, and the Mountain Jews among small and isolated tribes, partly Christain but mainly Moslem, the Bukharan Jews lived for most of their history in a society which was overwhelmingly Moslem. They, too, claim descent from the ten lost tribes.

We find in the Book of Esther a distant echo of the wide dispersion of Jews within the ancient world. We are told that Jewish communities were to be found in the "one hundred and twenty-seven provinces . . . from India to Ethiopia" of the Persian empire. It may be assumed that after the campaigns of Alexander the Great in Bactria and Transoxiana, and the consequent expansion of commerce between the lands of the Mediterranean basin and the Far East, the Jews established themselves as merchants and middlemen in the centers of these civilizations. One of these centers is the region of which we are speaking.

There is ample written evidence to the effect that pros-

perous and well-established Jewish communities existed in
this region during the period when it was under Moslem
influence. Prosperity and cultural expansion were restored
in the region after the dark age which followed the Mon-
gol invasions of the thirteenth century. Large cities were
rebuilt along the "Silk Road," which led from the Mediterranean to the Far East. International commerce was revived and educational, scientific, and religious academies
were established. From the fourteenth through the six-
teenth centuries, Samarkand and Bukhara were magnificent centers of culture. Their culture was, in fact, an integral part of the great Persian-Islamic civilization of the
Middle Ages.

During that period the Jewish communities grew and
prospered in the cities of the various principalities and
emirates; Bukharan Jewish poets and writers created a religious and secular literature in Hebrew and Persian; Bukharan Jews developed and adopted Persian with Hebrew
characters as their secular language; and, finally, they
began to settle in the large cities and to trade mainly in
cloth, silk, woven materials, and carpets.

Unlike the Georgian and Mountain Jews, who were also
merchants but lived among comparatively small and isolated communities, the Bukharan Jews were, for many
centuries, people of the great, colorful, and lively Oriental
bazaars, like their brethren in Isfahan, Shiraz, and Meshed
in Persia. They organized and financed caravans from
India and China to the Mediterranean ports and to Europe. They owned large stockpiles of wool and other raw
materials for industry and were an essential element in the
economy and in the internal and international commerce
of the region.

But with affluence and prosperity came assimilation to
and emulation of the social mores of the surrounding
wealthy Moslem society. During the eighteenth century, a
number of rabbis and scholars came to the Bukharan Jewish communities on a mission from the Jews of the Otto-
man empire. It was these men who saved Bukharan Jewry
and returned it to the mainstream of Judaism.

During the nineteenth century, the lands of this region
were conquered and annexed to the Russian empire. For
the first time the Bukharan Jews encountered the highly
developed cultural and religious civilization of Ashkenazi
Jewry. The Bukharan Jews were ready to absorb the new
trends which were then beginning to develop among the

Jews of Russia. A Bukharan Jewish cultural and national-Zionist renaissance took place in the late nineteenth and early twentieth centuries. Modern Hebrew schools were opened, youth movements were organized, sport clubs were established, and so on. A systematic emigration of Bukharan Jews to Palestine was initiated at the end of the last century. They went mainly to Jerusalem, where they built one of the first modern quarters outside the walls of the ancient city. In the twenties the new Soviet regime abrogated the Zionist movement, the Hebrew schools, and the youth movement, and closed down every existing Jewish institution and organization.

Once again, the family preserved the cultural, religious, and national traditions. And because the national movement had undergone extensive development among Bukharan Jews, they had something concrete to hold on to and to transmit from generation to generation—more so than has been the case among the other Oriental Jewish communities.

During the Soviet regime, young Jews began to enter the professions and now many are engineers, doctors, and technicians. At the same time, many Jews found their way back into government-owned trade and industry—cotton, wool, cloth, and carpets.

Today, when you visit the large government bazaar or the stores of Samarkand, you can see that most of the officials and salesmen are Bukharan Jews.

The Ashkenazi Jews of Central Asia

During the Second World War, the Bukharan Jews came into contact with tens of thousands of Ashkenazi Jews who had fled from the war zone and made their way into Central Asia. Of the hundreds of thousands of Jews who passed through that region, some tens of thousands stayed behind in the large cities of the republics of Uzbekistan, Tajikistan, and Turkmenistan. The Jewish communities there are now mixed and are made up of both Ashkenazi and Bukharan Jews.

The situation of the Jews in the Republic of Uzbekistan became acute after the war. A precarious racial balance prevails now in this, the central and most important of the

Soviet republics of Central Asia: the Uzbeks, an Irano-Mongolian people, comprise about half of the population; the rest are new European settlers (settlers have lived there since czarist times, but most were sent there by the Soviet authorities, mainly in Stalinist times). Since the Second World War they have occupied important and influential positions at top government, party, administrative, cultural, and economic levels.

The Uzbeks, who are, as it were, the "masters" of this republic, keep up a subdued, hidden, but ceaseless struggle for their due portion and place in every area of social and economic endeavor. This tension can even be sensed by a tourist who visits Tashkent or Samarkand for only a few days. The pride of the Uzbeks is manifest in their open use of their national language, their special dress, their peculiar architecture and other national symbols. Many of the Russians one meets there speak privately in contemptuous and ironic terms of the "Asians."

Tashkent, the capital, is a showplace for the various missions, most of them from Afro-Asian countries, and for tourists. Visitors are shown how Europeans and Asians can live side by side and in amity under the Soviet regime. The visitors are also told that the Asians, namely the Uzbeks, actually rule the Europeans since they constitute a majority in the Supreme Soviet of the republic, the municipalities, the courts, and the like.

But below the surface there are sharp inter-communal tensions, and the Jews, as usual, feel the strain from both directions.

The Bukharan Jews, who have not experienced serious anti-Semitism from the Uzbeks, now realize that the settlers from Russia and the Ukraine have brought this poison with them and have infected the Uzbek population. The Russians, and now also the Uzbeks, regard the Jews as competitors for positions of power and influence, particularly in the areas of commerce and culture. The Bukharan Jews thus find themselves, for the first time, placed in the "classical" position of the rest of Soviet Jewry: between the Russian hammer and the anvil of the national majority in the republic.

Among the hundreds of thousands of Ashkenazi Jews who passed through Uzbekistan as war refugees, there were several thousand who had been active in Zionist movements in Poland, Lithuania, Latvia, and other east

European countries. During their brief contact with Bukharan Jews, they inspired national feelings which on the surface appear to have subsided or been forgotten. But it would seem that they have not been forgotten at all.

On a visit to Tashkent, a Bukharan Jew persuaded me to be his guest for the Sabbath meal. I realized from the urgency of his invitation that he was not simply being hospitable but very much wanted me in his home for other reasons. I agreed and visited him on a lovely spring day. The whole family had gathered in the inner court which was surrounded by a brick wall, as is usual in the old houses of the town. There were grandfathers and grandmothers, fathers and mothers, sons and daughters and many grandchildren of all ages. We were seated at tables amidst fruit trees growing in the yard. The men wore European clothes but their heads were covered with square Bukharan caps, embroidered with golden and silver threads; the heads of the women were covered with the colorful and beautiful bands which are characteristic of that area.

When the meal ended and we were all warm with the heady wine, my host asked me to tell them about Israel.

I told story after story and was unable to satisfy the appetite of my audience. Other relatives had arrived in the meantime, and I found myself talking to several dozen people, all of whom were listening hungrily to every word I said.

In the course of my story-telling, I noticed three charming and gay old ladies who kept up an excited, whispered conversation. Finally, the boldest of the three asked me to sing "songs of Zion." She explained: "When we were young, about fifty or more years ago, there were Hebrew schools here which taught wonderful songs. But it is years since we sang in Hebrew. If our honored guest would sing us something, we might remember them again."

The other members of the family joined, especially the boys and girls: "Do sing us 'songs of Zion.' "

I am no singer, but how could I refuse them—especially the old ladies?

I tried to remember some of the songs which had been popular among the early settlers of Palestine and which I had heard sung by my parents and by the older generation. I started with a favorite song of the first Russian settlers in Palestine at the end of the nineteenth century: "To the mountain top, to the mountain top, who will beat a

path for the returning captives?" I did my best, but soon
realized that neither the words nor the tune conveyed anything to the old ladies. I tried another old song: "Hold
aloft the banner of Zion"—but this also failed to make
any impression. Then I recalled an old song that had been
popular among the youth of a few decades back: "Here in
the land our fathers loved." With the very first verse I saw
the eyes of the three old ladies light up; and when I
reached the refrain

> *Sing a song, song, song,*
> *Rejoice in joy, joy, joy*

their lips began to move in unison with mine. "That's it!"
the old ladies exclaimed delightedly. "That is the song we
learned. Please sing it again so that it will come back to
us." I sang it several times and with every repetition they
remembered more and more of the words and melody; it
was as though they were shedding years of accumulated
forgetfulness. Their voices seemed to become younger and
clearer.

As we sang this light and lovely song, I noticed that the
youngsters were now singing, too. Before long the whole
family caught the rhythm and words and we all sang together:

> *There in the land our fathers loved,*
> *Every hope will be realized;*
> *There we shall live and forge*
> *A life of joy and freedom. . . .*

Birobidzhan: a ghost town

My excitement increased as the Trans-Siberian train
neared Birobidzhan. I had heard about present-day Birobidzhan, about the utter failure of the experiment to establish an autonomous Jewish region in eastern Siberia. But it
is one thing to read and hear something and another to see
it with one's own eyes.

I reached Birobidzhan after visiting many Soviet cities
and towns and seeing Jewish life in various stages of humiliation and degradation. I had no illusions about the

Jewish Autonomous Region. Nevertheless, I experienced a peculiar feeling when I came down from the train and saw the large sign over the station building on which was written, in Yiddish with large Hebrew letters, the name BIROBIDZHAN. For a moment I was under the spell of those Hebrew letters and I felt that I was standing on Jewish soil.

The feeling accompanied me as I entered the nearby hotel and restaurant and when I saw the post office and other public institutions—all marked with Yiddish signs in the familiar Hebrew letters. The feeling persisted as I read the Yiddish street names and when I obtained (without any difficulty) the Yiddish paper, *Birobidzhaner Stern*.

But a few hours later, cold and cruel logic and the impact of the reality all around me overcame the effects of the signs and my own wishful thinking. Because from a Jewish viewpoint, the Jewish tourist who walks through Birobidzhan today sees only a city of signposts and ghostly shadows. There was life in the city, of course: children ran to school; loaded trucks passed; the movie houses showed films; housewives shopped in the markets; the city seemed as normal as any other provincial Soviet city with a population of a hundred thousand.

But there is no connection whatever between any of this everyday activity and the Yiddish signs.

You feel somehow that the signs have an existence of their own, a life belonging to other days; you see them as faithful witnesses to the great hopes, the deep yearnings, and the tremendous efforts that were once expended here and that were blown away by the cold Siberian wind.

After staying a day or two you begin to realize that the signs have no substance and that behind the "autonomy" there is a gaping Jewish void—and then the signs become irritating and depressing. Suddenly they remind you of the old movies of the wild west that you saw when you were young, and you begin to see yourself as a lonely rider entering a sleepy town at noon with the wind rattling the signs that hang along the single main street and announce: Bar, General Store, Restaurant, Hotel. But you ride on because you know that this is a ghost town. Robbery, insecurity, and hopelessness have driven the people away—and only the signs are left.

And when you leave Birobidzhan, even after speaking to living, healthy Jews, you feel as though you have left a Jewish cemetery where every legend reads: "Here lies a

Jewish dream, born 1928, died 1948, after a long illness and prolonged agony. May its soul rest in peace amidst the great pioneering schemes."

How was the Birobidzhan plan conceived? How did it grow? How and why did it die?

We have already said that the twenties, particularly the closing years of that decade, were witness to a sudden burst of flourishing activity in the life of Soviet Jewry. These were the years of the rebirth and flowering of Yiddish culture in the Soviet Union, the period when the Soviet government granted the Jews the same cultural rights as other nationals.

It was also the period of a vast, spontaneous wave of assimilation. Hundreds of thousands of Jews believed that they would live to see, through the gates flung open by the revolutionary society, the solution to the Jewish question, and that they themselves would be able to integrate fully into the new, supra-national, just society which would be established upon the ruins of the old regime.

The official Jewish leadership, the heads of the Jewish Section (*Evsektsiia*) which had been set up in the very center of the Communist party, as well as Yiddish writers and poets and others of the Jewish communist elite, were aware of the effects of assimilation. Given the very narrow latitude for action allowed them by the central authorities, they tried their best—in their own way—to safeguard the national identity and culture of the Jews.

They recognized full well the anomaly inherent in the social and economic structure of the Jewish nationality; namely, that it possessed no territory or peasant class of its own. It was along these lines that they sought a solution to the problem from the very start. They were hoping both to improve the Jewish social status and to create an alternative to Zionism, which stressed the need for territorial concentration outside the Soviet Union, in Palestine.

The plan for settling Jews on the land found willing adherents among some of the top Soviet leaders during the twenties. Special institutions were established for the purpose of settling Jews on the land and a movement for agricultural settlement was begun. Jewish villages were founded in the Crimean Peninsula and in areas of the Ukraine and Belorussia. They seemed to follow the pattern of the nascent Jewish agricultural colonization in southern Russia during czarist days.

The settlement of Jews in the Crimea was, comparatively speaking, quite successful. Over the years a few dozen Jewish settlements were established there, and some flourished. Though the collectivization program in Stalin's time weakened them, they nevertheless held on until the Second World War. When the Crimea was captured by the Germans, all of these Jewish settlements were destroyed and their people murdered.

During the twenties, the Jewish leaders realized that these schemes were very limited, since they were being carried out in areas that already had large non-Jewish populations, and that there could not be any possibility of "Jewish autonomy" or a "Jewish territory" in the Crimea and certainly not in the Ukraine or Belorussia.

Some dreamed, therefore, of extensive Jewish settlement in the new, empty lands of the Far East; of the creation of a Jewish-Soviet territory which, after the initial pioneering stage, would flourish and become a sort of "Jewish national home," or, in Soviet terminology, an "autonomous Jewish region," or, possibly in the distant future, a "Jewish republic" among all the other national republics of the Soviet Union.

The fulfillment of this plan, they thought, would also compensate for the absence of a specifically Jewish territory in the Soviet Union. Further, a Jewish center in which an independent Jewish communist culture might flourish would be a forthright answer to the Zionist tendencies current among Jews of the Soviet Union and at the same time serve as a source of inspiration to Jewish communism throughout the world.

These ideas fitted in perfectly with important and far-reaching plans then being drawn up by the Soviet rulers who intended quickly to settle the borderlands of eastern Siberia and China. These plans had both strategic and economic significance. This coincidence gave rise to the Birobidzhan plan.

The Birobidzhan region is named after the two rivers that encircle it: the Biro and the Bidzhan. It is a region of about 14,000 square miles in the southern part of the Soviet Far East, some 100 miles from Khabarovsk on the border between the Soviet Union and China. Its climate is very rigorous. The winters are cold, dry, and long. The summers are hot and rainy. The region is well watered with rivers, streams, and lakes, but due to the nature of the soil there are vast marshes. Forests cover much of the land and only a small area is fit for agriculture. The region also has iron, coal, graphite, tin, and copper deposits.

An expedition of scientists and technicians, most of them Jews, was sent to Birobidzhan in 1927, a distance of 5000 miles from Moscow, to determine the prospects for settlement. The expedition did not conceal the fact that there would be many difficulties, but most of its members were fired with enthusiasm over the pioneering aspect of the undertaking and recommended that the authorities make preparations to institute the plan.

The Jewish settlement organizations (the *Komzet* and the *Ozet*) adopted the commission's proposals, though quite a number of leaders in these organizations had doubts about the feasibility of the plan, chiefly because of the great natural difficulties of the area and the tremendous distance that separated it from the centers of Jewish settlement.

The pioneering leaders of the Autonomous Region

In March, 1928, the central Soviet authorities approved the principles of the plan and empowered the Jewish settlement organizations to proceed.

The first three years were the hardest. Only a few thousand Jews settled there, mostly artisans and workmen from little Ukrainian and Belorussian towns, and they had a terrible time getting acclimated to the desolate region. To appreciate the endurance and tremendous courage of these pioneers, one has to listen to the stories of that time which are told by the few of them who are still alive today.

Were it not for the small group of pioneering intellectual leaders among the Jewish communists who volunteered and went out with the workers to build the new towns and villages, the Jews would not have been able to continue their efforts. But the leaders, headed by Professor Liberberg of Kiev, knew how to stimulate the progress of the Birobidzhan plan. Living among the simple people, the Jewish writers and poets impressed upon them the extent to which they shared in an effort which was as significant to the Soviet Union as it was to the Jewish people.

Despite this, many of the first settlers were unable to endure the physical strain and arduous conditions, and left. Looking back from a perspective of over thirty years, it is possible to discard the political ideology of the plan and at the same time feel profound admiration for the Jews whose sweat soaked the soil of Birobidzhan. They deserve the respect accorded to pioneers. Many gave of themselves no less splendidly than the first pioneers in Palestine.

When the Japanese invaded Manchuria in 1931, the Soviet government gave top priority to the problems of settlement along the borders of China. The Jewish settlement organizations and the Jewish settlers were given new impetus by the government after their first three years of birthpangs and indecision. Three years later, in 1934, the Presidium of the Committee of the Soviet Union formally declared Birobidzhan a Jewish Autonomous Region (*Evrieskaia avtonomnaia oblast*). Many Jews in the Soviet Union regarded this as an act of great political significance. Its effects were felt not only by Jewish communists outside the Soviet Union but also by the Jewish people as a whole. This declaration no doubt won many Jewish friends for the Soviet government, particularly since the Nazis had already begun their persecution of Jews. The "Zionist" speech of the President of the Soviet Union, Mikhail Kalinin, was most impressive. He emphasized that the Jews needed to preserve their national character, and that this was possible only if they had a land of their own where they could establish a society based on agriculture and manual labor.

The following two years were the high point of the plan. To be sure, because results fell short of the hopes of the responsible organizations, the Soviets felt it necessary to send to Birobidzhan large numbers of Russians, Ukrainians, Belorussians, and other nationals. But from an economic point of view, there was rapid advance in the building of villages and towns. The city of Birobidzhan was declared the capital of the region; many new industries were founded; organizational and administrative cadres were established in which Jews occupied prominent positions.

During that same period, mainly in 1931–32, Jewish volunteers from abroad came to Birobidzhan in groups and individually. These were Jewish communists from the United States, Latin America, Palestine, and Europe who wanted to help as well as to settle in the region which was to become a Soviet Jewish republic in the not too distant future.

By the end of 1935 some fourteen thousand Jews lived in the autonomous region and constituted about a quarter of the population. The Jews had already established their own *kolkhozy* and *sovkhozy,* and were active in industry and manufacture, in public service and administration. There were Jewish kindergartens, primary and secondary schools, as well as vocational schools and research institutes. Most of the instruction was in Yiddish; some was bilingual, Yiddish and Russian. Initial steps were being taken to start a Yiddish publishing house, a Jewish press, a Yiddish theater, and various cultural and artistic groups.

Suddenly, in 1937, the fledgling region, which had just begun to take its first steps, received a savage blow from which it never recovered. A wave of purges swept like a storm over the entire Soviet Union and carried away the leadership of Birobidzhan. Some of its foremost figures were charged with being Trotskyites, nationalists, Zionists, nepotists, and so on. They were dismissed from their positions; many were imprisoned, exiled, or executed, including Professor Liberberg, the most beloved of all, who disappeared and was secretly killed. The purge swept the whole intellectual elite of Birobidzhan: the Jewish teachers, journalists, and writers, most of whom were discharged, arrested, and imprisoned. The foreign volunteers were accused of espionage, of conspiring with the Zionists and the international Jewish bourgeoisie to spy for the imperialist powers, of having come to that sensitive border area to commit sabotage. Many were imprisoned and put to death.

There is no doubt that Stalin and his cohorts had decided that the whole plan of settling Jews on the Chinese border in an autonomous Jewish region was basically wrong and should not be allowed to develop.

After the purges the plan was maintained through sheer inertia; there was even an increase in population. But it was a headless body whose progress was sporadic, aimless, doomed.

There was a new spurt of life and energy during and immediately after the war years. First, the Soviets exploited the publicity value of the Jewish Autonomous Region for the benefit of their Western allies. The Jews of Birobidzhan were suddenly given an opportunity to appeal to world Jewry to safeguard the future of the Jewish people by aiding the Red Army. Secondly, Jewish settlers again began streaming to Birobidzhan; some of them were refugees from the countries that had been annexed to the Soviet Union, others were fleeing from the German invaders. These included ardent communists who tried hard to provide the old plan with new leadership. Among the Jews who came to Birobidzhan during and immediately after the war there were prominent writers and spiritual leaders who attempted to revive its devastated Jewish culture.

After the war, when thousands of Jews were wandering like ghosts among the shambles of their homes in western Russia, it appeared that the government had reverted to the idea of a territorial concentration of Jews; Jewish volunteers were encouraged to move east; and Birobidzhan began to show signs of revival.

But in 1948, when Stalin's guillotine descended on Jewish culture throughout the Soviet Union, Birobidzhan was struck down again. This time the authorities were not content merely to exile and put to death the Jewish elite; they also uprooted every vestige of Jewish culture and education. Every Jewish school, publishing house, and theater was closed. The number of Jews in administration and local government was curtailed.

The Birobidzhan plan has not yet recovered from that blow. Birobidzhan is in its death throes as a Jewish Autonomous Region—but it is not yet dead.

What is the situation today?

The Jewish population of the Jewish Autonomous Region has never exceeded a few tens of thousands. According to the 1959 census, Jews numbered 14,269 out of a total population of 162,856, namely 8.8 per cent. The rest are Russians and Ukrainians. The meagerness of the Jewish population is clear evidence of its physical emasculation. Thousands of Jews abandoned the area after the 1948 purges, not in organized groups, of course, but as individuals. They simply picked up and left.

I talked with Jews in Khabarovsk, in eastern Siberia, who told me they had lived in Birobidzhan. They told me that they are better off both as Jews and as human beings in Khabarovsk, a city of half a million, than they had been in Birobidzhan. Khabarovsk offers better opportunities for improvement in the technical fields and is not so beset with mediocre provincialism. They are not taunted at every turn for their Jewishness. They are more anonymous in Khabarovsk and share the same fate as other Jews of the Soviet Union without having to bear the stigma associated with Birobidzhan. One constantly hears from the young people in Birobidzhan itself that they are anxious to move to the large Siberian cities which are developing rapidly and which offer infinitely greater opportunities for young people to integrate with the population and develop their talents.

In addition to the Yiddish signs, there are some other vestiges of "Jewishness" in Birobidzhan. Though the local government bureaus are managed largely by non-Jews, some few Jewish names are displayed here and there as regional representatives and elected officials. There is a small synagogue—a wooden shack in one of the suburbs. When I visited it on a Sabbath, I found about fifteen frightened old Jews inside. Sometimes a Jewish troubadour comes to Birobidzhan, but in this regard Birobidzhan is no different from any other city of the Soviet Union with a large Jewish population. And, as mentioned, the newspaper *Birobidzhaner Stern* is published. However, it prints only about a thousand copies, its format is small, and it is totally devoid of Jewish cultural content or information. When it occasionally publishes an item about Israel, the tone and content are as inimical as anything found in the general press. The Jews of Birobidzhan look down on it and most of them will not read it.

There has not been a single Jewish school in the Jewish Autonomous Region since 1948; nor has there been a single class for the teaching of Yiddish. There are no Jewish theaters and no institutions for the dissemination of Jewish culture. Two traces of the region's Jewishness remain: the absurd Yiddish periodical and the broadcasting of some Yiddish songs a few times a week.

A number of years ago, an American Jew visited this area. When asked how it impressed him, he replied that of the three words that make up the name "Jewish Autonomous Region" only one is real: the word "region."

Yiddish: a foreign element in Birobidzhan

In Moscow, I had heard that there was a central municipal library in Birobidzhan named after Sholem Aleichem. I was anxious to see it and to donate a few books to the only library in the Soviet Union with a Jewish name.

When I arrived at the two-story library building, I was

greeted by the director. It was evident from the first moment that this Jewish woman felt ill at ease over having to act as host to a Jew from abroad. As she took me through the lovely building, she kept showering me with details about the number of books the library had, the readers, and so on. But when I inquired about Yiddish books, she mumbled:

"Yes, the library also has a Yiddish section. It is part of the department of foreign books."

I asked to see the department. Amidst sections containing English, German, and French literature I found a bookshelf on which were about a hundred and fifty Yiddish books. Most of them dated back to the twenties and thirties: Yiddish translations of Marx, Engels, and Lenin, some old geography books, translations of Jules Verne, Mark Twain, Sholokhov, and a few other authors. And that was all.

I asked the director whether there were any other Yiddish books in the library. She said that there were quite a lot in the storeroom, but they were not taken out because the "readers are not interested."

A Jew of about sixty who happened to be nearby was trying to overhear the conversation. He heaved a deep "Oy" and directed a penetrating glance at me from sad eyes. The sigh and the look said more about the state of Jewish culture in the Jewish Autonomous Region than lengthy speeches and explanations. I went to the director to say goodbye and to thank her for her hospitality. I said: "Madam, I had heard about this library before I came and have brought three books as a gift."

The woman paled and said quickly: "Thank you, sir, but we do not need any more books. We have all we need."

I pretended to be offended and answered: "But, madam, you haven't seen the books. I am sure you'll be happy to have them when you do." I took the three volumes out of my briefcase. One was a luxurious edition of Sholem Aleichem's works in Hebrew translation, published in Israel; the others were *The Dairy of Anne Frank* in Yiddish and an album on the Dead Sea Scrolls by Professor Yigael Yadin.

She grew more agitated when she saw the books. She left quickly and returned with a lady colleague and said: "Please excuse me. I cannot read Yiddish, but this comrade knows the language."

The first book I showed them was Sholem Aleichem. They leafed through it and said: "But this book is not written in Yiddish; it is in Hebrew. We do not need it. We have no Hebrew readers."

I told them: "Ladies, I saw lovely exhibits of translations of famous Russian writers in Moscow and other cities in the Soviet Union. For instance, in Iasnaia Poliana there is a permanent exhibit of Tolstoy translations in dozens of languages. And if I am not mistaken, I saw a fine edition of Tolstoy in Hebrew. You might want to arrange an exhibit of translations of Sholem Aleichem some day and you would then have one in Hebrew."

They accepted the book and asked about the others. I mentioned the name of Anne Frank, but realized that it meant nothing to them. I told them briefly about Anne Frank, her book, and the tremendous publicity it had received throughout the world. They leafed through it and the director said: "But, sir, this seems to be a sad wartime story. Our readers are not particularly interested in this type of book." I said: "Madam, they are now showing a film of Anne Frank's life produced in the German Democratic Republic at the International Film Festival in Moscow. It won a prize from the Soviet organizers." She shook her head: "Are you sure they are showing this film in Moscow?" When I gave her my word of honor that this was so, she agreed to accept this gift as well.

"And what is the third book?" I showed them the album and briefly explained what the Dead Sea Scrolls were.

"But," they said, "not one of our readers is interested in the Bible and the archeology of the Middle East. This is a book for specialized libraries and not for ours. Won't you take it back?" I told them: "The Soviet Academy of Sciences is very much interested in this topic. Professors of the Leningrad University have published articles on the Dead Sea Scrolls in Soviet scientific journals. I hope there will be some readers in Birobidzhan who might be interested in these discoveries."

They asked whether I was certain that articles on the subject had been published in the Soviet Union. I answered that I was, and they agreed to accept the third book.

I left the building with a heavy heart. The fear lurking in the eyes of the two Jewish women when they accepted my books had clearly revealed the nature of the "autonomy" of the "Jewish region," its utter debasement and degradation.

When one leaves that city, with the Hebrew letters of the station's name disappearing from view, one asks himself why the government still maintains this fiction? Why is this administrative district still nominally the Jewish Autonomous Region? Why do they still publish a meaningless Yiddish paper? Why don't they remove the dual language signs and replace them with Russian ones? Why don't they let this small Jewish minority, which has neither influence nor means of expression, live in peace like the many other Jews in Soviet provincial towns? Why do they force them to remember, day in, day out, that they are living in the shambles of a Jewish utopia which was smashed to pieces long ago and of which nothing is left but some signs and shadows of the past?

There is no simple answer to this. Like other problems affecting the Jews of the Soviet Union, it has many elements.

First, the Soviet regime does not want to confess to an ideological failure; it hates to make such admissions. It does occasionally half admit to some disappointments in the economic and administrative fields. But it is another matter altogether to admit to the bankruptcy of a principle or a basic idea, for this would be like pulling a stone out of the base of a pyramid. At most the authorities will say, as they occasionally do, that they paved the way for the Jews and gave them a unique opportunity to create their own territory where they would eventually have been granted autonomous status, like the other nationalities, had they only invested in it the hard work necessary for a settlement of this sort. But the Jews, because they hate work and are such individualists, simply could not establish a healthy society. (This, almost word for word, was how Khrushchev explained the failure of the Birobidzhan plan to a correspondent of the French newspaper *Figaro*.)

Publicity is a second consideration. The Soviet regime is still capable at times of extracting a few drops of propaganda from the squeezed-out lemon of Birobidzhan, mainly for the benefit of the outside world. They can photograph a few children gathered around one of the Yiddish signs, and then talk about "the happy Jewish children in the autonomous region." Or they can take a picture of a Jew driving a tractor in one of the few *kolkhozy* where a handful of Jewish farmers may still be found. A montage of such pictures can serve as the basis for a feature article; then the whole package can be sent out to the Western world with the claim that everything is fine, that the Jews are well-off and lack nothing, not even a territory of their own, nor their own Jewish homeland.

Thirdly, it seems that the Soviet authorities feel subconsciously that it is worth holding on to the skeleton "because no one knows what can happen"; they might find themselves needing it in the near or distant future. A situation might arise when internal or external pressures might make it advisable to renew the scheme and send a stream of Jewish "volunteers" and emigrants into the area. Why break up the scaffolding, despite the fact that it is in such poor shape, when it might be necessary one day to add another wing to the structure?

I heard about this third possibility from many Jews, all of whom tremble whenever the name "Birobidzhan" reappears like a phantom in the Soviet press. They are afraid that they might be asked once again to sacrifice their sons and daughters to this Moloch. They do not feel at ease until the name fades once more into oblivion.

7

A Three-Pronged Struggle

Three basic questions

One must ask himself, first: What does the Soviet regime want of the Jews? Then: What do the Soviet Jews want? And finally: What is the position of world Jewry as regards the Jews of the Soviet Union?

These questions are indicative of the unequal struggle that is taking place today between the Soviet regime and those who are trying to safeguard the existence of Soviet Jewry.

Let me try to define the nature of this struggle and its prospects. I have already called attention to the fact that the Soviet regime is centralized, dogmatic, and based upon an all-encompassing ideology, and that the attitude of the central authority is decisive and affects every aspect of the life in the country. This is particularly true insofar as the Jewish question is concerned. Everything the government does or fails to do about the Jewish problem has great significance. Any hint of a possible change of attitude, for better or for worse, takes on far greater proportions than we can imagine. The economic trials can serve as an example: the executions that followed those trials and the publication of Jewish names at the head of the list of criminals plunged virtually all the Jews of the Soviet Union into a condition bordering on hysteria.

Every article in a major Soviet paper which defames Jews or the State of Israel causes a heart-throb to hundreds of thousands of Jewish readers, even if they know nothing, or next to nothing, about Jewish affairs and Israel, or even if they pretend that these are of no importance and do not affect them in the least. They are well aware, consciously or subconsciously, that they are affected every time the word "Jew" appears in Soviet literature or the press.

Furthermore, the non-Jew of the Soviet Union—the man in the street, or the party or government official, whether in the center of activity or in the provinces—shapes his attitude in accordance with the line or hints of a line that come from the authorities. This is true, in one way or another, of everything that happens in the Soviet Union, though in some areas of economic and social life one can discern pressures from below which influence and at times even shape the line decided upon above. To choose one example among many, in the matter of the production of consumer goods there is no doubt that pressures from below influence the policy of the central government. But this is not the case with the Jewish question: Soviet Jews cannot even attempt to bring serious, organized influence to bear from below. That is why it is so important to examine the governmental machinery that runs Jewish affairs and to uncover the nature of the fuel—political, ideological, psychological, and personal—that makes it function.

We must first find out who it is that deals with the Jews; then we must examine the lines along which the government shapes Jewish policy today. Finally, we must try to sort out the underlying causes and motivations of this policy.

Who controls Jewish religious and cultural affairs?

On the religious level the answer is simple enough. There is a Department of Religions whose function it is to supervise the existence and activities of all religions in the Soviet Union, including that of the Jews. This is an overall national body, administered from Moscow. It is controlled directly by the Council of Ministers of the Soviet Union, the central government. Because religion is a highly delicate and sensitive matter, it may be assumed that the administration of the department is in the hands of the highest officials in the political hierarchy and that they maintain an elastic and not too formal contact with those at the summit of the party or government who determine policy. At the same time, it may be assumed that the officialdom of this department, at all levels, is tightly connected and may even be linked administratively with the authorities who are in charge of internal security.

This is readily understandable, for the Soviet government regards religion, any religion, as a competing spiritual-social force, as a power which is a potential source of anti-Soviet feeling.

However, while the representatives of non-Jewish religions, with an established hierarchy of their own, are able to maintain contact with their counterparts in the hierarchy of the Department of Religions and thereby gain access to the highest echelon, the representatives of the Jewish communities know only the local officials in the cities and provincial towns. These are, for the most part, middle- and low-ranking officials, many of them poorly educated, who follow without hesitation the instructions from above which tell them how to deal with the religious Jews in their area. In many instances, these officials make a special effort to prove themselves reliable by adding their own personal callousness and cruelty to the manner in which they carry out the government's directives.

In a number of places, the local officials in charge of Jewish affairs are the people with strong leanings toward traditional native anti-Semitism. They find in this work a broad field in which to exercise their authority, and they give vent to their feelings by oppressing the old Jews. Many are ready to accept bribes to remove or soften the harsh government measures. The relationship between them and the Jews thus becomes a most dangerous one indeed to both parties. It is by the sufferance of these people that the Jewish religion exists in the Soviet Union. Every event and act in the Jewish community is subject to their wish and whim. Under the present circumstances there is no way in which religious Jews can confront the heads of the Department of Religions with any complaints, opinions, or suggestions regarding even the slightest improvements in conditions pertaining to Jewish religious life.

The other government bodies that deal with the Jewish religion are the numerous and varied atheistic organizations. These organizations, some of which are central all-

Soviet bodies, while others operate only within republics, districts, and towns, distribute propaganda material against all religions, including, of course, the Jewish religion. Some are disguised as scientific bodies and are known as "academies of science" of one kind or another. This is how in Kiev, in 1963, the Academy of Sciences of the Ukrainian Republic published the anti-Semitic pamphlet by Kichko, entitled, *Judaism Without Embellishment,* with caricatures in the style of the *Stürmer.*

Some atheistic organizations are branches of, or an organic part of, the Department of Progapanda and Information of the Communist party. They have easy access to all the publishing houses, clubs, and other communication media controlled by this department, whose activities penetrate every street and home in the Soviet Union.

Some atheistic bodies are assisted by the propaganda machinery of the workers' unions, of the municipalities, and of the communist youth organizations, the Pioneers and the Komsomol.

This, in effect, is the situation insofar as Jewish religion is concerned.

As regards affairs that bear upon Jewish nationality, these too are handled by low-ranking officials.

The publication of the few Yiddish periodicals and pamphlets is dealt with by the All-Soviet Association of Authors and Newspapermen and by the government publishing houses. The circulation of the *Sovietish Heimland* and the publication of fewer than six Yiddish books is negligible and inconsequential. Except for the work of the omnipresent censor, there is not much that needs to be done in connection with these publications.

Jewish concerts and singers are managed by theatrical organizations, in particular by Estrada, The Organization of Theatrical Artists, which is a branch of the Ministry of Culture. This organization, which is in charge of popular culture, decides on the type of performance Jewish artists can give and also supervises the ideological content of each performance. At times, Jewish amateur theatrical groups are supervised by local professional companies, or by municipal or provincial organizations of artists.

There is no doubt that these various methods of handling both Jewish religious affairs and the remnants of Jewish secular culture are manifestations of a wider strategy, which constantly affects the lives of more than three million Soviet Jews. The maintenance of ties between these Jews and those abroad or in Israel, the ability or inability of Jews to emigrate from the Soviet Union to Israel, the nature of the regime's reaction to world Jewry's struggle regarding such matters—none of these is the concern of the organizations we have mentioned but the result of decisions made on a much higher level. To be sure, it would not be altogether correct to regard the government as a monolithic whole with everything being decided finally and unalterably at the summit. Clearly there are differences within the central ruling body which show internal conflicts, tensions, and dissent. This is only natural and human. It may be assumed, therefore, that Soviet policy with regard to the Jewish question is also not unified and is subject to differing or possibly conflicting views.

Of one thing we may be certain: due mainly to the efforts of world Jewry the Jewish question in the Soviet Union is no longer only an internal matter. It is inseparably linked now with the problems of Israel and the Middle East. It affects the Soviet Communist party in the West. And it affects the relationship between the Soviet Union and many Western countries, particularly the United States.

At times one asks: Who deals with the "Jewish dossier" at the summit? Who is responsible for the shaping of strategy in this matter?

The situation was clear in Stalin's time, especially in his last years: the dictator shaped Jewish policy, and ideologists, such as Zhdanov, and heads of the security forces, such as Beria, carried it out, each in his own way. Zhdanov and his associates justified the policy on ideological grounds; Beria and his subordinates carried out the physical purging of Jewish institutions and invididuals.

This does not mean that only this trio dealt with Jewish affairs. All of those at the summit, and certainly all the leaders of the party, danced to Stalin's tune.

The situation was less clear in Khrushchev's time. He often felt compelled to answer nagging questions put to him by Western delegations and personalities about the situation of Soviet Jewry. His answers set the tone not only because he was the ruler, but also because he took a definite stand regarding the Jews and Judaism which he had inherited from traditional Russian anti-Semitism and the Ukrainian milieu in which he had grown up. Khrushchev's famous aphorisms on the "Rabinoviches," on their "lack of productivity," their "individualism," their "excess of intellectualism," were drawn from much deeper sources than communist dogma. But because he constantly consulted with his associates, it may be assumed that others shared in the shaping of Jewish policy—namely, Suslov; his second in command, Kozlov; the Minister of Culture, Furtseva; the head of the security forces, Shelepin; and others.

Khrushchev's heirs are young, more of the "technocrat" type, less colorful than he and less inclined to sprinkle their statements with popular sayings. Thus far they have been conducting their affairs in a manner that makes it difficult to determine who among them has the more decisive voice in Jewish affairs.

It is sometimes rumored that a specific committee or subcommittee in the Presidium of the party has been set up to deal with Jewish problems. But one cannot be certain. It is senseless to try to guess who might be involved. It seems more profitable to sum up the basic principles underlying Soviet strategy in Jewish matters.

The Soviet regime, which formally recognizes the Jews of the Soviet Union as a nationality, does not admit that there is any moral, national, historical, cultural, or religious affinity between this nation in the Soviet Union and the Jews abroad. This regime does not accede to the fact that such ties can be formed without its permission either by the Soviet Jews themselves or by Jewish institutions and organizations outside the Soviet Union. But there is no doubt that those who shape Jewish policy know that after almost fifty years of Soviet rule, actual ties still exist between the Jews of the Soviet Union and their relatives beyond Russia's borders. The men at the top also know that after the Second World War and the establishment of the State of Israel, Jewish national feelings among the Soviet Jews were strengthened rather than weakened, and that this is true of the younger generation as well—all this is in spite of the government's policies.

The government realizes that three reasons account for the peculiar position of its three to three and a half million Jews. To begin with, they are the only people who have so many relatives outside the Soviet Union. Secondly, a very large number of them are emotionally oriented to values and goals which are foreign to the Soviet Union. Thirdly, they are dispersed all over the country; they constitute a typically urban group and play an important role in Soviet science and technology.

The Soviet regime is well aware of the fact that the majority of the Jews live in countries which are outside the Soviet sphere of influence, mainly in the United States and Israel. Thus, it continues to regard the Jews of the Soviet Union as a security risk. This notion originated during Stalin's time. It was transmitted to Khrushchev, and to this day it continues to be the basis of Soviet strategy toward the Jews.

Why Jews cannot assimilate completely or emigrate

In the view of the authorities, the Jews must not be allowed to be completely absorbed into Soviet society. Had the government favored the complete assimilation of the Jews, it could have permitted them to change their Jewish names and to alter the Jewish nationality status stamped on their identity cards. For instance, it could easily have made it known, by means of the communication media at its disposal, that every Soviet citizen who is registered as a Jew could ask a specific official to change his national identity to that of the republic in which he lives, or to that of any other Soviet nationality of his choice.

Moreover, had the government really wanted to, it could have encouraged the Jews to do this; it could have waged a propaganda campaign through the press, radio, and television against the "anachronism" of Jewish nationality; it could have publicized the names and faces of Jews who changed their nationality; and so on. But the government takes the opposite course. It not only discourages such thorough assimilation, but perpetuates Jewish nationality from one generation to the next. It may be assumed, therefore, that this policy reflects the government's wish that the isolated Jew should not be completely absorbed into Soviet society; that constant supervision should be maintained over every Jew, wherever he may be, by means of his name and identity card.

The government reasons that the identified, isolated Jew is less likely to infect and is less harmful and dangerous than the one who changes his name and nationality. Such Jews, the authorities apparently fear, would remain Jews at heart, and there would be no administrative means of controlling them. He might possibly become a destructive agent and contaminate his environment with his innate traits: his individualism, skepticism, doubts, disloyalty. (Incidentally, the majority of Jews in the Soviet Union believe that the authorities are right in this matter. The change from the status of Jewish nationality might be detrimental in every way—both to the Jews and to Soviet society. The present impasse cannot be resolved by deepening the lie through the removal of Jewish identity.)

According to this logic, it is also not permissible to encourage the Jews to act in unison. They must not be allowed to establish cultural, social, national, or religious groups, for these would constitute an even greater danger. That is why they must not regain their national rights; they must not be given an institutional basis; they must not be allowed any tools or materials which they could use for the purpose of uniting and consolidating themselves; they must continue to live as isolated, scattered individuals, in a state of total disorganization and disintegration.

And now that the means of social consolidation in the secular sphere, such as education, culture, and language, have already been destroyed, it is necessary to eliminate the final remnant—religion.

According to this policy, no foreign Jewish influences must be allowed to penetrate the Soviet Union. All unnecessary and harmful contact with international Jewish bodies is forbidden. No Jewish "propaganda material," secular, national, or religious, must reach the Jews of the Soviet Union. They must not maintain any organized contact with Israel, its culture, language, literature, leaders, and values, for these are the nourishment, the fuel and energy which would bring about a rebirth of Jewish social feeling and arouse centripetal trends among the Jews.

To prevent the formation of these ties, the government emphasizes again an again, by means of its communication media and organs of propaganda, that they are forbidden and undesirable. The Jewish organizations in the United States and other countries of the Diaspora and, of course, Israel, are clearly tagged as "servants of capitalism and imperialism," as elements inimical to the Soviet Union. Isolated Jews in the Soviet Union are warned against any organized connections with them. The image of organized Jewry and Israel is besmirched and made unpalatable by means of horrifying accounts about life there and by the consistent depreciation of Jewry and Israel.

At the same time, to make it easier for Soviet citizens to spot the Jew in their midst, the real and potential danger that the Jews might pose to society if allowed to run amok must be made clear. That is why the authorities pillory individual Jews as "economic criminals," "profiteers," "parasites," "cheating and swindling rabbis and clerics," or as a mixture of all these. Through stories and caricatures in the press these Jews become prototypes, figures identified not only by the "Jewish nose" but also by their "Jewish character." So a potential scapegoat is ready at hand in case of need, one who will serve as a lightning rod for the fury of the mobs in times of crisis.

This brings us to a frequently asked question. If this is the true state of affairs, if this is what the Jews, or most of them, really are, why doesn't the government get rid of them once and for all? Why doesn't it allow them to emigrate to Israel or elsewhere; why doesn't it encourage Jewish emigration? It could easily spew out the Jews from the Soviet body and purify itself of this poisonous element.

The answer to this question is rather complex and involves ideological principles which affect the socio-political fabric of the country.

For fundamental ideological reasons, the Soviet Union is closed and forbids emigration. The underlying premise is that this land, which was the first to achieve communism and establish social and political justice, is the most modern and advanced country in the history of man—and all its peoples are content. Their satisfaction stems from their appreciation and awareness of the fact that they live in a finer, more humane, and better society than anyone else. Furthermore, according to this ideological premise, Soviet citizens know that by the very nature of their existence and efforts they fulfill a great mission: they are a symbol to untold millions of people who aspire to be like them and who wish to reach the same high standard of development and establish for themselves a similar just society. Is it conceivable, therefore, that large numbers of citizens within such an ideal society should be unsatisfied with their lives and ungrateful for their destiny? Why, then, should anyone wish to emigrate?

But besides the ideological reason there is a practical one as well. Despite their lack of sympathy for the Jews as a national group and for Jewish values as a culture and a religion, the Soviet authorities know quite well how to estimate the importance of the Jews as individuals scattered throughout the Soviet Union. They know that the Jews serve as important and vital catalysts in Soviet economic life; that they are a lubricant on the creaking wheels of the cumbersome and top-heavy Soviet economic machinery; that they serve as intermediaries and agents between consumption and demand, on the one hand, and production and supply, on the other.

The government is fully aware of the inestimable value of the tens of thousands of Jewish engineers with important duties in all branches of industry and technology. This is equally true of the Jews in medicine, teaching, and in several branches of communication and the arts.

The picture is even clearer in the field of science. The government knows that the Jews constitute a virtually inexhaustible reservoir of scientists who have made, and continue to make, a great contribution—far greater than their proportion—to the rapid progress of Soviet science. The regime pins its greatest hopes on scientific progress and achievement, which it regards as an ideological justification of its existence. Remove the Jews, and Soviet science would be robbed of its best people. Take the Jews out of Soviet technology, and a vacuum would be created which could not be filled. In addition, breakdowns, delays, and difficulties would inevitably result were the Jews to be taken from the fields of trade and commerce.

The Jews have often served as catalysts during their long history, for example, in medieval Spain. But the hatred and fanaticism of the Spanish kings, together with the influence of the Catholic Church and the Inquisition, resulted in the expulsion of Spanish Jewry in 1492. The same was true of Germany until the time of Hitler's "final solution" and the murder of the Jewish people.

The Soviet regime, however, neither annihilates peoples nor expels them. It does not want to kill the Jewish goose that lays the golden eggs. It is satisfied with isolating it from the rest of the country while giving it enough nourishment to continue laying these golden eggs and preventing it from having fruitful intercourse with its own kind, lest it lay eggs from which live chickens might emerge.*

* During his visit to Paris in December 1966, Soviet Premier Aleksei Kosygin stated at a Press Conference in response to a written question submitted in advance:

"If there are some families divided by the war who want to meet their relatives outside the U.S.S.R. or even to leave the

The story of the Khrushchev-Nasser dialogue

Thus far we have dealt only with the internal factors which prevent Jewish emigration from the Soviet Union. There are external factors as well, and these tend to complicate matters still more. Even if the Soviet government wanted to allow its Jews to emigrate, it would still have to take into consideration the fact that only one country is prepared to absorb them en masse—Israel. But at the moment the Soviets have vital political interests that are connected with Israel's position amidst the Arab countries in the Middle East.

The Soviets derive a twofold benefit from their attitude to the State of Israel and the prevention of Jewish emigration from Russia to Israel. Every Soviet gesture which favors the Arabs against Israel, every Soviet vote or veto against Israel, every anti-Israel article in the Soviet press is not only a potential killer of the national feelings of Jews in the Soviet Union but also a short-term investment which brings in immediate political dividends from the Arabs, who regard the Soviet Union as the only world power with a Jewish problem similar to their own. And similar it is indeed, but not identical. For, in contrast to the Arabs, the Soviets regard the actual existence of the State of Israel as being highly desirable, since this provides them with one more hidden asset in the arena of international diplomacy: the Soviet Union is the only country in the world which holds the key to a radical change in

U.S.S.R., we shall do all in our power to help them. The way is open to them and will remain open to them and there is no problem."

Significantly, this statement was reprinted in *Pravda* and *Izvestia* for domestic consumption as well as foreign, but the Soviet account omitted any reference to governmental assistance for potential emigrés or to the future character of his statement. There were indications that a large number of Jews carrying copies of the *Pravda* and *Izvestia* articles turned up at official bureaus throughout the Soviet Union to file for exit visas. While there are reports that in some cases such requests met with hostile responses, at this time of publication it is still not possible to determine whether the Soviet Union is prepared to translate the Premier's statement from word into deed.—*Publisher's note* the status of Israel through the possibility of increasing or even doubling its population.

Those who shape policy in Arab countries know that the Soviet regime, should it so desire, is capable of flooding Israel with tens of thousands of highly trained Jews. This capability constitutes a subtle, silent but nevertheless powerful diplomatic weapon which the Russians use with great effectiveness.

I heard this anecdote from Jews in the Soviet Union; though it is only a story, there is some truth in it.

When the Egyptian ruler, Nasser, visited the Soviet Union and met Khrushchev, they conducted long and intimate talks. At one of the talks the problem of the Egyptian communists was raised, for Egypt was at that time arresting and jailing communists. The discussion became deadlocked; the atmosphere grew heavy and strained. Then Khrushchev said to Nasser: "Suppose we let this ride for the time being and take up some noncontroversial issues."

"Go ahead," Nasser replied.

Khrushchev said: "I'd like to tell you about some data from the central statistical bureau of the Soviet Union. It might interest you."

"Please do," said Nasser.

Khrushchev went on: "My statisticians tell me that among the three million Jews living in the Soviet Union, there are about a half a million of military age, and those include several thousand trained flight engineers and pilots, several thousand weapons and armored car experts, a few thousand military engineers, several thousand military doctors, several hundred rocket experts and capable nuclear scientists, several thousand. . . ."

Nasser interrupted him and said: "Let's go back to the previous subject. I'm willing to promise. . . ."

For the sake of clarity I have tried to group principles of Jewish policy according to rational classifications on the assumption that Soviet policies are logically motivated, coldly reasoned, and that the men who shape these policies do so on purely rational grounds, according to the welfare of the Soviet Union. But it is not really as simple as all that, and the facts do not fit so neatly into definite categories.

Anyone who follows the statements and actions of the Soviet leaders who handle Jewish matters is aware that beneath their monolithic, reasoned, and rational exterior there are contradictions, hesitations, and things half-said and half-done. It may be assumed that some of the top leaders who deal with the problem understand that their Jewish policy is neither logical nor consistent and can lead to no solution. In all likelihood they appreciate the fact that their policy aggravates and perpetuates the problem. It is therefore utterly impossible to compare the Soviet regime to that of the Nazis, which actually planned and carried out the "final solution" of the Jewish problem. Negative as it is in this matter, the attitude of the Soviet regime is far more complicated and "complex-ridden" and therefore more human and pragmatic while less consistent and obvious.

The inner contradictions to which the Soviet authorities fall prey when they deal with the Jewish problem cannot be understood save by gaining an insight into the psychological motives, whether conscious or subconscious, which impel and guide them. Paramount among these is the factor of traditional Russian anti-Semitism.

The Soviet leaders are after all flesh and blood; they have been molded by their upbringing and home environment, school and society. One must remember that to this day, the Soviet leaders are people who rose by themselves from the lower or middle ranks of society and that they lack the finesse of an elite with a long ancestry. Most of them are natives of Russia, the Ukraine, and Belorussia, places where anti-Semitism is firmly rooted. Classical Russian literature shows the depth of anti-Jewish sentiment among the great Russian writers, such as Gogol, Dostoyevsky, Chekov. These authors wrote of what they saw and sensed in the Russian society around them.

The primitive Russian peasant, dominated during the czarist era by a feudal regime and by the Russian Orthodox Church, always regarded the Jews as Christ-killing aliens. They dressed differently, spoke an unintelligible language, prayed to another god, maintained "mystic" ties with their Jewish brethren everywhere and anywhere; they did not drink to excess; they were shrewd, deceitful, played tricks on the peasants and took advantage of them. The Ukrainian and, to some extent, the Belorussian peasant saw all this in the Jews—and more. In their eyes the Jew was the agent of the hated and overbearing Polish nobleman; the Jew did all the dirty work for this nobleman, collected taxes and fees, loaned the peasants money on usurious terms, and mercilessly exploited them.

The czars and the aristocracy had their own reasons for hating the Jews. Influenced by the Church, they regarded the Jews as Christ-killers; they, too, laughed at them and despised their language, customs, and faith. But at the same time they knew that the Jews were also an inexhaustible source of money, which they always needed. So they borrowed money from them and hated them the more for that. In the last century, the rulers began to despise the Jews because they regarded them, or many of them, as polluted carriers of Western culture and revolutionary radicalism, as the bearers of a foreign flame in Mother Russia. The Russian middle class, which began to develop at that time, hated the Jews because it saw them as competitors in trade. The Russian intelligentsia was also prejudiced by Russian and international anti-Semitic literature, by *The Protocols of the Elders of Zion,* which portrays international Jewry as a vast spider web whose threads encompass the whole world.

The Russian Orthodox Church had its own reasons for hating the Jews: not only were they Christ-killers but also they were spreading the seeds of atheism and disbelief among the Russian Orthodox faithful.

For the government, the aristocracy, and the Church, the Jews were a scapegoat and a lightning rod for the anger of the masses. They diverted all the bitterness and despair of the peasants and the depressed classes away from themselves and toward anti-Semitism. "Beat the Jews and save Russia" was the war cry of the czarist authorities and the Church.

The Jews of Russia, the Ukraine, and Belorussia lived for innumerable generations under the threat of spontaneous or planned pogroms. Whether the murderers were hungry and embittered peasants or the czar's Cossack horsemen, the end was always murder, rape, the knout, and terror. The closer the czarist regime came to its inevitable end, the more did it vent its fury against the Jews.

A new wave of pogroms was inaugurated by the antirevolutionary white armies during the Bolshevik revolution. New slogans were hurled at the Jews, accusing them of heading and leading the Bolsheviks and blaming them for all the suffering, the hunger, the epidemics, and the wars.

Then the Soviets triumphed and consolidated their position. They fought vigorously against anti-Semitism, which they outlawed. The security forces, where Jews occupied key positions, imposed severe penalties for anti-Semitic outbursts. But the war against anti-Semitism was short-lived. Had it lasted for some years, it might have brought about a gradual change and the eventual disappearance of traditional Russian anti-Semitism.

The situation worsened as a result of the first purges in the thirties. The masses interpreted the mock trials as proof that Stalin was sacrificing leading Jewish figures in his government to Moloch. That was how the suffering masses understood the attacks against Trotsky, Kamenev, Zinoviev, who were all Jews, and others on trial, many of whom were also Jews. Again the Jews became scapegoats. The prosecuting attorneys shouted: "Traitor!" at those who sat accused; the propaganda media trumpeted: "Destroyers of the motherland!" And the shouts and epithets fell on the attentive ears of the Russian masses.

The Nazis kindled the embers of hatred

The German invasion, the conquest of the Ukraine, Belorussia, and other huge tracts of Russia, and the presence of the Gestapo kindled again and stirred to a blaze the embers of deep anti-Semitism which had never been quenched. The Nazis found faithful followers in the occupied areas, mainly among the Ukrainians, who helped them carry out their crimes against the Jews. The Nazi anti-Semitic creed fell on fertile Soviet soil.

One might have expected that after the victories of the Red Army and the liberation of the native land, the Soviets would wage a vigorous campaign against the new wave of anti-Semitism. But no such campaign took place. No serious effort was made to explain to the masses the evil inherent in anti-Semitism. Nor did the authorities encourage the villages, towns, and cities to welcome the Jewish refugees who survived the Holocaust. The Jews were of no concern to anyone. A bitter fate awaited them: instead of a vigorous campaign against anti-Semitism, there were the dark years of Stalin—the uprooting of Jewish culture, the murder of Jewish writers, and the "doctors' plot."

It is against this historic, social, and psychological background that the forces which motivate Soviet policy makers must be evaluated. Soviet leaders would have had to exert great moral and intellectual efforts to overcome their primitive sentiments and see the Jews in a different light. But their hatred of the Jew was too deeply ingrained. The present wielders of power, as well as those next in line, are mainly younger people who grew up under the Soviet regime. And they, too, are not free of native anti-Semitism, for those who were youngsters at the time of the purges or the "doctors' plot" drank deeply of the anti-Semitic poison.

It is a vicious circle. The regime does not propagandize against anti-Semitism, and, due to motives we have described, its propaganda has anti-Semitic undertones under the guise of an atheistic and anti-Israel campaign; thus the anti-Semitic poison continues to be injected into each new generation in the Soviet Union.

The behavior of the minor officials in whose hands lies the fate of the Jews can now be understood in the light of past history.

These officials are not instructed to stop mistreating the Jews. On the contrary, many of them, reared in the tradition of native anti-Semitism, interpret in their own way the line of official policy in which they have been trained, and add to it their own measure of cruelty and insolence.

Many of the regime's officials who are responsible for Jewish affairs are motivated by three complexes derived from their prejudiced image of the Jew: *The-Protocols-of-the-Elders-of-Zion* complex; the crafty-and-fraudulent-Jew complex; and, finally, the Jew-as-Satanic-genius complex.

Many of these people, and this includes members of the intelligentsia, are spiritual and cultural leaders who know the true position of the Jews in the Western world; but they have unconsciously retained some of their forefathers' image of a mysterious "world Jewry" led by a hidden and powerful conspiracy. The antipathy which many Soviet leaders have toward international Jewish bodies derives not only from carefully thought out reasons but also from the fear or suspicion that, whether religious or secular, these bodies are the first encroachments of a giant spider which, concealed in some mysterious corner of Brooklyn or Jerusalem, weaves a web of intrigue throughout the world.

The picture of a "Jewish world leadership" which meets secretly and reaches decisions affecting the whole world, is familiar to them from their own organization. The Comintern, the Cominform, and the bodies which have taken their places, have been, and still are, organizations of this kind; with their headquarters in Moscow, they wield tremendous influence throughout the world. The people who rule from this world communist headquarters think and live in terms of international influence and intrigue.

I have heard it said in Moscow that a leading figure of the regime once remarked that there are three effective bodies in the world who know what they want and how go get it: the Communist party, the Catholic Church, and international Jewry. All the others are merely amateurs.

This image explains the obvious lack of proportion which characterizes the Soviet attitude toward the State of Israel, which it apparently takes to be the center of world Jewry. It explains also the reasons which motivate the heads of the regime to prevent the Jews in the Soviet Union from maintaining any ties with the "octopus" of world Jewry.

The crafty-and-fraudulent-Jew complex also arises from the depths of native anti-Semitism, from stories about the Jewish peddler, tax-collector, or usurer. It is undoubtedly a prime factor in the bizarre war which the regime wages against Jewish "economic criminals."

The Jew-as-Satanic-genius complex derives from the attitude of the common people toward the "Jewish mind," the "Jewish intelligence," the Jews as "talmudists" and as "great debaters." Jews are presumed to retain, even in Soviet Russia, some mysterious hypnotic power. This belief colors the attitude of the Soviets toward leading Jewish scientists, technologists, and thinkers in the Soviet Union and abroad.

It is rumored throughout the Soviet Union that the Jews of Israel have discovered a cure for cancer. Both the highly intelligent and the simple-minded believe this. I was asked about this by peasants in a *kolkhoz* as well as by doctors, who should know better. I met many non-Jews in the Soviet Union who did not even know where Israel is; but when I told them that I came from Israel, they immediately said: "So, you come from the place where they have discovered a cure for cancer."

My denials were often useless. I would tell them that many people die of cancer in Israel and would add that, as in the Soviet Union, we engage in cancer research in our scientific and medical institutes but have unfortunately not yet discovered even the cause of the disease let alone the cure. These denials would be met with skepticism and, sometimes, with ugly remarks: "You have discovered the cure for cancer, but you are clever and cunning enough to keep it a secret and only cure patients who pay fabulous sums." Some would even add: "You have cured our Shvernik of cancer. Our government asked yours to cure him and you agreed to do it for fifty thousand dollars."

One might perhaps go as far as to find the roots of the reverence and awe which Russians entertain for the "Jewish genius" in their subconscious awareness of the fact that the two leaders who transformed the fate of humanity and made such indelible marks on Russia were both Jews—Jesus and Marx.

Some of the finest and most enlightened Russians in czarist times stood by the Jews and defended them with great courage. But they were a mere handful and had little influence on the rulers and the people. Among the leaders of the revolution there were those who loved the Jews or those who at least had been able to rid themselves of anti-Semitism and view the Jewish problem without prejudice. One of these was Lenin. But in accordance with Marxist doctine, he regarded Judaism as a feudal remnant which was destined to disappear in a bourgeois society and certainly in a socialist society. Being a realist, however, he was aware that the millions of Jews in his own land would not disappear overnight. He knew, too, of the link between anti-Semitism and the black reactionaries whom he regarded as the source of anti-Soviet and anti-communist poison and against whom he waged relentless war.

A minority symbolized by Yevtushenko

There are certainly some leaders and young people in cultural, artistic, and scientific circles who dissociate themselves from the government's Jewish policy. They regard it as a vestige of Stalinist reaction, a regressive blend of primitive sentiment and distorted propagandizing which damages the reputation of the Soviet Union. The poet Yevtushenko is one such person. But they are still in the minority and have no significant influence upon the top echelons of Soviet leadership.

They know that Soviet Jews are badly dealt with and that this evil mars the image of the kind of Soviet society which they want to see. They understand also that in order to pluck out the evil, one must begin from the roots. This entails a vigorous campaign against every shade of native anti-Semitism. They know full well that an educational process of this kind would be a long and tortuous one. But precisely because of this, they say, it is imperative, for the good of the Soviets themselves, to begin to act now.

It would be a great day for Soviet Jewry if people of that sort reached positions of sufficient power and influence to institute what they regard as the correct policy.

If the answer to the question "What does the government want of the Jews?" has been involved and complicated, the answer to the other question "What do the Soviet Jews want of the regime?" is no less so. And this is mostly because the Jews have no one who can speak for them.

Occasionally, the regime issues "authoritative responses" from the rabbi of Moscow or other rabbis, from the heads of the various religious Jewish communities, from the editor of *Sovietish Heimland,* or from some "Jewish general." These responses, presumably coming from the Jews themselves, are supposed to supply answers to questions raised in the West about the fate of Soviet Jewry. The clichés are familiar. The rabbis declare, according to instructions dictated from above, that "We are quite satisfied with the facilities given us by the Soviet government in matters of religious observance," or, "We don't require religious articles from abroad, as we have all we need here."

Similar stereotyped answers are also given regarding cultural matters: "We are proud of Soviet civilization and contribute our share to its development. Our language and civilization is Russian and we identify ourselves willingly with this rich culture." Or, in a different vein: "We are happy to share in the creation of the splendid Soviet culture as expressed in the Russian language and are grateful to the Soviet Union for giving us a journal in Yiddish for those who still speak that language."

There is also a ready-made, stereotyped technique for handling matters concerning national life, Israel, and the Jews outside the Soviet Union. Jews, either as a group or as individuals, write letters to newspaper editors, saying: "We know the tricks of the Zionists. We have learned from our brethren, who returned from Israel, the enormity of the lie about the 'paradise' there which is promised to the Jews of the world. We dissociate ourselves completely from this deception. We warn comrade workers in the Soviet Union not to fall into the trap set by the Zionists and other Jews who are only tools of the organized imperialist bourgeoisie."

These statements are woven of rough yarn. It is not difficult for either a Jew or a gentile outside the Soviet Union to recognize the origin of this fabric.

The truth of the matter is that today the Jews of the Soviet Union are dazed, bewildered, angry; some have despaired. I would stress again that there is no Jew in Russia who is unaffected by the problem. Some feel that their Jewish heritage is a blemish which they would like to rid themselves of; they are like a hunchback dreaming that he might become normal. This daily confrontation with reality is heart-rending. No doubt there are Jews who dream that one bright morning they will wake up and find that all the complications growing out of their names, identity cards, and, particularly, their "Jewish faces" have suddenly disappeared.

The "Jewish face" (still a by-word in Russian: *zhidovskaia morda*) is much in evidence among Soviet Jews today. The identifying mark is not necessarily the "Jewish nose" but a mingling of traits, physical and psychological, peculiar to Jews in the Soviet Union and elsewhere. I came to recognize in the Soviet Union what one might call "Jewish eyes." In a mixed crowd of Jews and non-Jews, at a theater, movie house, or football game, one easily singles out those eyes which express a blend of anxiety, curiosity, intelligence, sensitivity, and the furtiveness of a trapped animal. The fact that the Jews are mainly urban and that their work is "clean" and "intellectual" serves to make them different in behavior and dress. There is also something which is defined as the "Jewish woman type," which differs in some respects from the "Slavic type." And after all the "Jewish nose" is not altogether a fiction.

On one occasion I traveled with an Israeli family by express train from Baku to Moscow. We soon became aware of the fact that two of our companions in the compartment were Jewish petroleum engineers who were going to the capital on business. They heard our Hebrew conversation, saw the Hebrew books the children held, stared at us, and listened openly to everything we said. Soon a lively conversation developed between us.

We spoke, of course, of Jewish affairs and Israel. They took a keen interest in our search for oil and our young petroleum industry, and we did our best to satisfy their hunger for honest information about Israel.

They could not take their eyes off the Israeli boy. One asked: "Do many of the children in Israel look like him? He looks like a real *goy*, just like a Swedish or Danish boy." We told them that many of our children look like him and that he was a normal Israeli boy. Much impressed, they repeated: "He doesn't look at all like a Jew; he looks just like a *goy*. . . ." The boy already understood some Russian and, feeling that he was being discussed, asked; "Father, why do they stare at me like that? What are they saying about me?" The father explained that they thought he didn't look like a Jew. The boy retorted angrily: "But I do look like a Jew. Why do they insult me?" The men saw that the child was angry and asked what he had said. We told them he was rather hurt because they thought he didn't look Jewish, and that he insisted that he did.

One of them stroked the boy's blond hair and said: "Yes, my child, you do look like a Jew, and it is marvelous to hear you say so. I wish we and our children could say that and as proudly."

A common denominator of all Jews, both of those who want to escape their Jewishness and those who maintain it, is the desire for change. The present situation is unbearably tense. It is like living between the Soviet hammer and sickle.

This state of absolute despondency is felt most acutely by some of the older Jews, who look back upon their past Jewish life and realize that it is utterly lost. As to the future, everything appears black; there is nothing but their sense of irreparable loss and the unlikelihood of change.

Not so long ago an old Jew wrote an "Obituary of the Jews of the Soviet Union" which reflects the hopelessness of Soviet Jewry. He said among other things:

We suffer from an incurable disease which no doctor and no medicine will help. We do not agonize day by day, but from one hour to the next. We are lost forever. We do not leave anyone to say *Kaddish* [prayer over the dead], or anyone to remember us in a *Yahrzeit* [annual commemoration of the dead]. There is no one to set a tombstone over us, and no sign of us will be left. We will be lost like the shadow of a passing bird and like a stone that is hurled into the abyss. . . .

I would have wanted to say *Kaddish* for myself and for my generation; in the last moments of my life to say my confession from the depths of my heart; to pronounce the *Yizkor* [memorial service by which relatives honor the departed], and the last *El Maleh Rahamim* [a memorial prayer], and leave a will. But, alas, there is no one to read my will and it would be useless effort. The Messiah will not come to the Jews of our generation in Russia. And if he should, he would be too late. He will come when there is no one left to save from the darkness of our exile. . . .

Again: "Why have you forgotten us?"

Many Russian Jews who are concerned about the problem of Soviet Jewry fail to understand why the Jews of the world have forgotten them and are doing nothing—so they think—to change the state of affairs. These Jews are fed Soviet propaganda, which always exaggerates the power and influence of world Jewry; they cannot understand why such a powerful body, which is so intimately tied to them and which shares their anguish, cannot hold out a helping hand. Above all these Jews desire closer ties between the Soviet Union and the Western world. They are certain that a further freezing of relations between East and West or a withdrawal by the Soviet Union into greater solitude would lessen the prospects of a change in the status of Soviet Jewry that might come about as a result of pressure brought to bear by Western Jewry.

This accounts for the question one hears repeated so often: "Why have you forgotten us?"

If we were to ask what kind of change Soviet Jews want, we would receive all sorts of answers. Perhaps one can come closer to a clear answer by asking some hypothetical questions. How would the Jews react if given the opportunity to decide their own fate? What would happen if the government declared: (a) Jews who wish to assimilate may do so by applying any day between 8:00 A.M. and 4:00 P.M. at the Registry Offices of the Ministry of the Interior in their own towns and changing their national status to that of the area where they live, or to any other in the Soviet Union. Jews can also change their family names; (b) Jews who wish to retain their present national status may do so. The government hereby declares that it will uphold all their cultural and national rights such as those enjoyed by other nationalities. The Jewish faith and its institutions will be granted all the privileges and facilities enjoyed by other religions; (c) Jews who wish to leave the Soviet Union and emigrate to Israel or anywhere else may do so, provided those countries are willing to accept them. They must first apply to the Israeli Embassy in Moscow, or to any of the other embassies, for their entry visas.

All of this is, of course, absurdly conjectural. All attempts to answer such questions are fraught with the dangers that pervade hypothetical inquiries of this sort. But I shall try to answer them anyway, on the assumption that such a situation could come about under present conditions, and that all three alternatives would be open to Jews simultaneously.

How many would want to be assimilated?

If Soviet Jews were given the opportunity to change their Jewish national affiliation with ease, I believe that many would do so, though it is very difficult to say how many. They would try to assimilate completely, forget the past, and commit themselves and their children to total assimilation, to a path from which there would be no turning back.

But this statement must be carefully qualified.

First, there is the matter of age. Few if any of the synagogue Jews, or of the older Jews generally, would flee from their status as Jewish nationals. None of the pious old Jews would follow this course, for it would be tantamount to announcing that they weren't Jews, and this they would never do. And those non-religious old Jews who lived as Jews for the greater part of their lives would also refuse to cast off their Jewishness as if it were an old garment, despite their having suffered for it all their lives.

The number of young and middle-aged Jews who would be ready to assimilate is far greater, but even they would not do it with ease. Many of the Jews who witnessed the Second World War and the Holocaust, as well as many of the younger Jews who grew up after Stalin's days, have developed Jewish feelings and sensitivities whose roots are so deep, precisely because they had no way out of their Jewishness, that they would regard a change of status as an act of treachery to themselves and to their way of life.

There would be Jews who would want to revert to the situation that prevailed in early revolutionary days, when they used Yiddish as their own official language and had their own culture. Though it was communist in content, it was a rich culture, with its own schools, newspapers, theaters, publishing houses, and so on.

The greatest problem would be that of leadership.

After the hard blows inflicted upon the Jewish intellectual elite, no new leadership has appeared that seems capable of rebuilding Yiddish culture. The survivors of the previous generation are too old, too shattered, too tired to start afresh. It is quite possible that there are young Jews in the Baltic countries, and in Bukovina and Moldavia, who would undertake not only to keep Yiddish alive but also to transform it once again into a living tongue and culture. If such people could be found and if, according to my assumptions, they were given the tools with which to carry out their mission, then tens of thousands of Jews would undoubtedly come to their aid and help them to revive Yiddish culture.

If the Jews were given an opportunity to teach their children Yiddish, even on a part-time basis like the American Sunday School, many would do so with joy.

Furthermore, as in the case of established Western Jewish communities in England, France, the United States, South America, and other lands of the Diaspora, the Soviet Jews would want to teach their children Hebrew and would regard it as their second language. If the Soviet authorities would open the door to the study of Hebrew, I have no doubt that modern Hebrew would be studied by thousands of Jewish youths in the Soviet Union.

There would be a renewed creativity in Jewish literature, poetry, history, and so on—in Russian. There was a varied and flourishing Russian Jewish literature before the revolution, and there is no reason to doubt that it could revive under favorable conditions. The possibility of religious revival would present serious difficulties. The few surviving rabbis are too old and would not have the energy to inaugurate a religious revival or to set up nationwide religious institutions and organizations. To renew and maintain Jewish religious and cultural life in the Soviet Union, ties would first have to be established with the centers of Jewry outside the Soviet Union, particularly with Israel. Only then would the Soviet Jews be able to train Yiddish and Hebrew teachers for a network of Jewish schools; only then could they begin to raise a new generation of religious leaders.

How many would emigrate to Israel?

It is not at all easy to find an answer to the question: How many Russian Jews would emigrate to Israel? To say, with every tourist or Israeli visitor to the Soviet Union, that "I met many Jews who expressed a desire to go to Israel," elicits the response: "Of course; only those who want to go to Israel approached and spoke to you. And how many of them were there? Not so many after all. And what do you know about all the other Jews?" To this I must reply by referring to the criterion I mentioned in my opening chapters. Many outsiders have had conversations with Jews of all ages, occupations, and walks of life throughout the Soviet Union. If out of all these encounters we get a picture of a large number who want to go to Israel, then that picture would be authentic.

In many cases it is not even necessary to ask Soviet Jews whether or not they wish to emigrate to Israel. For they themselves ask, in a thousand different ways, when they will be able to leave for Israel. Those who want to go to Israel often use the word *"peshkom,"* meaning "on foot." I heard that word very often indeed, sometimes in answer to the question: "How will you go?"; at other times as a slogan: "Let's go!" With the word *"peshkom,"* these Jews are saying: "We'd get out right now, if they'd let us, and we'd go on foot, we'd walk, from here to Israel."

But you do not always get *"peshkom"* for an answer. Sometimes there is another answer from someone who wants to emigrate. I talked to a middle-aged Jewish engineer from Kharkov and this is what he said:

"If I heard tomorrow on the radio or read in the papers that one could formally register for emigration to Israel and that a train would take Jews from Kharkov to Israel, I would not go to register and I would not go to the railway station."

Earlier he had told me that his family had been wiped out in the Holocaust, that he had only one brother left, in Israel, and was most anxious to join him there.

I asked him in surprise: "Why wouldn't you register and go?" He answered: "Because I don't know what would be behind such a registration, and I don't know where the trainload of Jews would go. We might be told that it was going south, to Odessa, to put us on a ship for Israel. But we might suddenly find that the train was traveling east, and that we had actually 'volunteered' to go to Birobidzhan."

Thirty years of Stalinist rule caused this type of reaction in Soviet citizens generally, and especially in Jews of this age group. Young Jews are not so intensely haunted by fear. Growing up in the post-Stalin era they only heard about rather than experienced for themselves the expulsions, imprisonments, exiles.

In Israel, when I related my experiences, the question always put to me was: "What will happen when the gates are opened?" I would reply that this is a highly involved question, but that I had the impression that many would emigrate. Pressed to give an exact number, I would say that no one could possibly give such a number; the situation is dependent upon factors that are constantly in flux. Despite this, however, it might still be possible to give some sort of approximate number. To do this, it is necessary to discuss separately the Jews of the western borderlands, the eastern borderlands, and those of the center.

As stated, some three hundred thousand Jews live in the western borderlands—in the Baltic countries, the Galician areas annexed to the Soviet Union, and in Bukovina and Moldavia. Given only a chink in the wall, the Jews of Riga, Vilna, Chernovtsy, Kishinev, and other towns in these areas would burst forth and emigrate. We have already mentioned the special motives that would impel them, namely their many relatives in Israel, their Jewish upbringing, and their strong sense of alienation from the society in which they live.

Many if not most of the Oriental Jews of the Soviet Union—the Bukharan, Georgian, and Mountain Jews, who number about two hundred thousand—would go to Israel if given the chance. They would be motivated by a profoundly religious and near messianic longing to return to Zion and Jerusalem, as well as by close family ties and the obedience of all members of the family to their leaders and elders. They would emigrate, I think, just as the Jews of Kurdistan and Yemen did: entire clans with their rabbis, teachers, and Scrolls of the Law.

The picture of the Jews in central Russia, who constitute the majority of Soviet Jews, is less clear. It is difficult to say how many of the synagogue Jews would have the courage to go, despite all their yearning for Jewish life and all their courage and devotion to Jewry. They are now in their declining years, old, feeble, weary. Some would go; others would be fearful and would choose to stay.

Some middle-aged people would undoubtedly decide to leave their homes and jobs and emigrate to Israel. Many would find the decision a hard one to make. There would also be young Jews, students and those who had just started out in life, who would be prepared to go. There is no doubt at all about that. As a matter of fact, it is possible that younger people might find it easier to decide to emigrate and build a new life in a new country. The young are generally braver, more inclined to adventure and to making long-range decisions. But it is difficult to say how many of them would go if they were given a chance, though I believe there would be many more than we think.

In sum, we are dealing with between half a million to a million Jews who, I believe, are now ready to emigrate to Israel. And I do not mean to say that this is all there will be. I am referring only to the first wave of emigration.

What of the other Jews, those still hesitant, fearful, indecisive, who will wait to see how things turn out? This will be answered only when the first phase is completed and the first wave has left.

The nature of the second wave is contingent upon a hundred and one factors: How will the first wave be absorbed? What sort of letters will they send back to the Soviet Union? What will be the fate of the tens of thousands of uncircumcised Russian Jews who will come to Israel?

What will be the attitude in Israel to those Russian Jews who have gentile wives? How will the professional and skilled workers find employment? What will happen to the thousands of doctors, engineers, and technicians? What will be the economic situation of the first wave? And so on.

Israel as described by "those who returned"

It appears that the Soviet authorities are well aware of the underground currents of national consciousness and pride that prevail among Jews generally and younger Jews in particular. It is enough to see the waves of enthusiasm and love that surround every appearance of young Israelis, or groups representing Israel at international festivals and congresses, to appreciate the real depth and strength of these feelings.

That is why the Soviet press, both central and provincial, and especially in areas with many Jews, frequently publishes articles about the harshness of life in Israel. In recent years, popular editions of books and pamphlets about Israel have begun to appear, all of them written by "experts" or "eye witnesses" who either lived in Israel for a while and returned to Russia, or who went as tourists for a brief stay and are now able to relate impressions and experiences from "genuine sources." In this manner the authorities try to tell the Soviet reader, and the Jews in particular, the "true facts" about life in Israel. They say that there is constant and severe unemployment in the country and hundreds of thousands are penniless, that newcomers are discriminated against in favor of oldtimers, and that immigrants from certain countries are disliked and treated with contempt. The *kibbutz* is described in some articles as a trick to exploit workers ("people work there all year round without getting a penny, not even carfare to Tel Aviv"). They also speak of the unbearable heat, the dirt and ignorance, and of the millionaires and capitalists who exploit the masses. Most articles describe Israel as an armed camp of imperialist aggressors.

Naturally, propaganda articles of this sort are also published every now and then about other countries, mainly the Western capitalistic ones. But I do not think that there is any other small country in the world which is the subject of as much propaganda as Israel and in such inverse ratio to its size and importance.

There is no doubt that this intensive, special attention is caused by Jewish national sentiment in the Soviet Union and is intended to combat it.

It is interesting—and typical of the situation—that the authorities, in many cases, get different, often contrary results from those they seek. To begin with, many Jews buy anything at all that is published about Israel. Any paper featuring an article on the subject, even if it is derogatory, is snatched up by Jews, and so are books and pamphlets. Jews—and gentiles—have acquired the special art of reading between the lines. They manage to find the information they want in almost every article. For instance, if an article speaks very resentfully about Israel's help to African countries, about the thousands of experts who are scattered over the whole African continent working as agents and tools of imperialism and neo-colonialism, the Jews deduce from this that Israel has the hydrologists, geologists, irrigation engineers, agronomists, doctors, architects, and highly-trained specialists and scientists in other technical areas which the developing countries need.

The book entitled *A Journey to Israel,* written by a Jewish tourist from the Soviet Union named Gregorii Plotkin, was published in many thousands of copies and has a photograph of two female soldiers carrying guns. The picture was intended to prove that all of Israel is an armed camp and that even girls are drafted into the army. I saw many Jews carrying the picture, which they had cut out of the book; they were proud of "these lovely and brave Israeli girls."

A young Jewish student analyzed for me the processes of inverted logic that are applied in reading Soviet articles about Israel:

"First they tell us that your poor and tiny country has two million people. Then they go on to describe how everybody suffers from the terrible and maddening heat and that people collapse like flies. They add, furthermore, that a large percentage of the population is unemployed and goes hungry. Then they suddenly relate that your country is full of the latest model tanks, jets, and rockets, and that your aggressive army is ready day and night to attack and defeat tens of millions of your neighbors in Egypt, Syria, and Lebanon. Then my friends and I put two and two together. How is it possible for two million miserable, exhausted, and hungry Jews to handle tanks, planes, and ships efficiently, and to produce nuclear scientists and mobilize several army groups for modern warfare? Something is not logical here. Either the Jews of Israel are not so miserable, pitiful, and hunger-ridden, or they are not so aggressive and do not have such a modern and well-equipped army. Or, possibly, the whole story is a fabrication and bears no relation to reality."

The Jews are not the only ones who mistrust such crude descriptions. Israel is slowly beginning to assume a different aspect even in the eyes of the young Soviet intelligentsia. Many Soviet scientists, Jews and non-Jews, have met Israeli scientists at international congresses. They have come to realize that Israel is represented in almost every technical and scientific field and that its people are highly skilled. Sports delegations from Israel have participated in several international events in the Soviet Union and outside, and have met Soviet athletes who liked them. This is true of painters, movie and theater actors, musicians, and other artists who have witnessed Israel's artistic and cultural creativity.

Igor Stravinsky visited the Soviet Union a few years ago. He was received with great warmth by innumerable admirers. During a television interview, which was watched by millions, he was asked about his future plans. Stravinsky told the interviewers, in all innocence, that he was returning to the United States where he would concentrate on a new musical composition on the subject of the sacrifice of Isaac, and that this work was to have its first performance in Israel, in Hebrew. And he added some words of praise about the Hebrew language and the high level of music in Israel. Stravinsky's remarks were a source of profound comfort to tens of thousands of Soviet Jews who saw that television program.

At times I found among non-Jews some strange and amusing fragments that ricocheted from the bursting of anti-Israeli propaganda shells. One day I took a cab from the Hotel Ukraina in Moscow to the Israeli Embassy at 16 Vesnina Street. On the way the driver asked me if I was from Israel. When I told him I was, he said, smiling: "Ah, *Izrail ochen khorosho*" (Israel, very good), and repeated it. I asked him in surprise: "What do you know of *Izrail*, and how do you know it is so *khorosho?*"

He told me a story:

"A few years ago, in 1956, I worked in a large Moscow factory. One morning, comrades came and told us to stop work and go out to a demonstration in front of the Israeli Embassy. All the workmen in the plant went. We were given banners on which were inscribed slogans like: 'Aggressors, keep your hands off Egypt!' We marched, singing, to the Israeli Embassy, gathered around the building, and shouted: 'Keep your hands off Egypt!' We threw some stones (not large), broke some windows (not many); then, after half an hour, we scattered and had the day off. Since then, I have a nice memory of *Izrail*. Yes, *Izrail, ochen khorosho.*"

When I returned to Israel I told one of the army commanders who had seen action in the Sinai campaign that he and his comrades had got a full day's holiday with pay for the industrial workers in Moscow.

The second largest concentration of Jews

The Jewish people (and despite all difficulties in defining the term "Jews," there certainly is a Jewish people) now number about fourteen million. Having lost a third of their number in the Holocaust, Jews now live in three large concentrations: about six million in the United States, about three to three and a half million in the Soviet Union, and about two and a half million in Israel. The others are scattered throughout the world.

The Jews of the Soviet Union, therefore, constitute the second largest concentration of Jews—about one-fourth of the total of today's Jewry.

The Jews are not only scattered over the five continents and in a hundred and one countries but are also divided among themselves. There are Orthodox, Conservative, and Reform Jews in the United States, and many with no congregational affiliations. There are Zionists and non-Zionists, Hasidim who study the Law all day in the religious schools of ultra-Orthodox rabbis in Brooklyn, and M.I.T. students in Boston. Jewish religious, social, and cultural institutions give the impression of being as innumerable as the sands of the sea.

The Jews of Israel are divided into a dozen political and

religious groupings. The Jews of Great Britain, France, Latin America, and elsewhere have their own institutions of every kind, religious, political, and educational.

The Jews also have a few dozen international organizations: congresses, federations, unions. To find one's way through this labyrinth of Jewish organizations requires a long thread and a strong searchlight.

Jews have always been inclined to quarrel and argue among themselves. But they are also capable of uniting and acting as a single body when confronted by certain ideas or principles.

Helping one's fellow Jews in their time of need is one of the fundamental principles of Jewish unity.

After the destruction of the Temple, the Palestinian exiles found refuge among their brethren in Mesopotamia, Persia, and Egypt. Those from Spain and Portugal who fled the murderous Inquisition were saved by the Jews of Turkey, North Africa, Italy, and Holland. The established Jewish communities of America helped the Jews of eastern Europe who landed in the United States at the end of the last century. The Jews of the world united against the czarist pogroms. Huge and powerful rescue organizations were established, such as the Alliance and the Joint Distribution Committee. Hundreds of thousands of Jews fought in the Allied armies during the Second World War. But they could not stop the Holocaust and the murder of millions of brethren. Guilt for having done too little too late weighs upon Jews to this day. At the end of hostilities, Jews throughout the world mobilized to rescue the remnants.

The high point of their relief and rescue work was the period of illegal immigration to Palestine in the years 1945–47 and the establishment of the State of Israel in 1948.

Jewish sailors and marines, demobilized from the United States Armed Forces, volunteered to pilot ships of illegal immigrants to the shores of Palestine. Everywhere Jews helped convoys of refugees to break through and reach their destination. They exerted the full weight of their influence throughout the world to arouse public opinion and to secure votes at the United Nations in favor of the establishment of the State of Israel. Jews from Finland and Sweden, South Africa and Rhodesia, England and France, Argentina and Brazil volunteered for service in Israel as soldiers, pilots, gunners, and tank drivers in the War of Independence. In North and South America, Europe, Australia, and dozens of other countries, Jews raised hundreds of millions of dollars to buy arms and equipment for the Jewish state.

Soviet Jewry is the greatest misfortune of Jews today.

During the first decade after the Second World War, the Jewish nation was still in shock from the Holocaust and was entirely engrossed in the task of aiding the survivors and in the struggle for the State of Israel. The Jews of the Soviet Union seemed to be overlooked. But it must be remembered that until the death of Stalin in 1953, the Jews of the world did not know the full truth about the situation of Soviet Jewry and were inclined to blame Stalin for all the evils of the Soviet regime. Some argued that the purge of the Jewish intelligentsia was merely part of the general purge; that while it was true that many thousands of Jews had been imprisoned or interned in camps in Siberia, they were but a fraction of the millions that Stalin sent into forced labor; that Jewish cultural, educational, and religious institutions were indeed being closed, but that Stalin was doing the same to all other such institutions.

It was during Khrushchev's regime that the world, and world Jewry, were given a window into the Soviet Union, were able to hear what Khrushchev himself had to say about the period of Stalin's rule, and were able to establish some degree of close contact with many Jews in the Soviet Union. And when the Jews of the world no longer needed to concentrate all their efforts upon the remnants of the Holocaust and the struggle for the State of Israel; when they began to look around and draw up a balance sheet of the existent body and soul of Jewry—then and only then did they come to realize that one-fourth of world Jewry had been almost completely cut off from the stream of Jewish life and from any sort of living contact with the Jews of the rest of the world.

When this situation became clear, many thought that the end had come and that the most active, dynamic, and fertile segment of the Jewish people, a segment which had once led the entire nation, was now totally lost.

In the course of the next few years, a few hundred, then thousands, and then tens of thousands of Jews and non-Jews visited the Soviet Union as tourists, businessmen, journalists, diplomats, artists, and students, and came back to tell of their meetings, conversations, impressions, and experiences with the Jews of the Soviet Union. These encounters began to weigh heavily on the conscience of Jews. They realized gradually—as all now do—that the situation of Soviet Jewry is complex, difficult, tragic, and unprecedented, but that it is not desperate, that something could be done because there are many Jews in the Soviet Union who are anxious not to be cut off from their people.

It is of interest to note that this picture of the true condition of Soviet Jewry was put together out of bits and pieces of information gathered from "below" rather than from "above." Jews visited the Soviet Union as tourists and met relatives from whom they had been separated for decades. Back home in London, New York, or Jerusalem, they told their families and friends what they had seen and heard. Members of athletic teams and scientific delegations to congresses and conventions in Moscow brought back a large store of Jewish experiences, which they then related to their families and friends. Jewish performers from the West who appeared before Russian audiences returned with stories of pathetic encounters with Soviet Jews.

It was only by weaving together all these stories and first-hand accounts that the Jews of the world, and the public in general, were able to put together a picture of what it was that had happened to the Jews of the Soviet Union.

It must also be remembered that not all of these visitors to the Soviet Union were anti-Soviet. I daresay that the contrary would be nearer the truth. Many of the tourists or members of delegations belonged and still belong to the Communist party or various socialist or liberal groups. They remembered that during the Second World War the Red Army had saved innumerable Jews, perhaps their own relatives among them. Many had retained from childhood strong sentimental attachment to the Russian people, language, and culture. These people were hardly disposed to see everything as black when they landed at Odessa or in the Moscow airport.

But a sensitive Jew who visits the Soviet Union even for a short time and meets relatives or other Jews who are eager to open their hearts, suddenly becomes aware, even against his will, that within the total spectrum of Soviet life Jewish affairs are like a streak of darkness—and from that moment on he can no longer see anything in the Soviet Union objectively; for this darkness is to be found everywhere, and it spoils and distorts the entire picture.

How to break the vicious circle

At the same time that individual contacts with Soviet Jews were making it evident that something was very much amiss there, Jewish organizations and institutions were trying to contact the Soviet authorities in order to discuss the situation with them. But here they came up against a stone wall. The Soviets refused to discuss the matter. Their position was, to begin with, that there was no Jewish problem in the Soviet Union; secondly, if there were some vestiges of this problem, the Soviet regime knew how to deal with them efficiently and effectively; thirdly, and this was possibly their main point, the whole subject was no concern of foreign Jewish organizations nor in fact of anybody, Jewish or non-Jewish. The entire matter, the Soviets claimed, was unquestionably an internal affair of the Soviet Union and no person or organization had the right to interfere. Consequently, the Jews of the world, or those who claim to represent them, are not in any way involved in this matter.

Not only did the Soviet regime close its ears and slam the door to the representatives of the Jewish world, but also among the Jewish leaders themselves there were those who were fearful of giving the matter too much emphasis because they were afraid of "what the gentiles might say."

This fear is as old as the Jewish exile. For generations the Jews maintained the dictum: "Do not provoke the gentiles." Taught by bitter experience, they were always afraid of making matters worse than they were. To raise an outcry, to protest, to stand up for their rights and lives, might make the gentiles all the angrier and provoke them into more violence and bloodshed. It was therefore best to absorb the blows, the humiliation, the dishonor—and remain silent. "Sha sha, don't make a row," frightened Jews would say when they learned of the bitter lot of their brethren in another town or another country. Rather than resort to open protest, the Jews developed a technique of peaceful intercession. This in time became the art of "Jewish diplomacy." The Jewish mediator would rush around discreetly and try through supplication, bribery, and self-debasement to moderate the ruler's decree.

But Jews have forgotten that this kind of diplomacy failed far more often than it succeeded, and that in most cases the policy of noninterference served only to make matters worse.

A few years ago when Jewish leaders began asking themselves what to do about the problem of Soviet Jewry, many said, "Sha sha." They claimed that every loud protest and outcry would serve to anger the Soviets and harm the Jews in the Soviet Union.

Only when all attempts at discussions with the Soviet authorities failed and when the burden of eye-witness accounts continued to grow—only then did Jewish organizations, some slowly, others more rapidly, begin to raise their voices in behalf of the Jews of the Soviet Union.

The Jews of the world have learned that the loud protest is the only way open to them. The problem of Soviet Jewry today occupies the top position in the order of priorities of the various bodies and organizations of world Jewry. Even the problems of the State of Israel are at times pushed aside because of the urgency of the question of Soviet Jewry.

What does world Jewry want from the Soviet regime? What are the goals that Jews have set for themselves in order to solve the problem of Soviet Jewry?

The desire that is shared by all Jews and with which those in the Soviet Union fully identify themselves is for the Soviet Jews to be given the opportunity to choose between several alternatives.

Bearing in mind the peculiar ideological and political difficulties of the Soviet regime in Jewish matters, the Jews of the world point to the communist regime in Poland. The Jews there had three alternatives after the war. Those who wished to assimilate into Polish society were allowed to change their family names to Polish names without any difficulty; their Jewish nationality was not registered in their identity papers. Those who wanted to preserve their Jewish nationality and culture, in Yiddish, were given the opportunity and the funds to maintain a national Jewish theater, a national book publishing house, as well as Jewish research institutes and educational bodies. Polish Jews who wished to emigrate to Israel were allowed to do so, and indeed tens of thousands did.

This solution did not tarnish the image of communist rule in Poland or undermine its ideological foundations. It did not arouse the anger of the people, and it helped to solve, almost entirely, the Jewish problem in Poland.

The Jews of the world constantly make it clear to the Soviet leaders that such a solution, or something similar to it, would release the Jews from the horrifying position in which they now find themselves, as well as relieve them of the feeling of being trapped.

A solution of this sort would not undermine the foundation of the Soviet regime. On the contrary, it might break the vicious circle the Soviets have created for themselves and the Jews. Because from the time that the Soviets began labeling the Jews in their midst a security risk and treating them as such, the Jews have begun to turn into an embittered and restless element of the population. This increases the wariness of the authorities and aggravates still further their relationship with the Jews; and the Jews react by growing more distrustful of the regime.

Accessible goals

Before the far-reaching goal of free choice is attained, the Jews of the world have simpler, intermediate goals which would be far easier for the Soviets to achieve.

The Soviets could stop closing synagogues; or allow the Jews to reopen those that were closed; or, more optimistically, allow new ones to be opened.

They could allow rabbis and heads of communities to meet and discuss common religious problems; or, optimistically again, permit the religious communities to establish permanent institutions like those of the Russian Orthodox, Moslem, and Baptist groups.

They could allow the rabbis to teach Bible, Talmud, and other religious subjects to young people in order to ensure the continuity of religious leadership after the passing of the older generation. The "yeshiva" of Moscow might then become a vital institution, similar to the seminaries of the other religious bodies in the Soviet Union, which are permanent and active institutions of learning and whose existence, as we know, does not in any way undermine the country.

They might allow the heads of the communities and their elders to participate occasionally in international Jewish religious conventions, something that is completely taken for granted by the heads of the Christian churches in the Soviet Union. This would not in the least tarnish the image of the Soviet Union in the world or diminish its prestige.

Later, the Soviets might possibly allow religious students to travel and attend courses in yeshivas and seminaries in Israel, the United States, or some other Jewish center. This is permissible to religious students of other religions, and no evil has befallen the Soviet regime because of it.

They could stop molesting the circumcisers and allow Jews to circumcise their sons openly and without harassment.

Let them permit the Jews to bury their dead as they wish. Russia is a vast land with ample room for everyone, both the living and the dead. The dead Jews will not interfere with "city planning." Let them be buried away from the towns, as long as their families can visit the graves as prescribed by tradition.

Let them permit the people of the religious communities to pay for and bake matzot for Passover, to buy some citrons and palm fronds for the Sukkot Festival, and be permitted to purchase from abroad some of the religious books and objects which they lack. This will hardly affect the Soviet balance of payments. And if the religious communities do not have the money, or if the Soviet government does not care to spend even one ruble for the Jews, let the Jewish communities abroad be permitted to provide their Soviet brethren with these items.

To proceed to another area: Let the Soviets be daring enough to open classes for the study of Yiddish and Hebrew for those Jewish students whose parents wish it. Or if this is too much, let them at least open evening courses in these languages in the Jewish communities. And if that is still too much, at least inaugurate classes where just a little is taught, perhaps only twice or even once a week!

The Soviets should not make themselves objects of mockery and the Jews objects of humiliation by stating that ten Jews cannot be found in any city or small town in the Soviet Union who want such instruction. The one half million Jews who registered Yiddish as their mother tongue have demonstrated that they want it. The 70 per cent of Soviet Lithuanian Jews who registered Yiddish as their mother tongue are certainly entitled to it. The tens of thousands of Jews who absorbed Hebrew in their youth and the thousands of young Jews who are presently studying it surreptitiously at home also want it.

The Soviets should know that until schools, classes, or any other form of instruction in the languages spoken by the Jews are allowed, they will be absolutely unable to convince the Jews of the world that they have changed their attitude toward their own Jews. The life and death of a people's culture are contingent upon the nature of its classrooms. The Soviets know this well. They have revived and breathed new life into various languages simply by opening a network of schools. And the Jews of the world know it, too. The few Yiddish books and newspapers, the occasional Yiddish show and concert which the Soviet authorities throw to the Jews are nothing but palliatives. One has to be thankful for them, but they are not even a beginning of a real cultural existence.

Let the Soviets allow the families torn apart by the war and the Holocaust to reunite. Let them permit parents to join their children, children to join their parents, brothers their brothers, and relatives their relatives. This, in my opinion, would affect only a few tens of thousands and would cause no significant change in either the Jewish or the Soviet demographic situation.

But before all else, the Jews of the world want the Soviet regime to change its general attitude to the Jews. The Jews do not expect the Soviets to adopt a philo-Semitic position. Their plea is for a Soviet campaign against internal anti-Semitism. This course is not contrary to the ideology of the Soviets, who have learned that anti-Semitism by its very nature is linked with dark and questionable elements in Russian society. If the Soviet authorities wish to root out anti-Semitism from the land, they must uproot it first from their own midst. Later, they should banish native anti-Semitism through education and propaganda.

But before going on to positive action, the Soviet authorities should desist from publishing pamphlets, articles, news items, and books which, under the guise of an atheistic and anti-Israel campaign, besmirch the Jews everywhere and debase all Jewish values. They should stop identifying Jews generally, and those of the Soviet Union in particular, as swindlers and deceivers. This discontinuation would augur a change in the distorted picture of Jews and Jewish life which is painted today in the Soviet Union.

The Jewish people do not now nor have they ever wanted to combat the Soviet Union. The opposite is true. The extreme rightist or leftist elements in Europe and America, those who hated the Soviets, were almost invariably anti-Semitic and without Jewish adherents. The Jews, by and large, have always been identified with the liberal, progressive, socialist trends in the political and ideological life of their countries. They were great leaders in the left-wing parties and even in the Communist parties of countries outside the Soviet Union.

But now virtually all Jews have come to the conclusion that it is impossible for them to concede in the matter of Soviet Jewry because they are fighting for a just cause, one that vitally affects three million of their brethren.

The Soviet authorities know now that until the situation of the Soviet Jews improves, the Jews of the world will raise their voice in protest. If it is still possible today to organize a demonstration in which all Jewish organizations, parties, and groups participate, it is because of this single problem: the Jews of the Soviet Union. Jews from all over the world are prepared to cry out until this problem is solved.

It is true that there is no tangible power behind the Jewish outcry. Didn't Stalin ask mockingly: "How many divisions does the Pope have?"

But the communist leaders know full well the great strength of a world movement—even one without divisions. They were themselves once such a movement.

The Israeli boy who blessed the Hanukkah lights

A Jewish boy lived in Moscow at the time when his father, a friend of mine, was there as a diplomat from Israel. When Hanukkah drew near—the last that my friend's family was to spend in Russia—the eleven-year-old boy asked permission to pronounce the blessing over the Hanukkah candles in the synagogue. It was three years since the child had had any contact with Israel, its scenery, customs, and holidays, and he was eager to get home. It was no wonder that at every religious or national holiday he was consumed with a hunger for the atmosphere of Israel.

The custom to have a boy recite the blessings over the Hanukkah candles is practiced in Israel and in many other Jewish communities. When I mentioned this to the synagogue elders in Moscow, they were eager to let the boy bless the candles after the rabbi's blessing.

Unlike the great holidays in the fall, Hanukkah is not known to many Jews in the Soviet Union. The elderly and aged do not attach great importance to the festival which symbolizes heroism in war, the overthrow of foreign rule by rebels and fighters, and the glorious feats of Jewish guerillas more than two thousand years ago. Most of the young people are not at all familiar with this festival and its significance in Jewish history. In the past forty years the symbols of Hanukkah have slowly been lost. Even the bravest of Jews in the Soviet Union would not dare to light the Hanukkah candelabrum at home to commemorate a national rebellion. The familiar spinning tops, pancakes, and other holiday customs have almost entirely disappeared.

Nevertheless, despite the bitter cold of the Russian winter, many hundreds of Jews converge on the synagogue in Moscow to witness the lighting of the first candle of Hanukkah. Most of them are old, swathed and wrapped up in their heavy black overcoats and dark woolen scarves which they do not take off even during the service. But here and there, particularly along the sides of the building, one sees beneath the fur caps the bright eyes of boys and girls luminous with curiosity.

That year, after the rabbi of Moscow had recited the blessing over the candles in the large ancient silver candelabrum set on the pulpit, the boy went up and blessed the little colored candles in the small bronze candelabrum he had brought from Israel. His hands shook and his voice trembled with emotion. He almost choked over the first words of the blessing, but recovered in the second verse. His voice rang out clearly.

Years passed. Then one day I visited my friend at his home in Israel. He told me that one of the teachers in the school which his son attends had asked the pupils to write a paper on the theme "Memories of My Childhood." My friend said that his son did not like to talk to his friends or even to his family about his impressions of Moscow. But for some reason he had decided to choose "Hanukkah in Moscow" as the topic of his paper. And this is what he wrote:

"In the fifteen years of my life I have traveled and seen much more than the average boy. I have visited twelve countries, including the Soviet Union. Not everyone is allowed to visit Russia. Luckily, my father was sent there on a mission for the State of Israel. That is how I came to live abroad where I absorbed impressions I shall never forget.

"The thing that impressed me most was the condition of the Jews in the Soviet Union. This is not clear or understandable to anyone who lives here and merely reads about it in the papers. Only by actually experiencing the atmosphere on the spot can one feel what happens to the Jews in that country. The Israeli delegates do not have much to do there, but a cheerful word can at times bring a ray of light into the hearts of the Jews.

"I occasionally visited the homes of boys of my own age. As I would come in, the parents' eyes would light up with a joy which is hard for me to describe. They would take me quickly to their living room. I would be treated most hospitably and would tell them about Israel and its activities, trying to counteract the anti-Israel propaganda that is heard over their radio and television.

"During our last Hanukkah in Moscow I was given permission to light my small candelabrum in the synagogue. My heart beat rapidly as I entered the synagogue. I could hardly see what was going on around me. I almost forgot all the blessings I had learned. After the traditional evening service, the rabbi lit the synagogue candelabrum, reciting the blessings in a dry voice. Then my turn came. I was frightened by the large crowd that had gathered there. I walked to the pulpit with trembling knees and lit the candles. Then the little flames gave me courage. I knew I had to say the blessings and to sing well while hundreds of eyes were focused on me. As I pronounced the blessings, I saw the eyes of the Jews lighting up and I began to sing "Hanerot Halalu." In the middle of the chant a mysterious conductor seemed to have given a signal—and the worshipers joined me in a tremendous chorus.

"When I left the synagogue, I was filled with the feeling of having helped, of having been a messenger of comfort who brought light and hope to his people."

Some time later I was present at a Hanukkah party in

Bet Hillel, a Jewish students club in one of the large universities in the United States. The building was new and roomy. A charming student chanted the blessings over the candles in a perfect Hebrew that was tinged with an American accent. Lovely girls handed out the traditional pancakes, and the entire group of about one hundred and twenty boys and girls sang festive songs in English and Hebrew. Between these songs I told them stories about Israel, including the one about the Israeli boy who lit the Hanukkah candles in the great synagogue of Moscow. When I finished my story, I noticed that the eyes of the students had become serious and sad; they were like the eyes of the young Russian Jews I had seen, the eyes I had come to know so well as a result of my experiences in the Soviet Union.

A lovely and very popular Israeli singer represented her country at one of the international movie festivals which have been held in recent years in Moscow and which have become major events in that city. The singer appeared among a host of famous stars in the city park. Preceding her were some of the greatest and amost famous movie and stage artists of the Soviet Union, who sang, danced, and played, as well as many famous stars from Europe, America, India, and Japan. The Israeli singer sang Hebrew folk songs, a Yiddish folk song, and a Russian song she had memorized without understanding the meaning of the words. She was received with tumultuous applause and calls of *"bis"* and "bravo" from the crowd of thousands, which doubtless included many Jews.

Dozens of Jews came to her after the performance, and probably some gentiles as well, congratulated her, gave her flowers, asked for autographs—in short, behaved as is customary in the presence of a famous star.

When the tumult subsided and she was on her way out, a man came over to her. He was young, dark-haired, and had beautiful eyes. He caught her hand and told her in fluent Russian how impressed he had been with her appearance and her Hebrew songs. The singer sensed what he was trying to convey and answered him with looks and with half-words uttered in the sort of simple, halting Hebrew that invariably serves to bridge a chasm of this kind. As the conversation came to a halt, it was obvious that the young man felt that he had been unable to express himself fully. He began to say again and again, *"Ia Izrail.*

Ia Izrail." (I am Israel.) To this day the singer does not know whether he meant to convey that his name was Israel or that his heart was with Israel, or both. After a minute he felt it was time to say goodbye to the singer. He caught her hand, pressed it hard, and uttered the only Hebrew words he could remember:

"Yom Kippur! Yom Kippur! Yom Kippur!"

The young singer overcame her tears and answered:

"Yom Kippur! Yom Kippur!"

Postscript

1969

During the very tense days prior to the Six-Day War the Ambassador of Israel gave a cocktail party in a restaurant at the International Food Production Exhibit in Moscow —as had been done by other countries.

To this party were invited the pavillion heads, the diplomatic corps, and government personnel. Somehow about fifty Jewish students who had been constant visitors to the Israeli pavillion succeeded in entering the restaurant where the party was taking place.

The honored guest at the party was the then Israeli Minister of Labor Yigal Allon, who was serving at that time in the USSR as head of the Israel delegation to the International Convention on Social Security. Suddenly, at one point during the party, the fifty students formed a circle about Yigal Allon and presented him with a gift: a fluent Hebrew rendition of "The Song of the Palmach."

This story is typical of much that has begun to take place among Russian Jews in recent years. There is, especially among the younger generation of Russian Jews, an increasing sense of Jewish identity, an inner identification with the battle for survival being waged by the State of Israel, and an audacious willingness to display these feelings publicly by means of mass demonstrations in front of synagogues on Jewish holidays.

The impetus for a return to Judaism has passed from the older generation to the younger. It is the young people who are now the flagbearers in the struggle for Jewish identity, for Jewish pride, and against degradation and forced assimilation.

During the past years there has been a significant trend in the Soviet Union toward foreign language study. The opening of the gates to thousands of tourists from Western lands, Soviet tourism to Western countries, and radio broadcasts from the West have all brought about an eagerness on the part of youth to study foreign languages.

Jewish youth share that eagerness, but at the same time they are seeking means to study Hebrew. Despite the lack of textbooks and teachers, they somehow manage to find their way to the Hebrew language. A veteran Jewish teacher, one of the few remaining from the 1920's, told me about the many young Russian Jews who make every effort to acquire Hebrew newspapers and books from city libraries and then come to him seeking his guidance in learning the Hebrew language. The old man expressed his delight at being privileged to see Jewish youth in Russia so miraculously and powerfully attracted to the study of Hebrew, something he regarded as a fitting response to those in the Soviet Union who had tried to kill Jewish culture.

A number of events that took place in the Soviet Union during and after the Six-Day War are also indicative of this new spirit among young Russian Jews.

An Israeli tourist who was in Uzbekistan on the eve of the Six-Day War told me the following story which I relate in his own words:

"In the morning of the fifth of June we left Tashkent in an Intourist car. We didn't know that the war had broken out. We arrived at a small town, parked the car, and asked a lad of about sixteen where the synagogue was. He glanced at us, noticed the Israel insignia on the lapels of our coats, and shouted: 'Representatives from Israel!' He proceeded to lead us to the synagogue. The Jews of the town began to stream out of the houses and stores all along the street. Soon we found ourselves at the head of a parade of some three hundred people.

"We reached the synagogue. About two hundred people stood around the entrance. The synagogue filled swiftly. We stood on the pulpit of the crowded synagogue and responded as best as we could to the many questions that were put to us by the people: 'Will there be a war?' 'Does our El-Al (they used the word "our") function as it should and is it secure from aerial attack in case of war?' 'Why does Israel not require political support in the U.N. of the

African states that receive aid from her?' Someone asked why the water desalinization project wasn't progressing, and outlined the pressing importance of this project to the country. There were those who wanted to know whether Israel's textile manufacture would not be hurt by the cut-back in British textile imports. They asked why Elat wasn't being developed into an international tourist attraction. The questioning went on for two hours.

"On the evening of the same day we returned to Tashkent and learned that the war had broken out. At 7 P.M. Radio Moscow reported that heavy fighting was taking place between the Arab and Israeli armies, that Haifa was in flames, Tel Aviv and Jerusalem had been severely shelled, and the Syrian army had advanced beyond Nazareth. There were accounts of Israeli pilots taken prisoner after eighty-two Israeli planes had been destroyed that morning. We were thunderstruck. We tried to tune in a Jerusalem station, and succeeded—but all we heard was the dry official statement about 'heavy fighting on the borders of Israel' without additional details. We tried to contact Moscow by phone; it proved to be impossible. I sought a telephone conversation with Israel and was told there was no connection. We wanted to return to Moscow and were told that there were no more flights out of Tashkent that day. We then went to the synagogue for the Ma'ariv service. The synagogue was completely filled. People prayed aloud and with great feeling. I had never experienced such emotion-filled prayer before. The service lasted a full hour. There were many young people among the worshipers. When the service ended we saw that people were confused; no one wanted to leave and yet they hesitated to approach us. And then, suddenly, someone gathered courage and approached us and shook our hands without a word. Immediately, the congregants began to pass before us in a long line, each one in turn shaking our hands, a few individuals whispering words of blessing and hope.

"The next day at 5 A.M. we were able to tune in the Israel radio station and learned that three hundred enemy planes had been destroyed. We understood that the outcome of the war had already been decided. We dressed and went to the synagogue to share our feelings. When we arrived we found the synagogue almost completely filled. It became clear that, like us, the people there had not slept at all—and that they too had listened to Radio Israel in the early morning. Many said to us: 'Our lives were not easy until now and will undoubtedly be more difficult from here on, but it is vital that yours be good.' "

Another friend told me of all that happened in Moscow and in other major centers of the Soviet Union during those eventful days:

"Jewish students in Riga; a group of engineers and doctors in Gorki Park in the heart of Moscow; and thousands of Jews in the Israel Pavillion that was part of the food-produce fair then going on in Moscow—all of them bombarded every Israeli they saw with the questions: 'What is to become of *us?*' 'Will *they* be allowed to slaughter *us* and push *us* into the sea?' It was 'us' rather than 'you,' and their tearful faces expressed their pain and concern. We, the Israelis, attempted to calm them and repeatedly spoke of our confidence in the strength and competence of Israel's defense forces.

"On Shabbat, the tenth of June, 1967, word was spread of Israel's victory. The Jews of Moscow were ecstatic with joy. In May, 1948, when Israel was declared a state, it was mostly the adults and the aged who rejoiced; the younger generation was unable to comprehend what took place. But now, in June, 1967, it was the young people who seemed happiest and who gave open expression to their joy.

"On that Sabbath, called 'The Great Sabbath' by Jews in synagogues, we strolled through the neighborhood of the Moscow synagogue. Jewish youths recognized us as Israelis and began to follow us. We walked like that for a long time—accompanied by a crowd of young Jews who followed us openly and fearlessly through the streets of Moscow."

These days did not last. The entire Soviet propaganda apparatus opened up with a vicious anti-Israel campaign: newspapers, radio and television speakers, lecturers at popular meetings—all of Russian officialdom seethed with hatred toward Israel.

On the tenth of July, the Soviet Union severed diplomatic relations with Israel. The Israeli Embassy in Moscow was ordered closed. A police and military cordon was placed around the Embassy building until the Israeli diplomats left.

Tourists from Israel and other countries who happened

to be in the neighborhood of the Embassy at that time saw the tight guard and saw, too, the large group of young people who came to stand across the street from the Embassy in order to demonstrate by their presence what was in their hearts. Foreign reporters who witnessed this silent demonstration could not believe their eyes.

The break in diplomatic relations severed the living tie between Israel and the more than three million Jews of the Soviet Union. But there is every indication that the sense of Jewish identity continues to grow among them and especially among the younger generation.

Other SIGNET Fiction and Non-Fiction
You Will Want to Read

☐ **THE SOVIET UNION: The Fifty Years edited by Harrison Salisbury.** The top Moscow hands of **The New York Times** trace the progress of the Soviet Union from troika to Sputnik during the past fifty years as they examine Russian daily life, art, science, military capabilities, sports, religion, and diplomacy, to mention only a few topics. (#Y3679—$1.25)

☐ **IN MY FATHER'S COURT by Isaac Bashevis Singer.** A delightful memoir of the unique way of life of the pre-World War I Warsaw ghetto, recalled with humor and sensitivity in 49 vignettes by a renowned author, "one of the great literary artists of our time." **Saturday Review.** (#Q3306—95¢)

☐ **TREBLINKA by Jean-Francois Steiner.** An international bestseller, the powerful story of a group of Jewish prisoners who led a successful armed rebellion against their Nazi captors in a model death camp. (#Q3445—95¢)

☐ **DOCTOR ZHIVAGO by Boris Pasternak.** This celebrated novel—a bestseller and center of political controversy—has been hailed as a literary masterpiece throughout the world. By the great Russian writer and Nobel Prize winner. An MGM motion picture with an all-star cast. (#Y4058—$1.25)

MENTOR Books of Special Interest

☐ **A HISTORY OF THE JEWS (Revised Edition) by Solomon Grayzel.** This comprehensive history of the Jewish people weaves a rich tapestry of personalities, places, and events. Includes 24 maps.   (#MW870—$1.50)

☐ **A HISTORY OF RUSSIA (Revised Edition) by John T. Lawrence.** A brilliant chronicle of Russia's lands and people, from its ancient beginnings to the present day.
(#MY923—$1.25)

☐ **TEN DAYS THAT SHOOK THE WORLD by John Reed.** The classic work on the Russian Revolution, written by an American journalist who witnessed at first hand the epochal beginnings of the Communist state in November 1917.   (#MQ947—95¢)

☐ **RUSSIA AND AMERICA: Dangers and Prospects by Henry L. Roberts.** A penetrating analysis of our relations with Russia, in view of the sinister global tensions created by atomic discoveries. The author is Director of the Russian Institute at Columbia University.
(#MT589—75¢)